Trade Union Finance

There are few contemporary studies on the finances of unions. Indeed, little research exists on the internal operations of unions in the United States. This book provides a comprehensive analysis of the financial resources and performance of the largest national unions. It discusses the theoretical and practical relevance of the topic, which goes directly to the formation, maintenance, and potential advancement of labor organizations. Financial capacity and performance create incentives for unions to mobilize at the grassroots level and launch major drives to improve their position in society. Understanding how unions raise and spend money provides insight as to their administrative orientation and organizational capacity.

Given its topical breadth and depth, the book stands apart from the extant literature on unions in society. It is unique in the range of financial information presented, how data are analyzed, and its treatment of such important matters as compensation and benefits, operating budgets, political activism as measured by expenditures from treasury-based funds, and political mechanisms funded by members through voluntary donations. The authors show not only the scope of union financial wherewithal and how it varies across labor organizations but also how such indicators compare to corporate entities who employ the rank-and-file.

The book provides a wealth of information on how to analyze the finances of unions and to use this information to prepare for collective bargaining and other aspects of labor-management relations. It informs employers and other observers about how unions are able to represent members and their ability to withstand strikes.

Marick F. Masters is a Professor of Business at Wayne State University, Detroit, Michigan, USA.

Raymond F. Gibney is an Associate Professor of Management, School of Business Administration, Penn State Harrisburg, Middletown, Pennsylvania, USA.

Routledge Studies in Labour Economics

Labour Market Institutions and Productivity
Labour Utilisation in Central and Eastern Europe
Edited by Beata Woźniak-Jęchorek and Michał Pilc

Economic and Social Perspectives on European Migration
Edited by Francesca Fauri, Debora Mantovani and Donatella Strangio

Foundations of Modern Slavery
Profiles of Unfree and Coerced Labor Through the Ages
Caf Dowlah

Universities and the Labour Market
Graduate Transitions from Education to Employment
Magdalena Jelonek

The Dynamics of Marginalized Youth
Not in Education, Employment, or Training Around the World
Edited by Mark Levels, Christian Brzinsky-Fay, Craig Holmes, Janine Jongbloed and Hirofumi Taki

The Digital Economy and the European Labour Market
Edited by Maria Urbaniec

Digital Labour Markets in Central and Eastern European Countries
COVID-19 and the Future of Work
Edited by Beata Woźniak-Jęchorek and Kamilla Marchewka-Bartkowiak

Trade Union Finance
How Labor Organizations Raise and Spend Money
Marick F. Masters and Raymond F. Gibney

For a full list of titles in this series, please visit: www.routledge.com/Routledge-Studies-in-Labour-Economics/book-series/RSLE

Trade Union Finance

How Labor Organizations Raise and Spend Money

Marick F. Masters
and Raymond F. Gibney

Routledge
Taylor & Francis Group
LONDON AND NEW YORK

First published 2023
by Routledge
4 Park Square, Milton Park, Abingdon, Oxon OX14 4RN

and by Routledge
605 Third Avenue, New York, NY 10158

Routledge is an imprint of the Taylor & Francis Group, an informa business

British Library Cataloguing-in-Publication Data
A catalogue record for this book is available from the British Library

Library of Congress Cataloging-in-Publication Data
Names: Masters, Marick Francis, 1954- author. | Gibney, Raymond, author.
Title: Trade union finance : how labor organizations raise and spend money / Marick F. Masters and Raymond Gibney.
Description: 1 Edition. | New York, NY : Routledge, 2023. | Series: Routledge studies in labour economics | Includes bibliographical references and index.
Identifiers: LCCN 2022047483 (print) | LCCN 2022047484 (ebook) | ISBN 9781032371382 (hardback) | ISBN 9781032371399 (paperback) | ISBN 9781003335474 (ebook)
Subjects: LCSH: Labor unions--Finance--United States. | Labor unions--United States--Accounting.
Classification: LCC HD6486.2.U5 M37 2023 (print) | LCC HD6486.2.U5
(ebook) | DDC 331.880973--dc23/eng/20220929
LC record available at https://lccn.loc.gov/2022047483
LC ebook record available at https://lccn.loc.gov/2022047484

ISBN: 978-1-032-37138-2 (hbk)
ISBN: 978-1-032-37139-9 (pbk)
ISBN: 978-1-003-33547-4 (ebk)

DOI: 10.4324/9781003335474

Typeset in Bembo
by SPi Technologies India Pvt Ltd (Straive)

Contents

Figures

Tables

Authors

Marick F. Masters is a Professor of Business at Wayne State University, Detroit, Michigan, USA.

Raymond F. Gibney is an Associate Professor of Management, School of Business Administration, Penn State Harrisburg, Middletown, Pennsylvania, USA.

Introduction

Unions have suffered a long-term decline in membership and attendant economic and political power. This decline begs the question of the financial health of unions. Money plays an important role in the formation and maintenance of unions as organizations. Opponents of organized labor often seek to enact policies which would hinder the ability of unions to raise money. The purpose of this book is to examine several questions about the financial position of unions. The book examines the financial resources and performance of 53 of the largest national unions in the United States over the years between 2006 and 2019. In essence, we analyze the balance sheets and income statements of these unions on aggregated and disaggregated bases. The book is organized into 16 chapters which cover how unions raise and spend money as well as how they manage money. It provides extensive information on how to analyze the finances of unions and to use this information to prepare for collective bargaining and other aspects of labor-management relations. The book addresses unions' financial capacities to withstand strikes. It also examines how more munificent unions might finance growing efforts to organize workers in traditionally non-union sectors and companies, such as Amazon, Apple, and Starbucks.

Organized labor in the United States faces challenges on many dimensions (Greenhouse 2019; Chaison 2006; Rosenfeld 2014). Declining membership erodes power at the bargaining table and in politics. Systemic economic, political, and technological forces undermine labor's base. Opposition groups mobilize to delegitimize unions. The societal deck seems stacked against labor. No clear path to revival emerges amidst structural deconstruction.

The withering plight of labor in America begs the question of its financial health. Anti-unionists seek to not only delegitimize but also defund labor unions (Lafer 2017). Financial erosion and destabilization lessen a union's capacity to service members and organize new ones. Ironically, anti-union activists gain momentum as unions recede. The temptation to exploit weakness proves irresistible. A vicious cycle ensues: union decay intensifies efforts to weaken labor even more institutionally, resulting in further erosion. The cost of simply maintaining the status quo rises, draining union energy and resources, contributing further to the downward spiral. Over time, the downturn reaches a point that raises questions about the viability of unions. Does labor deserve a seat at the corporate or

DOI: 10.4324/9781003335474-1

governmental decision-making tables? Or, is it so organizationally marginalized as to justify exclusion? Labor confronts this crossroads frontally today.

We address the financial condition of unions in the United States. Financial resources constitute a major component, along with human capital (members, officers, union employees, volunteers, allied groups, and community activists), of the institutional and operational factors that enable unions to exert influence and power (Willman, Bryson, and Forth 2020). The availability of money directly influences labor's capacity to acquire and deploy human capital with sufficient expertise, equipment, and other necessary support.

We focus on the wealth, revenues, disbursements, and financial performance of 53 major national unions in the United States, each with a total membership of over 5,000 in 2006. Our study covers the years between 2006 and 2019, providing a snapshot of the financial standing of these organizations on aggregated and disaggregated bases both before and after the Great Recession. It also examines several special topics, including how to analyze unions' financial data and reports; dues and other sources of member-based income (MBI); union political spending; union officers' and employees' compensation (including benefits); the relationship between membership and financial wherewithal; union corruption; the financial capacity of unions to withstand strikes; and the means by which more munificent unions might finance ongoing organizing efforts to unionize such corporate behemoths as Amazon, Apple, and Starbucks, which have opposed unions vigorously. We further comment on what the future of labor might look like if it were to succeed in organizing on scale magnitudes of order beyond recent contemplation.

Major Questions

Past research on union finances is sparse, notwithstanding the availability of relatively detailed data found in annual financial disclosure forms since the enactment of the Labor-Management Reporting and Disclosure Act (LMRDA, called Landrum-Griffin) in 1959. A paucity of scholarship exists with respect to both the empirical and theoretical dimensions of this subject, despite the accessibility of comprehensive data (Strauss 1975). Financial matters often only generate public interest when evidence of illegalities or improprieties surface (witness the extensive media attention paid to revelations of financial misconduct at the highest levels of the United Auto Workers [UAW] since the scandal first broke open in July 2017 [Goeddeke and Masters 2021a; 2021b]). Indeed, reported incidents of financial misfeasance or malfeasance sully the union image and may intensify public scrutiny, governmental prosecution, and regulation. In general, however, observers and scholars pay more attention to the role of unions in financing political campaigns than they do on the role of finances in the operation of labor organizations. While federal law prevents unions (and corporations) from contributing money to federal candidates and parties directly from their treasuries, it does permit them to establish political action committees (PACs), through which money collected on a voluntary basis from members and their families can be contributed to such candidates and parties, though within prescribed limits on the amount that can be donated (Congressional Research Service 2018). In its major ruling in 2010 in *Citizens*

United v Federal Election Commission, the US Supreme Court legitimized the use of union and corporate treasury funds to conduct electoral advocacy activities that were restricted under then-existing federal campaign-financing laws, leading to an explosion in the infusion so-called dark money into federal campaigns.

Several major questions guide our study:

- What financial information are unions required to disclose under federal law?
- How does one interpret the information unions report on financial disclosure forms, especially the LM-2 report?
- How does one analyze the financial position of a union?
- What are the implications of a union's financial position for collective bargaining and labor-management relations?
- What role does money play in the formation and maintenance of unions?
- How much does it cost employees to join a union?
- How much wealth do unions possess?
- How do unions invest their money?
- What are the current retiree-benefit obligations of unions?
- How do unions raise money?
- How do unions spend money?
- How much do unions spend on administration and compensation of officers and staff?
- To what extent can unions finance their operating budgets from recurring sources of revenue?
- To what extent are unions operated efficiently?
- To what extent are unions experiencing financial stress?
- What is the relationship between union membership and financial capacity?
- How much do unions spend on political action?
- To what extent is there corruption in the finances of unions?
- How can unions raise more money from their existing base?
- How can unions finance the new wave of unionizing directed to selected corporate giants such as Amazon, Apple, and Starbucks?
- What might labor look like if it were to massively structure to leverage money and derive economies of scale?

Sample, Data, and Measures

We examine the aggregated financial resources of 53 national labor organizations filing annual disclosure LM-2 reports with the US Department of Labor (DOL), where they are maintained by its Office of Labor-Management Standards (OLMS), for the years between 2006 and 2019, computing two-year averages for the financials (2006–2007, 2008–2009, 2010–2011, 2012–2013, 2014–2015, 2016–2017, 2018–2019). Unions with $250,000 or more in annual receipts file the LM-2 forms; labor organizations with smaller annual receipts file less detailed LM-3 reports. We chose the sample to include discrete national unions with at least 5,000 members in 2006 which have remained in existence as stand-alone entities through 2019. The LM-2 forms are available online from the DOL's OLMS website.

Sample

We report the 53 nationals and their respective memberships over seven two-year intervals in Table I.1. The overall sample includes unions which reported a total of nearly 18.80 million members in 2018–2019 (averaged over the two years). Over the seven-interval stretch, the unions' total membership climbed modestly from 18.38 million members in 2006–2007 to 18.79 million in 2018–2019 after having dropped 3.1 percent to 17.816 million in 2010–2011. In 2018–2019, six unions had two-year membership averages over one million, with another five reporting between 500,000 and one million. Ten unions showed averaged membership between 200,000 and 500,000. Twenty-one unions had under 100,000 members, with six of these at under 20,000.

The unions' average membership ranged from a low of 336,155 in 2010–2011 to 354,606 in 2018–2019. Twenty-nine unions had lower membership in 2018–2019 than at the beginning interval. Ten unions, including the AMA (−65.4 percent), UNITE (−33.7 percent), BAKERY (−30.6 percent), and the UMW (−28 percent), had at least 20 percent fewer members at the end compared to the beginning of these seven intervals. Nine unions, in contrast, gained more than 20 percent in membership from the same points of reference.

Data

In addition to reporting data on the union membership, which are included in the financial disclosures, we examine the specific categories of assets, liabilities, receipts, and disbursements which are enumerated. The line items reported in the LM-2 form appear in Chapter 2, which discusses how to read and analyze union financial information available under the LMRDA.

Measures

Two types of financial measures are reported: resource and performance. The resource measures include assets, liabilities, receipts, and disbursements, aggregated across unions or reported individually by each separate national organization. Performance measures include operating capacity, liquidity, survivability, stress, and efficiency. Again, these data are displayed on an aggregated basis across the 53 unions for the seven two-year intervals; they also appear on a disaggregated basis to show the variability among these nationals. Chapter 2 discusses how these performance ratios are calculated and interpreted.

Organization of Book

The remainder of the book is divided into 16 chapters. Chapter 1 addresses the question of why money matters to such non-profit organizations as labor unions. It focuses on the role of money in the formation and maintenance of unions. As organizations, unions need money to perform certain services, as reliance exclusively on in-kind assistance or volunteers is impractical if an entity is to operate

Table I.1 Membership by Interval

Union	*Members*							*% Change from 2006–2007 to 2018–2019 (%)*
	2006–2007	*2008–2009*	*2010–2011*	*2012–2013*	*2014–2015*	*2016–2017*	*2018–2019*	
Air Line Pilots Association	61,275	55,742	59,588	48,999	50,833	56,188	61,813	0.9
Air traffic controllers	14,610	15,160	16,138	16,195	16,464	17,252	18,496	26.6
Aircraft Mechanics Association	10,239	3,683	2,807	3,142	3,218	3,380	3,546	−65.4
Allied Pilots Association	11,040	9,516	9,354	9,694	12,304	14,498	14,332	29.8
Auto workers	5,01,679	3,93,114	3,78,666	3,86,964	4,06,053	4,23,417	3,97,266	−20.8
Bakery, tobacco, and grain	93,341	88,168	83,500	76,888	71,492	67,278	64,773	−30.6
Boilermakers	64,110	63,960	60,126	56,399	54,742	52,145	49,264	−23.2
Bricklayers	95,121	93,585	83,702	77,049	72,909	73,591	73,477	−22.8
Carpenters	523,471	492,415	437,451	413,428	430,011	435,348	436,769	−16.6
Communications workers	639,809	521,277	486,130	471,058	625,717	644,845	644,489	0.7
Directors Guild of America Inc	13,551	14,394	14,733	15,251	16,035	17,039	17,988	32.7
Electrical Workers IBEW	698,458	706,481	670,560	660,083	660,494	668,839	675,150	−3.3
Elevator constructors	26,411	29,153	27,865	25,411	25,185	27,056	28,706	8.7
Engineers, operating	400,638	405,045	386,668	380,174	375,913	378,930	398,242	−0.6
Engineers, professional and technical	60,502	63,768	67,829	61,931	60,419	59,465	58,502	−3.3
Firefighters	280,698	294,882	295,330	294,385	297,848	306,228	316,837	12.9
Food and commercial workers	1,307,529	1,315,220	1,288,539	1,273,235	1,271,477	1,256,092	1,239,213	−5.2
Government Employees AFGE	232,463	257,000	284,658	300,422	312,784	329,076	328,131	41.2
Insulators	20,801	22,204	21,005	21,905	22,212	22,308	22,404	7.7
Iron workers	130,678	138,208	124,814	121,794	126,110	128,159	129,194	−1.1
Journeymen and allied trades	49,863	57,076	56,244	55,292	58,034	65,353	77,458	55.3
Laborers	642,483	650,789	595,474	564,532	547,329	578,976	572,995	−10.8

(*Continued*)

Table I.1 (Continued)

Union	*Members*							*% Change from 2006–2007 to 2018–2019 (%)*
	2006–2007	*2008–2009*	*2010–2011*	*2012–2013*	*2014–2015*	*2016–2017*	*2018–2019*	
Letter Carriers, National Association	288,078	288,826	281,683	267,415	274,250	290,442	289,086	0.4
Letter carriers, rural	109,729	112,956	108,134	103,441	103,628	110,995	115,754	5.5
Longshore and Warehouse Union	38,466	41,592	44,963	37,180	34,693	35,542	36,156	−6.0
Longshoremen's Association	43,500	43,500	21,750	43,500	39,132	36,282	32,142	−26.1
Machinists	647,632	627,741	588,870	573,685	569,094	564,134	576,502	−11.0
Mine workers, united	83,081	77,817	78,135	73,869	72,639	65,321	59,795	−28.0
Musicians	89,660	88,886	88,722	79,650	77,074	74,580	72,797	−18.8
National Education Association	2,967,654	3,225,520	3,185,929	3,036,061	2,958,047	2,977,900	2,989,225	0.7
Novelty and Production Workers	17,296	14,440	14,397	16,419	19,200	17,993	16,906	−2.3
Office and professional employees	103,966	105,706	100,409	1,00,286	103,435	108,757	94,745	−8.9
Painters	130,588	129,136	1,12,320	104,540	105,242	109,876	111,988	−14.2
Plasterers and cement masons	42,551	42,921	39,819	38,203	38,228	41,744	44,262	4.0
Plumbers	329,603	344,864	337,778	330,016	330,255	338,933	352,072	6.8
Postal workers, American	279,704	258,069	248,548	242,271	243,048	246,427	229,583	−17.9
Roofers	23,401	23,241	22,139	21,195	20,776	21,540	22,450	−4.1
Seafarers	36,927	33,896	32,203	30,661	29,436	29,292	29,469	−20.2
Security police, fire professionals	19,858	26,149	25,308	17,656	17,031	17,006	18,061	−9.1
Service employees	1,633,729	1,832,386	1,919,195	1,872,170	1,890,858	1,910,260	1,940,557	18.8
Sheet metal, air, rail, and transportation workers	149,945	148,678	137,667	168,648	205,399	203,341	204,964	36.7
Stage and picture operators	106,876	111,604	1,12,464	115,364	120,484	130,168	142,371	33.2
State county and municipal employees	1451,892	1,484,179	1,444,436	1,382,617	1,321,127	1,323,192	1,333,579	−8.1

Steelworkers	726,741	665,858	605,946	606,727	590,613	565,369	578,501	−20.4
Teachers	827,281	872,763	880,511	1,207,850	1,605,294	1,568,027	1,681,160	103.2
Teamsters	1,410,806	1,383,469	1,318,331	1,257,977	1,292,419	1,276,724	1,356,978	−3.8
Transit Union	182,461	189,234	190,880	191,278	193,142	198,489	200,816	10.1
Transport workers	116,414	121,572	118,152	115,582	116,445	126,938	137,187	17.8
Treasury Employees Union	77,720	81,111	85,601	82,159	78,564	79,854	79,914	2.8
Unite Here	459,857	303,506	231,683	257,015	264,104	276,676	304,888	−33.7
University Professors	41,103	41,184	39,590	37,594	38,582	40,952	44,305	7.8
Utility workers	50,000	50,000	50,000	50,000	50,000	45,395	44,745	−10.5
Writers Guild West	18,276	19,118	19,972	20,962	21,661	22,971	24,124	32.0
Average	**346,859**	**348,693**	**338,428**	**336,155**	**346,065**	**348,690**	**354,606**	**2.2**
Total	18,383,552	18,480,752	17,936,702	17,816,207	18341,471	18,4,0,568	18,794,114	

independently and with the autonomy necessary to respond to routine matters of any sizable scale as well as exigencies that inevitably arise. Maintaining a union requires assembling the capital necessary to acquire the expertise and skills needed for effective representation. How well a union manages its money is not only relevant from a fiduciary perspective but also in generating sufficient money to finance organizational upgrades and updates. This first chapter also reviews past research on union finances in the United States, United Kingdom, and Australia and provides a framework to illustrate the role of finances in union formation and maintenance.

Chapter 2 on "Financial Reporting and Analysis" discusses that data unions are required to report under the LMRDA, particularly on the LM-2 form, which provides the most comprehensive disclosures unions make under federal law. It informs on how to read the disclosure information available to provide insight into the financial capacity and health of the unions under study. Chapter 2 further discusses the various financial measures used to summarize data for a similar purpose. We examine how one might analyze the financial position of a union in understanding its bargaining and political position.

Chapter 3 portrays the "big picture" of union finances, including aggregated assets, liabilities, receipts, and disbursements of the sample of national labor organizations. We also present disaggregated data to show patterns of inter-union variation in how they invest money and the extent to which they have liabilities. Chapter 4 examines the income unions derive from members through dues, fees, and other assessments. It also shows the unions' dues rates for selected years.

Chapter 5 examines the unions' balance sheet, reporting major categories of assets and liabilities. Chapters 6 and 7 examine the disaggregated data on union revenues and disbursements, while Chapter 8 reports on the measure of union financial performance.

Chapter 9 examines union finances on a per-member basis to permit comparison across labor organizations. In Chapter 10, we report on union political spending, covering electoral spending reported under federal election laws and made available online through Opensecrets.com. The data supplement information available from the unions' LM-2, which do not report on union spending made from non-treasury sources, such as voluntary contributions to PACs. Chapter 11 deals with the relative amounts unions spend on compensation and benefits for officers and employees. Chapter 12 reports on union corruption. It examines the extent to which there is evidence of such corruption and includes a discussion of the recent revelations of scandal at the UAW, which raises the question of when a government takeover of a union may be warranted due to systemic corruption. Chapter 13 provides data on the top ten unions ranked on each of the financial dimensions. It examines the concentration of union financial resources among the top ten over the several two-year reporting periods. Chapter 14 addresses in more detail the financial capacity of unions to withstand strikes. In recent years, an uptick in strikes has occurred, leading some to speculate that ongoing global economic problems centered on chokes in the supply chain triggered by the COVID-19 pandemic may create a climate more conducive to labor conflicts. Chapter 15 discusses how unions might leverage their financial wherewithal to support nascent organizing efforts in such corporate giants as Amazon, Apple, and Starbucks, where start-up organizing has shown some promise in achieving success winning representational rights. Chapter 16 looks at what labor might look like if unions were to massively restructure to leverage their money and garner additional economies of scale, which would free up more money to invest in start-up drives.

1 Why Money Matters

This chapter examines why money matters to unions given their non-profit status. In practice, unions need money to build the organizational capacity to represent their members. Such capacity and its effective usage provide a rationale for workers to join and support the organization. Several theories illuminate the question of why money matters, including perspectives on collective mobilization, administrative and representational orientation, strategic choice, and resource dependency. How unions raise, spend, and manage money influences their success in formation and maintenance, which is a continuing consideration rather than a set of one-off decisions. We provide a systems-based conceptual framework on the role of money in unions *qua* organizations. A review of the available research on the topic of union finances in the United States, the United Kingdom, and Australia reveals that few studies provide a systematic analysis of the financial resources and performance of unions on a disaggregated basis. Aggregated data by definition mask the variation among unions in their financial resources and performance, though the aggregated trends provide a basis for making important inter-union comparisons.

Labor organizations operate as non-profit entities. Technically, the US Internal Revenue Code (IRC) classifies them under section 501(c) (5), which renders them tax-exempt. Under the IRC, labor organizations constitute "an association of workers" with their primary purpose being to improve working conditions and advance occupations.

Given the lack of a profit motivation, the question arises as to why money should matter to labor organizations. The answer involves theoretical and practical considerations. Taking the latter first, unions need money to perform basic functions vital to their organizational survival. These functions include representing employees at the bargaining table and in grievance procedures, electioneering and lobbying, litigating, and organizing new members. When a labor organization grows beyond a small group of loosely connected individuals into a sizable collectivity in these various decision-making forums, it requires the resources necessary to operate in a credible manner, including sufficient personnel, expertise, technology, equipment, and space. Volunteers and in-kind assistance (such as the provision of office space and transportation on a no-charge basis) will carry any group only

DOI: 10.4324/9781003335474-2

so far without meeting major operational constraints. Acquiring and maintaining these resources to build sufficient infrastructure for purposes of mobilization and representation costs money, the effective management of which matters for reasons of organizational performance and fiduciary obligation.

While the practical need for money is self-evident, it does not explain the broader role of finances in the formation and maintenance of the union organization. What role does money play in this capacity? This question involves considerations at both the individual and organizational levels as to the incentives available to induce and maintain membership.

Theoretical Perspectives

The finances of labor organizations play a role in the formation and maintenance of unions in several ways. Financial matters enter the recurring calculation of the costs and benefits of joining and sustaining a union that individuals make. They also pertain to the choices that collectivities or organizations—inchoate and mature—make in inducing and maintaining membership through the provision of benefits at an acceptable price.

The resulting cost–benefit calculus requires solving a three-order problem that unions perpetually face (Willman and Bryson 2009). The first order pertains to overcoming the inertia or natural resistance to joining a group. The second-order problem considers how to price the cost of union membership, which will depend to a certain extent on the nature and level of benefits anticipated. The third-order considerations relate to setting organizational priorities and allocating resources accordingly in order to fulfill the mission. In a nutshell, there is no cost-free method of forming and maintaining a union, regardless of the degree to which it relies on volunteers, donations, or in-kind assistance. Even the tasks of assembling, equipping, and deploying *volunteers* require resources which cost money. A simple organization incurs expenses for which payment must be made. The lack of money imposes severe limitations on organizational capacity both in terms of providing benefits and mobilizing for such provisions.

Collective mobilization theory provides an explanation for how unions can overcome the initial barriers to joining and involving individuals in sufficient numbers to launch a viable organization. At their very inception, unions must offer a menu of incentives appealing enough to offset the costs of joining. In this regard, one central consideration involves the type of benefits to offer, which often boils down to their exclusive or collective nature. Exclusive benefits accrue to only those who bear the costs of membership. Collective benefits accrue to individuals regardless of whether they pay the cost of membership. By definition, collective benefits tempt recipients to free ride: a rational decision in one's self-interest suggests that it is logical to reap the collective benefit, to which one by definition cannot be excluded, without incurring the cost. Unions, as suggested, may seek to offset this temptation by offering exclusive or, so-called selective, benefits. However, they still must garner sufficient resources to provide such benefits to overcome the initial barriers, inertia, or resistance to joining. In the absence of the capacity to fund the provision of selective incentives, unions must appeal to other motivations, which may involve conformity with social norms, the potential realignment of the political power structure so as to generate a more equitable distribution of resources, or the remedy of societal grievances which motivate action. In short, sufficient impetus must exist to impel a person to take some risk or incur some cost to join a union at a stage when tangible benefits are only potential or uncertain in delivery. Some individuals arguably derive personal satisfaction from participating in a group effort to benefit a wider set of people. Since such satisfaction is a benefit which accrues to people individually, it may provide sufficient motivation to warrant joining a union and participating in its activities. Furthermore, the personal satisfaction one might derive, unlike certain material benefits, does not reduce the amount available to others. In fact, the benefits may prove contagious in that positive attitudes may spread across people engaged in a common pursuit. Thus, the very collective nature of these more intangible rewards actually serves to motivate individuals to overcome the tendency to free ride from a purely rationalistic standpoint focused exclusively on material goods which by nature are fixed in quantity.

At the same time unions need to formulate a portfolio of enticements, they must work to minimize the costs of membership, especially before any initial benefits are available. Therefore, unions need to find ways to defray some of the initial costs of union formation (e.g. donated office space, volunteers, pro bono expertise, and subsidized transportation). They also must seek to limit the costs incidental to joining a union, particularly if employers or other forces in a community mobilize resistance. In this vein, unions must often provide representation to current or prospective members who suffer retaliation or injury as a result of their initial pro-union efforts. Unions essentially attempt to protect workers who go out on a limb in organizing drives from adverse treatment. Such protection serves to signal to workers that it may be worthwhile to take some risks in forming the union because the organization has its back.

To form a critical mass, unions must possess the capacity to communicate effectively. Acquiring this capacity, in turn, requires the expenditure of time and money and often necessitates hiring qualified personnel. Unions need the technology and expertise to exploit the rapidly changing media of communications. If unions can communicate an appealing menu of benefits, including helping members who are vulnerable to employer retaliation, they go a long way toward obviating the first-order problem.

Once unions solve this widely challenging first-order problem, a second-level challenge arises over how much to charge for ongoing membership, especially in the form of dues and related fees. As suggested, this calculation depends substantially on the degree of effort required to attain desired benefits, given the difficulty in procuring their attainment. Individuals certainly cannot be expected to pay more than they can afford or anticipate receiving in net benefits, even allowing for the inclusion of multifaceted and non-pecuniary incentives. A relevant factor in calculating the price of membership is the ontological nature of the union organization, particularly with respect to its administrative vis-à-vis democratic orientation. Providing exclusive benefits through bargaining or securing collective benefits through political action may demand the mobilization of considerable resources. An innate tendency to rationalize administratively or bureaucratically results from pressures to build this organizational capacity.

The potential tensions between administrative and democratic orientation are often juxtaposed as intrinsically centrifugal. In this formulation, rising demands for services pressure unions to increase paid staff—and to bureaucratize. "Rationalization" raises the cost of doing union business. As Barbash (1969: 153) states: "The most pervasive way in which rationalization has taken hold in the union's internal management is the continuing replacement of the volunteer by the paid full-time officer." In increasingly complex employment relations systems, unions represent members (and non-member employees in bargaining units) in many legally and technically complicated situations that require expertise and due diligence. The professionalization of union services is a necessary response to this reality (Clark 1992). Growth in staff—clerical and professional—raises the need for more managers, which adds layers to the operation. However, bureaucracy in and of itself need not displace rank-and-file involvement or democratic participation. The efficient and effective operation of union business arguably gains from acquiring the organizational capacity to provide the benefits associated with union membership and participation. Schumpeter (1947: 206) observes aptly in regard to the reconciliation between administrative rationalization and democratic practice "that bureaucracy is not an obstacle to democracy but an inevitable complement to it." Nonetheless, the innate forces behind bureaucratizing impel unions to raise more money to fund the organizational infrastructure (Willman, Bryson, and Forth 2020).

As member-based collectivities, labor organizations logically expect dues, or other forms of member-based income (MBI), to offer a major source of revenue. They may complement this stream of funding with grants, governmental contracts (directly or, indirectly, through employers), and alliances that expand their operational capacity.

At all times, even when in a state of relative stability or growth, unions must make decisions about how to allocate resources—in order to solve the third-order problem. Operationally, this problem relates to how to allocate the resources that flow into a union to maximize benefits. Budgeting and financial management go to the heart of translating organizational goals and strategies into action. If unions fail to put resources behind their expressed goals, then they will accomplish little more than uttering platitudes. A failure to follow up with operational commitments invites cynicism and revolt.

From a strategic-choice theoretic perspective, unions set strategies and attendant goals to drive the distribution of financial and other resources. Money implements strategy. Strategy, at least in a formulated state, should dictate resource allocations, but gaps between goals and actions occur all too frequently in the normal course of organizational affairs.

How unions allocate money also depends on environmental and organizational factors which affect the availability and accessibility of resources. Resource dependency theorists argue that organizations respond to dependencies by trying to shape conditions that support the continual flow of needed resources or to alter the terrain so as to provide alternative sources. Thus, unions whose members depend on lawmakers as employers will arguably seek to exert their political clout to create favorable workplace settings and conditions for the public employees they represent. Similarly, unions which depend on favorable trade balances to protect members' jobs may lobby against bilateral or multilateral trade agreements which pose a threat. Somewhat unholy alliances between corporations and unions which gain from protectionist trade policies may result from common dependencies.

In sum, financial considerations permeate in the formation and maintenance of labor organizations. Delicate balances are continually struck between financing the provision of benefits and controlling the costs of operations in order to induce membership—current and prospective. The determination of relative costs and benefits of membership in complex environmental and organizational contexts raises numerous practical judgments, which further elaborate the significance of financial matters in the business of unionism. These judgments, for example, pertain to whether or not a union should mount a new organizing campaign or invest heavily in the fortunes of a presidential candidate.

Conceptual Framework

We develop a conceptual framework in two stages. The first involves putting financial affairs into a systems context within which all unions operate. The second concerns demarcating the different levels within the system at which unions conduct their operations. Integral to the formation, maintenance, and operation of a union, financial matters occur in the same contexts that encompass the employment relations system. Accordingly, various environmental and organizational factors impinge on union finances, which, in turn, affect the range of activities undertaken by any given labor organization (see Figure 1.1). These factors shape the level of financial resources a union can assemble and how money is managed. Financial determinations, in turn, affect the nature and scope of union activities aimed at achieving certain outcomes at the bargaining table, in politics, in the courts, and on worksites. These outcomes recycle back into the contexts in which unions operate in order to complete the circle of relevant activities. A circular flow of interactions and transactions governs financial operations. Anti-unionists seek to disrupt this flow in order to minimize the capacity of unions to perform on economic, legal, and political dimensions.

The centerpiece of this model involves financial resources, performance, and management. Resources include the inflow of money on recurring and non-recurring bases from assessments on members (and non-member represented employees covered by union-security agreements), returns on investments (US treasury securities stocks), and receipts from business transactions, including the sale of assets and consumer products (e.g. credit cards) plus property rentals. The financial picture of a union, therefore, involves examining revenue streams and the balance of assets and liabilities which require careful management.

Financial performance includes operational capacity, liquidity, survivability, stress, return on assets, and efficiency. The return earned on expenditures and investments bears on performance. Financial management deals with how unions allocate revenues, with insight provided by the extent to which recurring sources

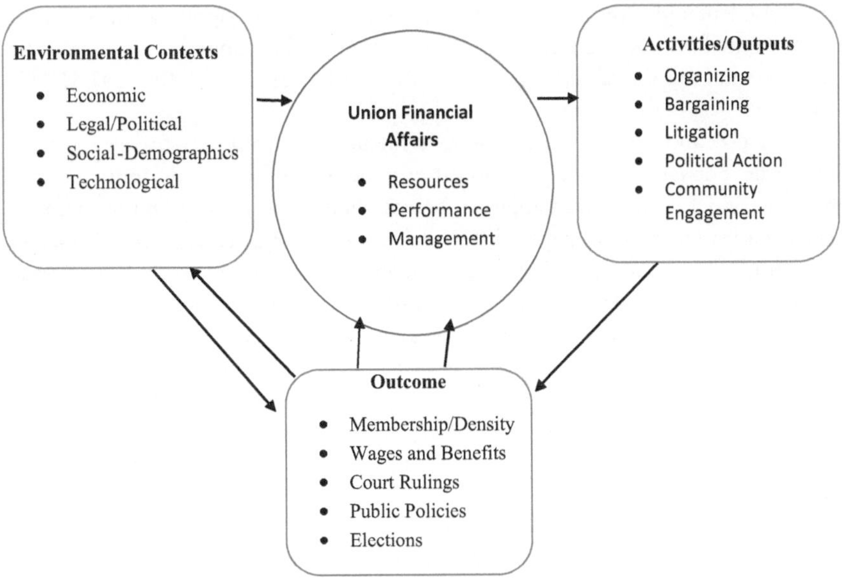

Figure 1.1 Conceptual Framework on the Role of Union Finances.

of revenue cover operating expenses, the administrative efficiency of expenditures, and the weight placed on representation, bargaining, political action, and organizing.

The availability of financial resources directly affects the range of activities unions may conduct. Specific resource allocations reflect union priorities and operational requirements. To varying degrees, unions engage in activities relating to the work site representation of members and represented employees, electioneering and lobbying, litigation, public relations, member education and communications, and organizing. Unions pursue these activities to affect various outcomes which define their relative position in society. These outcomes include membership and density, wages and benefits, court rulings, elections, public-policy enactments, and public opinion.

In a systems framework, unions operate within environmental contexts. Labor and product markets affect how unions function. Subsumed in the environmental area is the industrial and occupational composition of the workforce, which bears directly in the role of unions given their harmony or disharmony with certain employment trends. Other relevant factors include unemployment, the demand for employers' products and services, and the financial condition of governmental entities which employ union members. The interrelated legal and political contexts also impact financial affairs. As mentioned, Right-to-Work (RTW) laws and kindred measures aimed at eroding labor's position may negatively impact both union membership and financial capacity. Curbing union bargaining rights, for example, may shrink the potential appeal of unions. Disallowing dues checkoffs raises the cost of collecting dues from members. Anti-union legislative initiatives force the mobilization of potentially expensive resistance campaigns. Anti-union forces also entangle unions in costly litigation over their rights, as occurred in efforts to disallow the legitimacy of agency shops in the public sector, which the US Supreme Court invalidated in its June 27, 2018, decision in *Janus v. AFSCME, Council 31.*

The social and technological contexts further impact union financial affairs. Reflecting changes in societal populations, demographic trends influence the groups to which unions must appeal. The cost–benefit evaluation on union membership varies across demographic lines, including race, gender, and age. Minorities and women may gain more economic benefits from union representation because of their generally lower pay levels. By raising wages and reducing income inequality, unions offer more relative advantage to those groups. An aging workforce also changes the incentives to join a union. Labor has traditionally emphasized seniority-based personnel practices and retirement security through pensions and retiree healthcare. The appeal of seniority-related practices, wage increases, and retirement benefits may vary across age groups, which can influence the organizational priorities of unions.

Technology may lead to the elimination of certain kinds of work among unionized workers as have taken place extensively within the manufacturing sector through robotics and automation. The resulting job losses adversely impact the revenue flow into union coffers and may force the allocation of more resources to organize new members to replenish the depleted ranks.

The outputs that result from the acquisition and expenditure of funds reflect the governing and administrative decisions of the labor organizations. The priorities manifested in these allocations correspond with the mix of preferences of union officers, staff, and rank and file. To varying degrees, the outputs fall into organizing, community engagement, electioneering, lobbying, collective bargaining, grievance handling, striking, and litigating.

Ultimately, unions engage in these activities to obtain favorable outcomes. Recruiting and retaining members so as to increase density and attendant power vis-à-vis employers is one clearly desirable outcome. Raising wages, providing for job security, enhancing healthcare, retirement, and other benefits comprise another significant realm of preferable outcomes. Securing favorable court rulings and public-policy enactments that protect and expand labor rights and standards add to the mix. These outcomes, in turn, affect directly the financial condition of the organizations and the contexts within which they operate. For example, the number of union members influences the revenue intake of the labor organization and the cost of representation. It also affects density in an industry, which influences bargaining power relative to unionized employers. And union membership and its density influence the political environment, which, through the powers of appointment and election, shape legal developments through the judiciary at all levels of government.

Dependent to varying degrees on environmental conditions and the activities of other organizations, unions in the employment relations system operate at three distinctive levels in order to achieve their goals (Katz, Kochan, and McKersie 1986). As shown in Figure 1.2, the levels are the (1) macro-political, legal, and economic points of decision-making, (2) organizational, and (3) work site.

Level	Union Activities
Macro-Political, Economic, Legal	Electoral Participation Lobbying Litigation Alliance Building
Organizational	Collective Bargaining Corporate Campaigns
Work Sites	Grievance Procedure Workers' Compensation Informal Consultation

Figure 1.2 The Levels of Union Activities to Influence Employment Relations System.

At each, unions pursue a variety of activities to protect and advance their institutional interests as well as the goals they seek for members and the broader society.

To influence macro-level conditions, unions engage extensively in political action, legal advocacy, and alliance building. More specifically, they participate in elections through making contributions to campaigns and parties (via political action committees [PACs]), electioneering advertising, and voter education and mobilization. Labor's competitive advantage in this regard is its capacity to mobilize large numbers at the grassroots to convey political messages to rank and file on a personal basis. In the political context, unions also engage extensively in lobbying lawmakers at all levels of government. In addition, they keep a watchful eye on various governmental agencies that make decisions about labor-management relations (e.g. the National Labor Relations Board, Federal Labor Relations Authority, and numerous equivalent state bodies), trade, and other significant policy matters. As to legal advocacy, unions may instigate or respond to litigation involving the determination of the respective rights of employers and employees. For example, they participate in litigation associated with determining the employment status (i.e., employee or independent contractor) of various types of workers, including drivers for the companies of Uber, FedEx, and Amazon. Alliance building is another important sphere of activity at this level, where unions work with civil rights organizations, churches, and an array of other advocacy groups to influence decision-making and increase support for union-related efforts to organize members and win bargaining campaigns against recalcitrant employers.

At the organizational level, the focus shifts to collective bargaining and ancillary activities that directly impact the terms and conditions of employment for represented employees. Conducting a labor negotiation involves much more than merely designating a union officer to sit at the table and bargain for the best deal possible. Meticulous and expensive (in terms of time and potentially money) preparation is involved, as today's negotiations treat complicated matters regarding benefits (ranging from healthcare and retirement to paid sick time and family and medical leave), productivity and quality, and incentive-based compensation systems such as profit sharing. The complexities of modern-day collective bargaining may require expertise in actuarial calculations, benefits administration, profit sharing, gainsharing, as well as compliance with a wide array of legal and regulatory standards.

Perhaps no level of activity is more salient on a day-to-day basis, however, than what occurs at the work site. This is the point where union members interact among themselves and with their elected officers and paid union staff. Individual complaints and grievances are handled here, and how these matters are conducted can make or break a union and its leadership. If unions mishandle the grievance procedure through problematic representation, they invite discontent and defection, if not outright opposition. The devil is very much in the detail and how person-to-person communications are managed. Competent leaders and staff are essential to this task.

Previous Research

The body of literature on union finances is both sparse and disparate. The public availability of financial data mandated by the Labor-Management Reporting and Disclosure Act (LMRDA) never spawned the deep interest in the subject that some anticipated. As George Strauss (1975: 131) commented "Although the Landrum-Griffin Act required unions to file voluminous financial and other reports, relatively little use has been made of this potentially rich lode of data."

The more recent availability of the financial reports at no cost through online technology has done little to precipitate new interest in relevant research. While the decline in unions has undoubtedly contributed to this continuing paucity of research, it has not diminished the salience of the topic. Money becomes even more vital when organizations face existential threats as unions do today.

Published research in this area divides by geography and time. Geographically, research covers the United States, the United Kingdom, and Australia. Across countries, research on union finances tends to the empirical rather than theoretical. It also tends to be more institutional than quantitative, though a few hypothesis-testing analyses have emerged more recently. We present a summary in Table 1.1 on the relevant studies by country.

The United Kingdom

Research on the finances of unions in the United Kingdom covers data from 1936 to the most recent decade. Roberts' study (1956) examines selected years between 1936 and the early 1950s. It examines the income, political funds, and expenditures of all unions in the United Kingdom registering financial reports and the 18 largest national unions. Data reported include income from membership subscriptions, funds collected for political purposes, overall expenditures, and disbursements on selected benefits (such as sickness and funerals) and on working expenses (administrative costs). Results, in aggregate, show that union funding was higher both per capita and overall in the early 1950s than in 1936 but that subscription revenue from members rose more slowly than expenditures. Also, "working" expenses increased considerably as a share of overall spending, with disbursements on "friendly" benefits falling commensurately over the approximately 25 years.

Three major studies treat the subject using data from the early 1950s through the late 1980s (Latta 1972; Willman 1990; Willman, Morris, and Aston 1993).

Table 1.1 Selected Literature on Finances among Unions in the United States, the United Kingdom, and Australia

U.S. Studies	*U.K. Studies*	*Australian Studies*
Sakolski 1906 ***The Finances of American*** Trade Unions, (1905) 16 international, dues, and selected spending in 1905.	Roberts 1956. All registered unions and 18 largest unions, 1936–1950 (selected years): revenues (fees, contributions), benefits (sick, funeral, superannuation), branch, district, executive finances (amount spent, salaries, rent, etc.), political funds, expenditures	Wielgosz 1974. Sample: 125 federally registered unions reporting to the Industrial Registrar in Australia. Time period: 1971; data: assets and liabilities and their distribution; income
Kozmetsky 1950 Accounting practices; financial reports; uses of financial reports; in-depth case studies of ILGWU and USW; interviews with 27 international unions' officials; 100 financial reports (1946–1949)	Latta 1972. Trade Union Finance, Returns of unions of over 30,000 members in 1970; time period covered 1960–1970; 39 unions, 8.2 million or 82 percent of membership of affiliates of Trade Union Congress; income derived from contributions; average contribution per member, excluding political fund; per capita contributions; investments (municipal bonds and equity, rent and mortgages, bank interest, total investments); expenditures on benefits; working expense; per capita assets; political fund to pay; primarily, for affiliation fees with Labour party	Huntley 1976 and 1979. Sample: Australia's top 100 unions; time period: 1976, 1979; data: assets; membership subscription rates
Taft 1946. Dues and Initiation Fees in labor unions; 10 internationals; 250–300 locals	Willman 1990. The financial status and performance of British trade unions 1950–1988: all British trade unions registered, solvency, subscription dependency, acid test, shortfall, subscription proportion, return, net worth, regression analysis of per capita net worth with strikes, UE, shortfall, and return as predictors	Griffin and De Rozairo 1983. Sample: 137 unions filing with the Industrial Registrar in 1989; selected sample of 26 unions 1980; time period: 1980 and 1989; data: assets; membership subscription rates; financial performance ratios

(*Continued*)

Table 1.1 (Continued)

U.S. Studies	*U.K. Studies*	*Australian Studies*
Belfer 1949. Financial Resources of Trade Unions. 53 financial reports of trade unions of 107 of the largest surveyed, data circa 1947	Willman, Morris, and Aston 1993, Union Business: Trade Union Organization and Financial Reform in the Thacker Years, aggregated; 56 unions with 20,000 members in 1984 for disaggregated; net worth, subscription income, per capita measures, income, assets, expenditures, administrative costs; survey of finance officers of unions on income, investments, debt, financial management; survey of general secretaries; 53 item survey on finances and financial practices; time period 1950–1989, depending on measure.	
Belfer 1953. Trade Union Investment Policies: union assets, how they are distributed across various categories (cash, bonds, stock, real estate, mortgages, savings accounts, loans, special investments in controlled institutions) in circa 1952.	Willman and Bryson 2006. Accounting for Collective Action: Resource Acquisition and Mobilization in British Unions; all unions: solvency, reserves, income, expenditure (1990–2004); TUC affiliates over 100,000 members 2003–2004; off-budget resources, 1984–2004.	
Applebaum 1964. Financial Structure and Characteristics of labor organizations in a metropolitan area (Milwaukee, WI); data on 1961 year for 296 local unions on dues rates, initiation fees, cash and investments, assets, receipts, disbursements; statewide totals of 1348 locals for 1960) these data are aggregated across locals.	Willman, Bryson, and Forth 2020. Longitudinal analysis of British unions' aggregated financial state and case study one union. Union expenditures exceed member-based income, given in part because of the cost disease these organizations face. A natural creep in costs exceeds the rate of inflation. Unions must counter this trend by either liquidating assets or raising their dues/subscription rates.	
Applebaum 1965. An Analysis of the financial structure of local labor unions; Milwaukee and vicinity, 1961–1962 data, 111 locals 1961 and 1995 locals 1962; receipts, distributions, assets, liabilities, net assets, aggregated data.		

Applebaum 1966. Officer Turnover and Salary Structures in local unions; data on local unions (97) in Milwaukee area filing LM-2s for 1960–1962 inclusive; total and average salaries paid to highest paid officials; aggregated data.

Applebaum 1969. A Comparison of Officer Turnover and Salary Structures in Local Unions, 1960–1962 and 1963–1966 inclusive 97 locals in first period and 93 in second period; Milwaukee area, LM-2 filings, receipts, disbursements, payments of officers (aggregated) total and average salaries, selected years in relevant periods.

Troy, The Finances of American Unions, 1962–1969, aggregated assets, liabilities, net assets, same data per member, breakdown by local, intermediate, (regional, national and international), distribution of assets and liabilities, equity investments, dividend income, breakdown of receipts (recurring/nonrecurring) breakdown of disbursements (recurring, nonrecurring).

Strauss 1975. Union Financial Data, introduction to symposium

Allison 1975. Financial analysis of a local union. 500 local unions from CT, MA, RI which are affiliates of internationals; LM-2 1970–1972; 17 internationals; solvency, liquidity, debt burden, reserves, basic expenses as percentage of total receipts, expenditures on administrative expenses, education, per capita payments, professional fees as percent of total receipts.

(Continued)

Table 1.1 (Continued)

U.S. Studies	*U.K. Studies*	*Australian Studies*
Troy 1975. American unions and their wealth, 1962–1969: total assets, net assets, per capita assets and net assets, aggregated, total assets by local, central, national; breakdown of assets and liabilities (consolidated), consolidated investments in stocks, membership and receipts per union member.		
Applebaum and Blaine 1975. Compensation and Turnover of Union Officers, 1962–1967: random sample of 2,018 local unions in Ohio and WI.		
Ehrenberg and Goldberg 1977. Officer performance and compensation in local building trades unions; data from cross-section for 11 crafts in 68 cities in 1971; monthly dues, net local union assets, total annual dues collected, and the chief business agent's salary from LM-2 forms. Mean annual salary; mean salary/membership; estimates of salary with independent variables including total assets, total annual dues, and union members.		
Sandver 1978. Determinants of pay of large local union officers; 100 large local unions with over 1.6 million members; LM-2 data for years 1962; 1967; 1973; salary determinants include total assets, membership, dues, receipts/member, bargaining structure, wages.		
Sandver and Heneman 1980. Analysis and prediction of top national union officers total compensation; 100 largest national unions, 1962; 1967; 1973; mean compensation for top three of officers; independent variables include dues, total assets, total liabilities, cash disbursements, number of locals bargaining control.		

Sheflin and Troy 1983. Finances of American unions in 1970s; consolidates balance sheets 1962; 1969; 1976; assets and liabilities breakdowns; real assets and liabilities; distribution of assets across regional levels, consolidated income and expenditure breakdowns, current and real income.

Bennett 1991. Private sector unions: myth of decline; finances of private sector unions 1960; 1970; 1976; 1987; nominal receipts; real receipts; nominal receipts from dues, fees, fines, taxes, work permits (real and nominal) for each year above/same real receipts; per capita nominal receipts; union PAC receipts in nominal and real dollars, 1975–1976 and 1987–1988.

Masters and Atkin 1997, The finances of major U.S. unions; total assets and revenues, all unions, private sector unions, federal/postal only; 1995 [nominal and real]; concentration of assets in top unions, financial performance measures of 28 major unions, 1979–1993; operating income, net worth, per member measures of each

Latta (1972) examines the finances of a disaggregated sample of 39 unions with over 30,000 members in 1970, comparing selected data to averages for all registered unions in this period. Covering the years between 1960 and 1970, the study reports the unions' share of income derived from member contributions; average contributions per member; income from investments as a share of overall income; expenditures on benefits and working expenses as a percentage of overall disbursements; and the unions' per capita assets. Latta (1972) found that 21 of the 39 unions had less assets per capita in 1970 than in 1960. He also revealed that several of the unions reported expenditures exceeding income in several years. The third finding was that expenditures on working expenses rose faster than they did on benefits, reflecting the rise in the scope and volume of services provided by unions.

Willman (1990) updated the research by Roberts and Latta, examining the financial resources and performance of all UK unions registering financial reports for the years between 1950 and 1988. He reports the unions' real (inflation-adjusted) net worth (total assets minus total liabilities), real total income, and real total expenditures. He also calculates several measures of financial performance: solvency (total income divided by total expenditure); subscription dependency (subscription income divided by total income); acid test (total net worth, divided by total expenditure); shortfall (subscription, which includes dues and taxes of members income divided by total expenditure); subscription proportion (real per capita subscription income divided by real weekly pay); and return (total other income, i.e., non-subscription, divided by total net worth).

Willman (1990: 318) found that the unions maintained financial health and stability from 1950 to the mid-1960s but experienced "financial decline during membership growth from 1967 to 1981..." In seeming irony, however, the unions recovered somewhat in the 1980s, during a period of membership losses. During the entire time span (1950–1988), union income derived from members' subscriptions fell from 89 to 82 percent. Also, over the nearly 40 years, real total expenditures and administrative costs rose steadily, but spending on so-called friendly benefits was relatively stable, resulting in a sizable shift in the expenditure composition from the members "benefits" side to administrative expenses. In addition, while real income and expenditure per capita rose during the period of membership growth, real net worth per capita fell significantly. In terms of financial performance, the unions' condition deteriorated materially during the years between 1966 and 1970 on the acid test and shortfall measures, reflecting the decline in net assets (or worth) and the rise in expenditure relative to subscription income. The performance of the unions on the net worth relative to expenditure (acid test) indicator continued to fall sharply in the late 1970s, leading Willman (1990: 324) to conclude "that the financial problems of the late 1970s were so severe that unions were required to pay more attention to financial matters—hence the partial recovery in the 1980s..." Still, net worth relative to total expenditure hit a post-World War II low in the late 1980s. In addition, by 1988, the unions' shortfall position had fallen to the lowest point experienced since the 1966–1970 period, and overall solvency (at 1.05) hit another low point.

Willman, Morris, and Aston (1993) updated and extended the analysis of union finances in the United Kingdom. Their study updated aggregated data to include 1989, presented disaggregated information to show patterns of inter-union variation, and reported the results of a survey of union officials on financial management practices. It revealed that the unions in the United Kingdom, overall, showed a deteriorating financial position in 1989 compared to earlier years (1950–1988), with the unions' acid test and solvency ratios declining to record post-World War II lows. The unions' shortfall also fell to the lowest point over this period, reflecting a relative drop in subscription income compared to total expenditures. Willman et al. (1993) argued that unions shed assets during this post-war time period to cover expenditures that exceeded subscription income. Overall, Willman et al. (1993: 200) concluded that,

> In the aggregate, UK unions have suffered long-term financial debilitation in the post-war period. Although solvency has been maintained [though with shrinking reserves after expenditures]…, the real net worth of trade unions has fallen, particularly during periods of membership growth.

Based on their survey data, Willman et al. (1993) found that the management of union finances has grown both more centralized and professionalized. Unions had also grown more reliant on employers to collect their dues through automatic checkoffs. However, the unions had further (Willman et al. 1993: 201) displayed vastly different patterns in union financial wherewithal and practice. The results of their regression analysis of per capita real net worth demonstrated that strike activity, shortfall (subscription income relative to total income), and return (or total other income relative to net worth) were negatively correlated with per capita net worth. Thus, as the unions' income went down relative to expenditures and net worth, their per capita wealth rose.

Willman and Bryson (2009) conducted a study covering the finances of unions in the United Kingdom during the 1990–2004 period. They reported that aggregated union revenue from members rose faster than average earnings during this period but fell short of increases in expenditures. The solvency of the unions (total income relative to total expenditure) fell more or less continually from 1.06 to 0.99 between 1997 and 2003–2004. The unions' aggregated reserve ratio (total funds divided by total expenditures) also fell during the period between 1998 and 2003–2004, albeit unevenly. The reserve ratio dropped to 1.06 at the end of the period, compared to 1.15 in 1998 and 1.18 in 2000–2001.

Willman, Bryson, and Forth (2020) examined aggregated trends in union revenues and expenditures in the United Kingdom, coupled with an intensive case study. They found that unions in the United Kingdom, like other non-profits, suffer from a cost disease syndrome, which means that there are inherent organizational pressures which raise operational costs beyond the rate of inflation. Unable to generate enough money from members' subscriptions to cover these spending increases, unions may rely upon other sources of revenue, ranging from the liquidation of assets to raises in dues rates. This reality of cost creep makes it essential that unions improve their financial performance in terms of operating efficiently and generating sufficient income from sustainable sources.

The United States

In the United States, research on union finances is similarly limited. It may be classified into pre-1960 and post-1960 periods, which allows for the differentiation in the comprehensiveness of data covered before and after the enactment of the LMRDA of 1959. Before that year, researchers typically surveyed labor organizations directly to obtain information about their finances. Since then, they have relied on disclosures available from the US Department of Labor. The published studies in the post-1960 period include a stream of several articles which address the question of officers' compensation (see Applebaum 1966, 1969; Applebaum and Blain 1975; Ehrenberg and Goldberg 1977; Sandver 1978; Sandver and Heneman 1980; French, Hayashi, and Gray 1983).

Pre-1960, a mere handful of studies addressed union finances. Sakolski's (1906) dissertation on *The Finances of American Trade Unions* examined the dues and selected expenditures of 16 national unions in circa 1905. Taft (1946a,b) reported on the dues and initiation fees of ten internationals and between 250 and 300 local unions. Belfer (1949) studied the financial reports of 53 of the largest unions in the United States, reporting data from circa 1947. Kozmetsky (1950) expanded research to examine not only financial data but also unions' accounting practices, based on an inspection of 100 financial reports and interviews with officials at 27 international unions. He found that unions varied in terms of accounting practices used, but they provided detailed reports on income and disbursements that are generally audited. At the same time, the unions' reports did not reflect clearly on activities engaged in by unions nor the costs of supporting these activities; functional breakdowns did not exist. Furthermore, based on the interviews, union leaders did not use the financial data to guide administrative decision-making.

Belfer (1953) examined the investment policies of 42 national unions in the early 1950s. He reported how union funds were distributed across various asset categories, such as cash, bonds, and real estate. He found that unions invested nearly 73 and 11 percent, respectively, in cash and bonds. This led him to conclude (Belfer 1953: 346–347) that "trade unions today pursue an extremely conservative investment policy. Almost 85 percent of their assets are in cash, government bonds, and savings accounts."

Beginning in the 1960s, two streams of research emerged in the still relatively under-studied area of union finances in the United States. One, as mentioned, focused on the salaries of union officers while the second concerned the overall financial resources of unions. Applebaum (1966, 1969), and Applebaum and Blaine (1975) examined the compensation of top officers in various samples of local unions in Wisconsin and Ohio. In the last article, Applebaum and Blaine (1975) reported on the compensation and turnover of over 2,000 locals in Ohio and Wisconsin covering the 1962–1967 period. They found a negative association between the salary paid to local officers and turnover rates, suggesting that higher pay is correlated with lower levels of turnover.

Ehrenberg and Goldberg (1977), Sandver (1978), and Sandver and Heneman (1980) conducted statistical analyses of the correlates of different samples of union officers (local building unions, large local unions, and the largest national unions, respectively). Across these samples over different time periods (1971 for Erhenberg and Goldberg; 1962, 1967, and 1973 for Sandver, 1978; and Sandver and Heneman, 1980), they found a common body of correlates of compensation, including dues and assets, suggesting that ability to pay is a determining factor. Sandver and Heneman (1980) also found modest support for the hypothesis that job complexity, as revealed in the number of local unions affiliated with a national organization, is positively correlated with compensation. French, Hayashi, and Gray (1983) analyzed the compensation of presidents of 195 national unions in 1976. They found that unions' financial wealth, officers' job compensation, and tenure were correlated primarily with pay. However, financial wealth was not significantly correlated with officers' compensation among small- and mid-sized unions.

The second stream of post-1960 research focused on the financial resources and performance of unions across all levels, but primarily the local and national. Applebaum (1964, 1965, 1966, 1969) and Allison (1975) addressed the finances of local unions in different states or regions. In four articles, Applebaum (1964, 1965, 1966, 1969) reported on the finances of local unions in the area of Milwaukee, Wisconsin, covering the 1961–1967 period. In his 1969 article on "A Comparison of Officer Turnover and Salary Structures in Local Unions," Applebaum reported turnover levels for several sets of officers (e.g. President, Vice President, and Financial Secretary-Treasurer for the periods of 1960–1962 and 1963–1966), finding that almost 55 percent had a least one change during the latter period compared to just over 40 percent earlier. Applebaum (1969) also found a positive association between union membership and financial gross receipts, on the one hand, and the salary paid to all officers and the highest-paid officers across both time frames, on the other.

Allison (1975) examined the financial performance of more than 500 local unions of 17 nationals covering the 1970–1972 period. She focused on several accounting ratios: solvency, liquidity, debt burden, reserves, and basic expenses as a percentage of total receipts. In addition, Allison (1975) examined how the local unions allocated spending across such functions as administration, education, and professional fees. In presenting the data, Allison (1975) aggregated the locals (1) by their international parent and (2) by major industry category: construction, durables, non-durables, utilities, services, and Teamsters. Key findings revealed that substantial variation existed in financial performance across the internationals' aggregated locals and also in spending patterns. Within this varied performance, however, the locals across internationals tended to be relatively unburdened by debt and score highly in terms of liquidity (or current assets relative to current liabilities). However, union dues generally just barely exceeded basic expenses or, in several instances, actually fell behind (e.g. this applied to the locals affiliated with the carpenters, sheet metal workers, longshoremen, and rubber workers). In addition, spending patterns varied considerably across the unions' major industries: administrative costs were considerably higher as a percent of total receipts for the industries of construction (40.7 percent), Teamsters (39.5 percent), and services

(36.3 percent) than the others (durables, 30.9 percent; utilities, 31.8 percent; and non-durables, 11.5 percent).

Troy (1975a, 1975b) and Sheflin and Troy (1983) documented the financial resources of all labor organizations across local, intermediate, and regional/national levels covering the 1962–1976 period. They examined the distribution of assets at these organizational levels and the breakdown of aggregated finances by the categories reported in the balance sheets (and income statements) of all unions. They showed stability in the distribution of assets across organizational levels for the selected years reported (1962, 1969, and 1976); close to 50 percent was held at the local level; 5–6 percent was held by intermediate organizations; and 44–47 percent retained by the regional/national organizations.

Sheflin and Troy (1983) reported that the net assets of all unions climbed in nominal amounts from about $1.56 billion in 1962 to over $3.35 billion in 1976. Inflation-adjusted, however, net assets rose from $2.2 billion to $2.5 billion over this 15-year span. On a per-member basis, real net assets declined from $133 to $128. In addition, Sheflin and Troy (1983) showed that total union income from all sources rose, in real terms, from over $1.6 billion to about $2.2 billion, rising from just under $100 per member to slightly above $113 between 1962 and 1976. During this period, the share of total income generated by dues or per capita taxes increased from 63.4 to 72.8 percent. Sheflin and Troy (1983) further revealed that the percentage of unions' assets held in cash ranged from 30.2 to 32.4 percent during the period, with another 32.7 to 38.8 percent held in US Treasury Securities and "Other Marketable Securities." However, within the category of securities, the balance shifted significantly from Treasuries (which fell from 22.9 to 8.4 percent over the 15 years) and the "Other" group (which jumped from 15.5 percent in 1962 to 24.3 percent in 1973). By far the largest share of liabilities rested in the catchall "other" category.

Masters and Atkin (1997) studied the distribution of financial resources in 1995 across organizational levels, namely national, intermediate, and local [which is a somewhat different categorization from Sheflin and Troy (1983) and Troy (1975a, 1975b)] and the concentration of such resources among 155 consolidated unions. They found a roughly similar distribution of total assets across organizational levels as did Sheflin and Troy (1983), with almost 43 percent at the national level compared to 47.4 percent at the local in 1995. Masters and Atkin (1997) also found a significant concentration of union assets among the largest organizations in terms of membership. Almost 61 percent of the total assets of labor were held by the 17 largest unions in 1995. Masters and Atkin (1997) further showed that the real total assets of all unions in 1995 was $6.6 billion (inflation-adjusted) compared to $6.97 billion in 1976 (Sheflin and Troy 1983).

Australia

Just a handful of studies have treated the finances of Australian unions. Wielgosz (1974) examined the assets and revenues of unions filing with the Industrial Registrar, finding that, overall, the unions were not particularly well situated. He concluded that Australian unions had less wealth and income than their US and

UK counterparts. Blue-collar unions had more wealth per capita than their White-collar kindred. Australian unions, as was the case in the United States and the United Kingdom, held most of their assets in relatively liquid form. Most of their revenues came from membership dues, and these payment rates tended to be low. Moss (1983) reported on the finances of a sample of 24 public service unions in Australia as part of a Master of Business Administration (MBA) Research paper. Huntley (1976, 1979) reported on selected financial data on the top 100 trade unions in Australia. He observed that between 1976 and 1979, the unions' general financial position had improved, with their funds rising faster than inflation and wage increases, a finding at variance with the results of a later study by Griffin and De Rozairo (1993). The unions invested a considerable amount of these additional funds in fixed assets such as property for offices.

Griffin and De Rozairo (1993) examined the finances of Australian unions in 1989, comparing them to a smaller sample in 1980 and Wielgosz's (1974) earlier results. They found that the unions' financial situation, overall, deteriorated in the 1970s even though membership rose. Per capita assets fell during that decade, and expenditures outpaced income, as staff and property acquisitions contributed to higher levels of spending. Griffin and De Rozairo (1993), however, observed that the financial position of labor as a whole had improved since then, despite declining membership. White-collar unions, in particular, showed noticeable improvement with income and assets and less debt than their blue-collar counterparts.

Altogether, the studies in the United Kingdom and the United States permit a few major observations. First, there is substantial variation in financial wherewithal, performance, and practice/management across unions. Second, certain patterns emerge, including a correlation between (1) financial strength and officers' compensation; (2) union membership and financial wealth. Third, in the United Kingdom, the financial position of unions improved on certain dimensions in the 1980s but generally deteriorated over the post-World War II period until the early years of the 21st century. In the United States, the unions' overall assets declined between the latter half of the 1970s and mid-1990s. Fourth, it would appear that union financial resources are somewhat concentrated among a relatively small number of labor organizations with large memberships.

Conclusion

The topic of union finances involves important theoretical issues concerning the formation and maintenance of labor organizations. Unions need to offer a sufficient menu of benefits to overcome the initial barriers to joining a collectivity. The provision of benefits eventually requires the financing of an organization's capacity so that deliverable goods and services are affordable. Money is also the critical factor that translates the strategies of unions into practical action. Unions depend on money to organize new members, represent members at the bargaining table, litigate disputes, and engage in elections and lobbying.

The financial wherewithal, performance, and management of unions operate within a systems framework. Managing the inflow and outflow of money depends on a variety of environmental contexts, with the result being the capacity to fund activities related to the mission of a union. These multifunctional activities are intended to promote certain outcomes which affect both the inflow of resources and the contexts surrounding labor organizations. Unions which optimize their financial wherewithal, performance, and management position themselves better to achieve positive results and resist attack. Within this employment systems context, unions orchestrate their activities at three distinctive levels of decision involving: macro-political/economic, organizational, and work site. The capacity of unions to fund operations at these levels is important in influencing the scope and type of benefits they provide.

To date, the available research on union finances is quite limited. At a time when unions face existential threats to delegitimize, destabilize, and defund them, we know remarkably little about how they perform financially. How did unions manage financially during the Great Recession? How has their financial wealth and performance changed while under relentless attack? How do unions raise and spend money? How capable are they of withstanding interruptions in recurring sources of revenue? These questions beg for answers. They pertain directly to the continued relevance and import of the labor movement in American society.

2 Financial Reporting and Analysis

Federal law requires that unions make extensive financial and other informational disclosures to their members and the public. The US Department of Labor (DOL) compiles these reports and makes the data available to the public, broadening accessibility through online public disclosures. To comply with the Labor-Management Reporting and Disclosure Act (LMRDA) of 1959, unions periodically file disclosure forms with the DOL, including the LM-2, which reports extensively on the unions' balance sheets, income statements, and sundry financial transactions and obligations. We examine the disclosure requirements of the numerous reporting forms, focusing especially on the LM-2. The chapter then turns to specify the financial measures we cover, including those on assets, liabilities, revenues, and disbursements. We conclude with a review of how to analyze the LM-2 reports in order to assess the financial position of a union and how such information is useful to understanding how to deal with unions a bargaining counterparts or interest-group competitors.

Federal law imposes extensive requirements on unions in terms of their internal operations and financial reporting (Estey, Taft, and Wagner 1964). It grants union members a "Bill of Rights" to participate in union elections and governance. Federal law also imposes fiduciary obligations on unions and their officers. In addition, it requires the periodic disclosure of information on the unions as organizations and on their financial operations. Unions make these relevant reports to the US DOL, which makes them available to the public. Currently, the DOL, through its Office of Labor-Management Standards (OLMS), assembles and reports the disclosed data through a digital online public disclosure room (https://www.dol.gov/agencies/olms/public-disclosure-room).

We review the financial and informational disclosure requirements imposed on labor organizations under the LMRDA of 1959. A summary of the specific data the unions must disclose is provided. We also discuss how to read the main financial reports unions make and to interpret the relevant data. This chapter covers several measures of financial wherewithal and performance to provide insight into relevant capacity and efficiency. We further identify how financial data, as reported in various summary measures, implicates unions in terms of their bargaining, contract administration, legal representation, and political activism.

DOI: 10.4324/9781003335474-3

LMRDA

Congress enacted the LMRDA (commonly called the Landrum-Griffin Act after its two principal congressional sponsors) on the heels of a series of highly publicized hearings in the 1950s exposing illegal and unethical conduct in several major unions in the United States (Estey, Taft, and Wagner 1964; Strauss 1975; Masters 1997). In Sections 1 and 2 of the law, Congress declared its basic findings behind and purposes of the enactment (see Table 2.1). As shown in Section 2, lawmakers had found evidence of several instances of unethical and illegal conduct among selected unions, which required legal intervention to protect the rights of rank and file and the interests of the public. Section 1 recognized the guiding objectives of the LMRDA to be extensive financial reporting and disclosure and the prevention of further abuses of power.

In Section 201 of the law, Congress mandated that labor organizations regularly report to the US DOL its assets and liabilities, receipts and disbursements, compensation of employees and officers, and loans made to officers and employees. LMRDA has required unions and the DOL to make these financial reports available to union members and the general public. Thus, for more than 60 years, labor organizations of all sizes covered by the legal ambit of LMRDA have had to report comprehensive data on their finances, which can be inspected by rank and file and the public in general. In promulgating forms for unions to use in making these reports, the DOL has required the reporting of detailed schedules on financial transactions, including union payments to vendors, gross salaries and allowances allotted to employees and officers, and benefits paid as part of their compensation structure.

In addition, LMRDA established a "Bill of Rights" for union members to participate in matters of governance and the election of officers (Section 101). Among other things, it granted union members "equal rights" to participate in their organizations' elections and meetings, required that dues and assessments be established according to democratic procedures, gave rank and file access to negotiated collective-bargaining agreements, and mandated a full hearing of the charges that might be levied against union members under duly established constitutional procedures.

Section 501 of the LMRDA established the fiduciary obligations of labor organizations and officers and others entrusted with managing their finances. It specifically has obligated responsible parties "to hold its money and property solely for the benefit of the organization." Thus, the fiduciary requirement extends beyond adhering to the legal requirements prohibiting bribery, embezzlement, fraud, or other forms of illegalities to requiring the management of money to the benefit of the organization and its members.

Major Reporting Forms Required under the LMRDA

A partial list of these reporting forms appears in Table 2.2. Operating under the authority of the LMRDA, the OLMS of the DOL has issued several different disclosure forms which unions much file periodically. It has also promulgated guidance on how to complete these forms. Accordingly, the OLMS has issued

Table 2.1 Key Selected Provisions of LMRDA

Provisional	*Statutory Requirements*
Subject	**Public Law 86-257, September 14, 1959, 73 Stat. 519–546, as amended** **29 U.S.C. 401-531**
Purpose	Section 1. To provide for the reporting and disclosure of certain financial transactions and administrative practices of labor organizations and employers, to prevent abuses in the administration of trusteeships by labor organizations, to provide standards with respect to the election of officers of labor organizations, and for other purposes. Section 2(b). The Congress further finds, from recent investigations in the labor and management fields, that there have been a number of instances of breach of trust, corruption, disregard of the rights of individual employees, and other failures to observe high standards of responsibility and ethical conduct which require further and supplementary legislation that will afford necessary protection of the rights and interests of employees and the public generally as they relate to the activities of labor organizations, employers, labor relations consultants, and their officers and representatives.
Bill of Rights	Section 101. Union members have equal rights to nominate candidates for union office, vote in union elections, and participate in union meetings. They may also meet with other members and express their opinions. Unions may impose assessments and raise dues only by democratic procedures. Unions must afford members a full and fair hearing of charges against them. Unions must inform their members about the provisions of the LMRDA. Members may enforce Title I rights through a private suit against the union but may be required to exhaust internal union remedies for up to four months before filing suit. Union members and non-union employees may receive and inspect collective-bargaining agreements. This right may be enforced by the individual or by the Secretary of Labor.

(*Continued*)

Table 2.1 (Continued)

Provisional	*Statutory Requirements*
Reporting and disclosure	Section 201. Every labor organization shall file annually with the Secretary a financial report signed by its president and treasurer or corresponding principal officers containing the following information in such detail as may be necessary accurately to disclose its financial condition and operations for its preceding fiscal year– (1) assets and liabilities at the beginning and end of the fiscal year; (2) receipts of any kind and the sources thereof, (3) salary, allowances, and other direct or indirect disbursements (including reimbursed expenses) to each officer and also to each employee who, during such fiscal year, received more than $10,000 in the aggregate from such labor organization and any other labor organization affiliated with it or with which it is affiliated, or which is affiliated with the same national or international labor organization; (4) direct and indirect loans made to any officer, employee, or member, which aggregated more than $250 during the fiscal year, together with a statement of the purpose, security, if any, and arrangements for repayment; (5) direct and indirect loans to any business enterprise, together with a statement of the purpose, security, if any, and arrangements for repayment; and (6) other disbursements made by it including the purposes thereof, all in such categories as the Secretary may prescribe.
Fiduciary obligations	Section 501. (a) The officers, agents, shop stewards, and other representatives of a labor organization occupy positions of trust in relation to such organization and its members as a group. It is, therefore, the duty of each such person, taking into account the special problems and functions of a labor organization, to hold its money and property solely for the benefit of the organization and its members and to manage, invest, and expend the same in accordance with its constitution and bylaws and any resolutions of the governing bodies adopted thereunder, to refrain from dealing with such organization as an adverse party or in behalf of an adverse party in any matter connected with his duties and from holding or acquiring any pecuniary or personal interest which conflicts with the interests of such organization, and to account to the organization for any profit received by him in whatever capacity in connection with transactions conducted by him or under his direction on behalf of the organization.

Table 2.2 Brief Descriptions of Reporting Forms Required under the LMRDA by the US DOL

Form LM-1 Labor Organization Information Report
The Labor-Management Reporting and Disclosure Act, as amended (LMRDA), requires public disclosure of information concerning the structure, practices, and procedures of labor organizations. The Secretary, under the authority of the LMRDA, has prescribed the filing of the Labor Organization Information Report, Form LM-1, for labor organizations… Every labor organization subject to the Labor-Management Reporting and Disclosure Act, as amended (LMRDA), the Civil Service Reform Act (CSRA), or the Foreign Service Act (FSA) must file a financial report, Form LM-2, LM-3, or LM-4, each year with the Office of Labor-Management Standards (OLMS) of the US Department of Labor. These laws cover labor organizations that represent employees who work in private industry, employees of the US Postal Service, and most Federal government employees. Labor organizations that include or represent only state, county, or municipal government employees are not covered by these laws and, therefore, are not required to file. If you have a question about whether the labor organization is required to file, contact the nearest OLMS field office listed at the end of these instructions. II. What Form To File Every labor organization subject to the LMRDA, CSRA, or FSA with total annual receipts of $250,000 or more must file Form LM-2.
Form LM-2 Labor Organization Annual Report
Every labor organization subject to the Labor-Management Reporting and Disclosure Act, as amended (LMRDA), the CSRA, or the FSA must file a financial report, Form LM-2, LM-3, or LM-4, each year with the OLMS of the US DOL. These laws cover labor organizations that represent employees who work in private industry, employees of the US Postal Service, and most Federal government employees. Labor organizations that include or represent only state, county, or municipal government employees are not covered by these laws and, therefore, are not required to file. If you have a question about whether the labor organization is required to file, contact the nearest OLMS field office listed at the end of these instructions. II. What Form To File Every labor organization subject to the LMRDA, CSRA, or FSA with total annual receipts of $250,000 or more must file Form LM-2.
Form LM-3 Labor Organization Annual Report
Every labor organization subject to the Labor-Management Reporting and Disclosure Act of 1959, as amended (LMRDA), the CSRA, or the FSA must file a financial report, Form LM-2, LM-3, or LM-4, each year with the OLMS of the US DOL. These laws cover labor organizations that represent employees who work in private industry, employees of the US Postal Service, and most Federal government employees. Labor organizations that represent or include only state, county, or municipal government employees are not covered by these laws and, therefore, are not required to file. If you have a question about whether your organization is required to file, contact the nearest OLMS field office listed at the end of these instructions. III. When To File Form LM-3 must be filed within 90 days after the end of your organization's fiscal year (12-month reporting period). The law does not authorize the US DOL to grant an extension of time for filing reports for any reason. The penalties for delinquency are described in Section VI of these instructions. If your organization went out of existence during its fiscal year, a terminal financial report must be filed within 30 days after the date it ceased to exist. See Section XII of these instructions for information on filing a terminal financial report. II. What Form To File Every labor organization subject to the LMRDA, CSRA, or FSA with total annual receipts of less than $250,000 may file the simplified annual report Form LM-3, if not in trusteeship as defined in Section IX of these instructions.

(*Continued*)

Table 2.2 (Continued)

Form LM-4 Labor Organization Annual Report
Every labor organization subject to the Labor-Management Reporting and Disclosure Act of 1959, as amended (LMRDA), the CSRA, or the FSA must file a financial report, Form LM-2, LM-3, or LM-4, each year with the OLMS of the US DOL. These laws cover labor organizations that represent employees who work in private industry, employees of the US Postal Service, and most Federal government employees. Labor organizations that represent or include only state, county, or municipal government employees are not covered by these laws and, therefore, are not required to file. If you have a question about whether your organization is required to file, contact the nearest OLMS field office listed at the end of these instructions. II. What Form To File Labor organizations with total annual receipts of less than $10,000 may file the abbreviated two-page annual report Form LM-4, if not in trusteeship as defined in Section VIII of these instructions. The term "total annual receipts" means all financial receipts of the labor organization during its fiscal year, regardless of the source, including receipts of any subsidiaries and any special funds.
Form LM-10 Employer Report
The Labor-Management Reporting and Disclosure Act of 1959, as amended (LMRDA), requires public disclosure of specific financial transactions or arrangements made between an employer and one or more of the following: a labor organization, union official, employee, or labor relations consultant. Pursuant to Section 203(a) of the LMRDA, every employer who has engaged in any such transaction or arrangement during the fiscal year must file a detailed report with the Secretary of Labor. The Secretary, under the authority of the LMRDA, has prescribed the filing of the Employer Report, Form LM-10, for employers to satisfy this reporting requirement. These reporting requirements of the LMRDA and of the regulations and forms issued under the Act only relate to the disclosure of specified payments. The reporting requirements do not address whether specific payments, transactions, or arrangements are lawful or unlawful. The fact that a particular payment, transaction, or arrangement is or is not required to be reported does not indicate whether it is or is not subject to any legal prohibition. II. Who Must File Any employer, as defined by the LMRDA, who has engaged in certain financial transactions or arrangements, of the type described in Section 203(a) of the Act, with any labor organization, union official, employee or labor relations consultant, or who has made expenditures for certain objects relating to activities of employees or a union, must file a Form LM-10. An employer required to file must complete only one Form LM-10 each fiscal year that covers all instances of reportable activity even if activity occurs at multiple locations
Form LM-15 Trusteeship Report
The Labor-Management Reporting and Disclosure Act of 1959, as amended (LMRDA), the CSRA, and the FSA require public disclosure of certain matters pertaining to a trusteeship which a labor organization imposes on a subordinate body. The Secretary, under the authority of the LMRDA, the CSRA, and the FSA has prescribed the filing of the Trusteeship Report, Form LM-15, to satisfy the requirement to disclose information on the imposition of a trusteeship and to semiannually disclose the status of the trusteeship. II WHO Must File Every labor organization subject to the Labor-Management Reporting and Disclosure Act of 1959, as amended (LMRDA), the CSRA, or the FSA which has established a receivership, trusteeship, or other method of supervision or control, suspending the autonomy otherwise available to a subordinate labor organization under its constitution or bylaws, must file trusteeship reports with the OLMS of the US DOL.

Form LM-15A Report on Selection of Delegates and Officers

The Labor-Management Reporting and Disclosure Act of 1959, as amended (LMRDA), the CSRA, and the FSA require public disclosure of certain matters pertaining to a trusteeship which a labor organization imposes on a subordinate body. The Secretary, under the authority of the LMRDA, the CSRA, and the FSA has prescribed the filing of the Report on Selection of Delegates and Officers, Form LM-15A, to satisfy the requirement to disclose matters relating to the selection of officers of the parent body imposing the trusteeship and the selection of delegates to a convention of the parent body imposing the trusteeship. II. Who Must File Every labor organization subject to the Labor-Management Reporting and Disclosure Act of 1959, as amended (LMRDA), the CSRA, or FSA which has established a receivership, trusteeship, or other method of supervision or control, suspending the autonomy otherwise available to a subordinate labor organization under its constitution and bylaws, must file trusteeship reports with the OLMS of the US DOL You must file Form LM-15A, Report on Selection of Delegates and Officers, with a semiannual Trusteeship Report, Form LM-15, or a Terminal Trusteeship Report, Form LM-16, if the following occurred during the period covered by the Form LM-15 or the Form LM-16: } a convention or other policy-determining body met to which the trustee labor organization sent delegates or would have sent delegates if not in trusteeship;

Form LM-16 Terminal Trusteeship Report

The Labor-Management Reporting and Disclosure Act of 1959, as amended (LMRDA), the CSRA, and the FSA require public disclosure of certain matters pertaining to a trusteeship which a labor organization imposes on a subordinate body. The Secretary, under the authority of the LMRDA, the CSRA, and the FSA has prescribed the filing of the Terminal Trusteeship Report, Form LM-16, to satisfy the requirement to disclose matters relating to the termination of a trusteeship. II. Who Must File Every labor organization subject to the Labor-Management Reporting and Disclosure Act of 1959, as amended (LMRDA), the CSRA, or the FSA which has terminated a receivership, trusteeship, or other method of supervision or control, suspending the autonomy otherwise available to a subordinate labor organization under its constitution or bylaws, must file a Terminal Trusteeship Report, Form LM-16. This report must be filed whenever the following occurs (1) the subordinate labor organization is restored to the autonomy otherwise available to it under its constitution and bylaws and the constitution and bylaws of the labor organization which imposed the trusteeship, or (2) the subordinate labor organization loses its reporting identity through dissolution, merger, consolidation, or otherwise.

The Labor-Management Reporting and Disclosure Act of 1959, as amended (LMRDA), the CSRA, and the FSA require public disclosure of certain matters pertaining to a trusteeship which a labor organization imposes on a subordinate body. The Secretary, under the authority of the LMRDA, the CSRA, and the FSA has prescribed the filing of the Report on Selection of Delegates and Officers, Form LM-15A, to satisfy the requirement to disclose matters relating to the selection of officers of the parent body imposing the trusteeship and the selection of delegates to a convention of the parent body imposing the trusteeship. II. Who Must File Every labor organization subject to the Labor-Management Reporting and Disclosure Act of 1959, as amended (LMRDA), the CSRA, or FSA which has established a receivership, trusteeship, or other method of supervision or control, suspending the autonomy otherwise available to a subordinate labor organization under its constitution and bylaws, must file trusteeship reports with the OLMS of the US DOL You must file Form LM-15A, Report on Selection of Delegates and Officers, with a semiannual Trusteeship Report, Form LM-15, or a Terminal Trusteeship Report, Form LM-16, if the following occurred during the period covered by the Form LM-15 or the Form LM-16: a convention or other policy-determining body met to which the trustee labor organization sent delegates or would have sent delegates if not in trusteeship;

(*Continued*)

Table 2.2 (Continued)

Form LM-20 Agreement and Activities Report (Consultant)
The Labor-Management Reporting and Disclosure Act of 1959, as amended (LMRDA), requires public disclosure of agreements or arrangements made between any person, including labor relations consultants and other individuals and organizations, and an employer to undertake certain activities concerning employees or labor organizations. Pursuant to Section 203(b) of the LMRDA, every person who undertakes any such activities under an agreement or arrangement with an employer must file a detailed report with the Secretary of Labor. The Secretary, under the authority of the LMRDA, has prescribed the filing of the Agreement and Activities Report, Form LM-20, to satisfy this reporting requirement.
Form LM-21 Receipts and Disbursements Report (Consultant)
The Labor-Management Reporting and Disclosure Act of 1959, as amended (LMRDA), requires public disclosure of agreements or arrangements made between any person, including labor relations consultants and other individuals and organizations, and an employer to undertake certain activities concerning employees or labor organizations. Pursuant to Section 203(b) of the LMRDA, every person who undertakes any such activity under an agreement or arrangement with an employer must file with the Secretary of Labor a detailed report of receipts and disbursements annually for each fiscal year during which payments were made as a result of any such agreement or arrangement. The Secretary, under the authority of the LMRDA, has prescribed the filing of the Receipts and Disbursements Report, Form LM-21, to satisfy this reporting requirement. These reporting requirements of the LMRDA and of the regulations and forms issued under the Act only relate to the disclosure of specific agreements, arrangements, and/or activities. The reporting requirements do not address whether such agreements, arrangements, or activities are lawful or unlawful. The fact that a particular agreement, arrangement, or activity is or is not required to be reported does or does not indicate whether it is or is not subject to any legal prohibition. II. Who Must File Any person who, as a direct or indirect party to any agreement or arrangement with an employer to undertake activities of the type described in Section 203(b) of the Act, must file a Form LM-21 for any fiscal year during which a payment was made or received as a result of the agreement or arrangement. A
Form LM-30 Labor Organization Officer and Employee Report
The Labor-Management Reporting and Disclosure Act of 1959, as amended (LMRDA or Act), requires public disclosure of certain financial transactions and financial interests of labor organization officers and employees and their spouses and minor children. See 29 C.F.R. 404.1-404.9 (reports by officers and employees of labor organizations). The purpose of disclosure, among other things, is to publicly identify an actual or potential conflict between the personal financial interests of a union officer or employee and his or her obligations to the union and its members. The LMRDA establishes the basic rights of union members, including equal voting rights, freedom of speech and assembly, and other essential safeguards for union democracy, among other protections; establishes financial reporting and disclosure requirements for unions, union officers and employees, employers, and labor relations consultants; regulates union trusteeships; details procedural requirements for the conduct of union officer elections; and establishes a fiduciary duty on union officers, employees, and other representatives. Pursuant to Section 202 of the LMRDA, and subject to certain exceptions, if you are a labor organization officer or employee (other than an employee performing exclusively clerical or custodial services), who has, directly or indirectly, held any legal or equitable interest in, received any payments from, or engaged in any transactions or arrangements (including loans) with certain employers or businesses or labor relations consultants during your fiscal year, you must file a detailed report with the Secretary of Labor

(Secretary). See Part X of these instructions for a detailed discussion of the types of financial matters that must be reported. You are not required to file a report unless you or your spouse or minor child held a reportable interest, received a reportable payment, or engaged in a reportable transaction or arrangement during the reporting period. As discussed in Part X, you are not required to report insubstantial payments or gifts, as there defined. The Department's OLMS has developed guidance to assist with LMRDA compliance. Guidance to assist with completion of the Form LM-30 is available on the OLMS website: www.olms.dol.gov. For additional OLMS contact information, see the final page of these instructions. The reporting requirements of the LMRDA and of the regulations and forms issued under the Act relate only to the public disclosure of specified transactions and interests. The reporting requirements do not address whether such transactions and interests are lawful or unlawful. The fact that a particular transaction or interest is or is not required to be reported is not indicative of whether it is or is not subject to any legal restriction; this must be determined by provisions of law other than those prescribing the reports. Failure to file a required report may subject an individual to civil or criminal penalties, or both. See Part VIII of these instructions. II. Who Must File Any officer or employee of a labor organization (other than an employee performing clerical or custodial services exclusively), as defined by the LMRDA and these instructions, must file Form LM-30 if, during the past fiscal year, the officer or employee, spouse, or minor child, either directly or indirectly, held any legal or equitable interest, received any payments, or engaged in transactions or arrangements (including loans) of the types described in these instructions.

Form S-1 Surety Company Annual Report

The Labor-Management Reporting and Disclosure Act of 1959, as amended (LMRDA), requires public disclosure of financial information from any surety company which issues a bond required by the LMRDA or the Employee Retirement Income Security Act of 1974 (ERISA). The Secretary, under the authority of the LMRDA, has prescribed the filing of the Surety Company Report, Form S-1, for surety companies to satisfy this reporting requirement. II. Who must file Form S-1 must be filed by any surety company having a bond in force which ensures the following: (1) a welfare or pension plan covered by the ERISA; or (2) any labor organization or trust in which a labor organization is interested covered by the LMRDA. A single report for a group of surety companies will not be accepted.

Source: US Department of Labor, Office of Labor-Management Standards website. https://www.dol.gov/agencies/olms/Regs/Compliance/formspage

three basic sets of reporting forms covering (1) organizational operations; (2) general financial data involving the unions' balance sheets and income statements, plus accompanying details, such as the compensation of individual employees and union officers and the relative amounts of time they spend on such union functions as representation, union administration, general overhead, contributions, and political action; and (3) specialized reports on the activities of labor relations consultants to be filed by labor unions and employers and on labor organizations under trusteeship. Table 2.2 describes the central requirements of these selected disclosure forms.

How to Analyze Union Financial Reports

We discuss in more detail the nature and scope of the data reported in two of the major disclosures filed by labor organizations of all sizes covered by the LMRDA: the LM-1, LM-2., LM-3, and LM-4 forms, the latter two of which are abbreviated disclosures. In so doing, we report on how the OLMS presents the data on the LM-2 reports in its online public disclosure room. We identify several measures of financial wherewithal and performance which analyze the position of unions on this dimension.

Table 2.3 outlines the reporting provisions included in forms LM-1 through LM-4.

Table 2.3 Reporting Provisions of Forms LM-1, LM-2, LM-3, and LM-4

Form LM-1: Labor Organization Information Report
A three-page report including 19 questions, several of which are multipart. Questions pertain to basic information about the name and location of the organization, major policies and practices, dues rates and fees, and the nature of the organization (whether it is local or national and whether it includes the private sector, federal, or postal employees).
Form LM-2: Labor Organization Annual Report
Labor organizations with annual receipts equal to or greater than $250,000 file this 26-page report. It covers 69 items in the background and Statements A (assets and liabilities) and B (receipts and disbursements). Background items include questions on dues, fees, and assessments, whether the union sponsors a political action committee (PAC), and annual membership. Twenty separate schedules are included which detail information about assets, liabilities, receipts, and disbursements, plus the compensation paid to individual employees and officers. Schedules 11 and 12 also report the amount of time officers and employees to spend on representation, union administration, general overhead, political action, and contributions.
Form LM-3: Labor Organization Annual Report
Labor organizations with between $10,000 and $250,000 in annual receipts file this abbreviated financial disclosure form. Six pages in length, it includes 55 items about the union's background, assets, liabilities, receipts, and disbursements. It provides for the itemization of individual officers' compensation. The form includes the same items as in Statement A of the LM-2 and a shortened version of the LM-2's Statement B.
Form LM-4: Labor Organization Annual Report
Covering labor organizations with annual receipts under $10,000, this is a two-page form with 18 questions which reports information about the union's name and location, its total assets, liabilities, receipts, and disbursements, its dues rates, and its total payments to compensate officers and employees, which each group aggregated.

Source: US Department of Labor, Office of Labor-Management Standards website.

LM-1 Form

The LM-1 form requires unions to report whether or not membership consists of members from (1) private industry; (2) the US Postal Service; and (3) the non-postal Federal government. It also requires the organization to report whether it is a local/branch, intermediate, or national/international. In addition, it must indicate where its annual receipts fall into the three categories: (1) less than $10k; (2) $10k–$ 249,999; or (3) equal to or greater than $250k.

In this LM-1 form, unions must further describe various organizational practices and procedures, including membership qualifications; assessments levied on members; participation in insurance or benefit plans; the process used to authorize disbursements of organizational funds; requirements associated with auditing financial transactions; procedures used to call regular or special meetings; procedures used to select officers and stewards; procedures invoked to protect the integrity of elections; how work permits are secured; procedures available to disqualifying officers, ratify contracts, impose fines, and authorize bargaining demands. As part of this disclosure in the LM-1, unions must submit copies of their constitution and bylaws as well as when and how changes have been made in these two sets of governing documents.

LM-2 Form

Unions under the LMRDA with $250,000 or more in annual receipts must file the LM-2 financial disclosure form, which is the most detailed of the three levels of financial reporting (LM-2, LM-3, and LM-4). The LM-2 consists of four main sections: (1) descriptive information about the union, including whether or not it sponsors a political action committee (PAC); its dues rates and other assessments; and its membership for the year of reporting; (2) statements A and B on totaled assets and liabilities (A) and receipts and disbursements (B); (3) 20 specific schedules which provide more details and selected summaries of assets, liabilities, receipts, and disbursements; and (4) an open-ended general information section where unions footnote details about selected data.

More specifically, as part of the first main section of the LM-2, unions report information about their location and address, key officers who must affix their signatures to the disclosure form, upcoming elections of union officers, dues rates and fees, membership totals, and whether or not the union has established a PAC. The bulk of the LM-2 form is dedicated to reporting information about union finances and relevant transactions. It includes two statements on assets and liabilities (Statement A) and receipts and disbursements (Statement B), which constitute summary forms of the balance sheets and income statements.

Table 2.4 itemizes the specific reporting requirements for Statement A. Seven asset categories are itemized, with information reported for the beginning and end of year periods. They include cash, accounts receivable, loans receivable, US Treasury Securities, Investments, Fixed Assets, and Other Assets.

Table 2.5 details the categories of receipts and disbursements. Thirteen categories of receipts are specified along with 17 disbursement classifications. The receipts

Table 2.4 Itemization of Assets and Liabilities Reported in Statement A of the LM-2

Assets	*Liabilities*
(at the beginning and end of the reporting period)	(at the beginning and end of the reporting period)
Cash	Accounts payable
Accounts receivable	Loans payable
Loans receivable	Mortgages payable
US treasury securities	Other liabilities
Investments	Total liabilities
Fixed assets	
Other assets	
Total assets	Net assets

Table 2.5 Itemization of Reporting Requirements in Statement B of the LM-2

Dues and agency fees	*Representational activities*
Per capita tax	Political activities and lobbying
Fees, fines, assessments, work permits	Contributions, gifts, and grants
Sale of supplies	General overhead
Interest	Union administration
Dividends	Benefits
Rents	Per capita tax
Sale of investments and fixed assets	Strike benefits
Loans obtained	Fees, fines, and assessments
Repayments of loans made	Supplies for resale
On behalf of affiliates for transmittal to them	Purchase of investments and fixed assets
From members for disbursement on their behalf	Loans made
Other receipts	Repayment of loans obtained
Total receipts	To affiliates
	On behalf of individual members
	Direct taxes
	Subtotal
	Withholding tax and payroll deductions
	Total withheld
	Less total disbursed
	Total withheld but not disbursed
	Total disbursements

side of the ledger includes revenues collected "on behalf of affiliates for transmittal to them" and revenues "from members for disbursement on their behalf." Disbursements include payments made "to affiliates of funds collected on their behalf" and payments "on behalf of individual members." Thus, both receipts and disbursements include intra-union financial transfers, which are incorporated into the totals for both general categories. Calculations of net receipts and net disbursements, as noted below, delete these intra-union transfers.

LM-3 and LM-4 Forms

These are abbreviated LM-2 forms which cover labor organizations with annual receipts between $10,000 and $250,000 (LM-3) and less than $10,000 (LM-4).

Financial Measures

Two types of financial measures are reported: resource and performance. The resource measures include total assets, total liabilities, net assets, total receipts, total disbursements, net receipts, net disbursements, working capital, member-based income, business income, operating budget, administrative budget, and compensation budget. Table 2.6 shows how these resource measures are calculated.

Table 2.7 shows how we calculate the performance measures: operating capacity, liquidity, survivability, stress, efficiency, return on assets (net receipts and member-based income), per-member net receipts, and per-member member-based income.

Implications for Union Organizational Operations and Effectiveness

Financial capacity directly affects the ability of unions to perform in terms of delivering goods and services to their members (and other relevant stakeholders). The sheer wherewithal of unions affects their potential but not the full measure. How well unions manage and spend their money is also relevant. In this regard, unions must make decisions about how much they want to rely on paid officers and staff to perform the work rather than tapping a reservoir of volunteers. Regardless, the mobilization of unpaid rank and file plus allied constituencies pushes out the outer boundary of capacity to perform. In addition, unions face decisions about the mix of services and goods they will provide, some of which may be offered on a user-fee basis to offset the costs of delivery. A union must

Table 2.6 Calculations of Resource Measures

Resource measure variable	*Calculation*
Net receipts (NR)	= Total receipts − (receipts on behalf of affiliates + receipts on behalf of members)
Net disbursements (ND)	= Total disbursements − (disbursements to members + disbursement to affiliates)
Member-based income (MBI)	= Dues + per capita taxes + fees
Business income (BI)	= Sale of supplies + interest + dividend + rent + investment
Administrative budget (ADBUD)	= General overhead + union administration + sale of supplies
Compensation budget (COMPBUD)	= Gross salaries and allowances to officers and employees + benefits
Current assets	= Cash + accounts receivable + securities
Working capital	= Current assets − current liabilities
Operating budget (OPBUD)	= Representational activity + political activity + contributions activity+ general overhead + union administration + sale of supplies

Table 2.7 Calculations of Financial Performance Measures

Performance measure variable	*Calculation*
Operating capacity	= Member-based income/operating budget
Liquidity	= Current assets/current liabilities
Survivability	= Net assets/operating budget
Stress	= Operating budget/current assets
Efficiency	= Member-based income/administrative budget
Return on assets (net receipts)	= Net receipts/total assets
Return on assets (member-based income)	= Member-based income/total assets
Per-member capacity (net receipts)	= Net receipts/membership
Per-member capacity (member-based income)	= Member-based income/membership
Per-member capacity (member-based income)	= Member-based income/membership

further determine its policies and practices regarding the compensation of officers and staff. The related financial determination is how much to charge rank and file to join the union and remain a member in good standing, thereby enjoying relevant rights and privileges. These matters involve philosophical and political as well as economic considerations. Few issues may provoke as much internal debate as the compensation of union officers, dues rates and increases, and spending priorities (e.g., political action, organizing, bargaining, education and training, etc.).

Put differently, financial data provide insight into the operations of a union. How much money a union has available to spend on operations influences the relative amount of time, expertise, and experience it can bring to bargaining, contract administration (filing grievances and taking them through the procedural steps to arbitration if necessary), political participation in electioneering and lobbying, and various other pursuits germane to serving the membership and institution. In this regard, employers with unionized workforces benefit from understanding the financial capacity of counterparts to afford experienced negotiators arbitrating grievances, organizing campaigns, political operations (sometimes in support of bargaining goals, especially in the public sector), strikes, and litigation (which requires either in-house legal expertise or outside counsel, neither of which is a trivial cost).

The data reported in LM-2 financial forms in particular offer information on such matters as how well the union is staffed to support bargaining-related activities and to withstand a strike (at least from a financial standpoint). We encourage union observers and employers to examine several aspects of the unions' finances to discern their capacity. In particular, data analysis should focus on estimating the:

- relative amount of money and time unions spend on representing employees rather than general administrative and overhead activities; and
- capacity to finance strike benefits and otherwise withstand a strike without hindering operations.

Table 2.8 specifies the financial data available to shed light on these capacities. In this regard, unions disclose the amount of time its officers and employees devote

Table 2.8 Financial Information Reported in LM-2 Forms Relevant to the Estimation of Unions' Functional Capacities

Function domain	*Financial information*
Bargaining and contract administration capacity	The percentage of time the union officials and employees spend on representational activities. The "officers and employees" report provided in the OLMS online public disclosure room details the compensation (gross salary and allowances) of each officer and employee, plus the amount of time that this person spends on representation, political action, and administration. This gives information on the portion of the compensation budget of the union devoted to these respective activities. In Statement B, the union reports its cumulative disbursements on representational activities, apart from this compensation. It includes information on the union's payments for the costs of lodging, meals, and transportation for officers and employees who are deployed to participate in bargaining-related activities.
Legal and financial analysis expertise	The "payee and payer" report the OLMS produces in its online public disclosure room itemizes the disbursements made for legal advice (e.g., outside counsel) and for financial-analytic services (e.g., corporate valuation, pension obligations, healthcare obligations).
Political Influence	The unions' overall political spending as reported in Statement B, plus the itemization of specific disbursements, provides useful information on the relative scope of its engagement in electioneering and lobbying. In addition, the amount of time officers and employees devote to politics, which is available in the "officers and employees" report, supplements this information. The itemization of political disbursements offers detail about the nature of a union's political operation and may reveal information about its ideological leanings, determined by the orientation of the providers who received payment for relevant services.
Strike capacity	Many unions maintain strike funds. These are usually tapped through the availability of relatively liquid assets, which appear in the estimation of "working capital." Union constitutions, available as part of LM-1 disclosures, may include provisions specifying these strike funds. For example, Article 16 of the UAW constitution describes the funding requirements for its strike fund. Incidentally, at the national level, the UAW retains the largest such fund among its peers in the US labor movement filing under LMRDA. A union may determine through policy how much money it will pay strikers, usually on a weekly basis, and whether it will also cover healthcare benefits during the strike. It is possible to estimate the amount of funds unions might deplete by multiplying the number of workers on strike by (1) the number of weeks on strike and then the sum of this amount by (2) the weekly payment. It is also important to note that unions lose dues revenues during a strike from their strikers. This adds a further "cost" to the strike.

to representational activities and the specific services they pay for bargaining activities. They also disclose their aggregated political expenditures, which gauges their general political orientation, and their itemized disbursements to contract relevant services. Through an examination of their payees, the unions provide information on their political ideology and partisanship. Disbursements that unions make to retain outside counsel and financial analysis are also available through the itemized schedules. Estimates of a union's "working capital" (current assets−current liabilities) indicate how much money it potentially has to provide strike benefits and offset the loss of dues revenues from strikers.

3 The Big Picture

This chapter portrays the aggregated financial position of the 53 unions over the 2000–2007 through 2018–2019 time period. The data show the unions experienced some downturn in financial resources during the great recession but ended up over these 14 years with substantially greater total and net assets. Their total and net receipts were also higher but by relatively smaller amounts. Overall, the unions' member-based income (MBI) increased by a significantly greater amount than their operating budgets. Across the national organizations, administrative and compensation expenditures climbed by 15 and 18 percent, respectively, comparing 2018–2019 to 2006–2007. Over the entire time period, the unions' aggregated financial performance according to the five ratios improved in each instance. On a per-member basis, the unions' financial position generally improved in terms of available resources.

In this chapter, we take a panoramic look at the aggregated finances of the 53 nationals in our sample, which, as noted, comprised the overwhelming majority of union members in the United States over the period studied (2006–2007 through 2018–2019). The chapter reports aggregated trends in:

- financial resources, including total and net assets, receipts, and disbursements;
- breakdowns of the major categories of assets, receipts, and disbursements;
- member-based income (MBI) and the unions' aggregated operating, compensation, and administrative budgets;
- current assets and liabilities;
- per-member net receipts and MBI and spending on operations, compensation, and administration; and
- financial performance.

Trends in Aggregated Assets, Receipts, and Disbursements

Figure 3.1 reports the unions' aggregated total and net assets. It shows that the unions' total assets climbed 52 percent from 2006–2007 to 2018–2019, reaching slightly over $10.265 billion. The unions experienced a slight 1 percent drop in

DOI: 10.4324/9781003335474-4

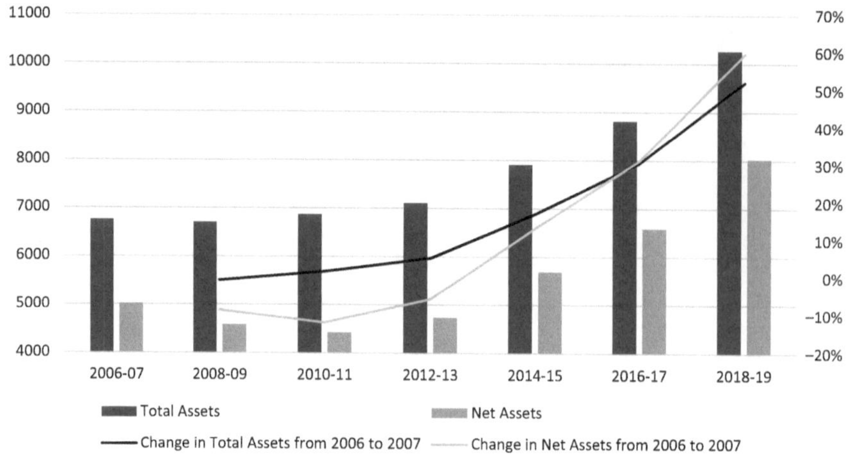

Figure 3.1 Total and Net Assets.

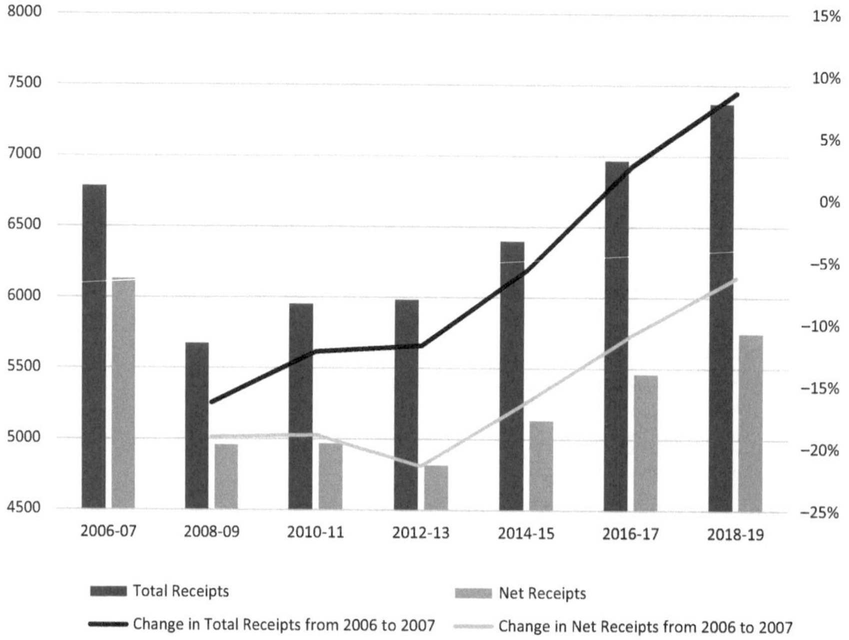

Figure 3.2 Total and Net Receipts.

total assets in 2008–2009 from the beginning of the reported span. Aggregated net assets grew 60 percent from beginning to end, but fell 12 percent from $5.02 billion in 2006–2007 to $4.42 billion in 2010–2011. The 53 nationals ended the period with just above $8 billion in net assets.

Total and net receipts appear in Figure 3.2. Aggregated total receipts rose 9 percent comparing end to beginning to almost $7.37 billion. This increase occurred

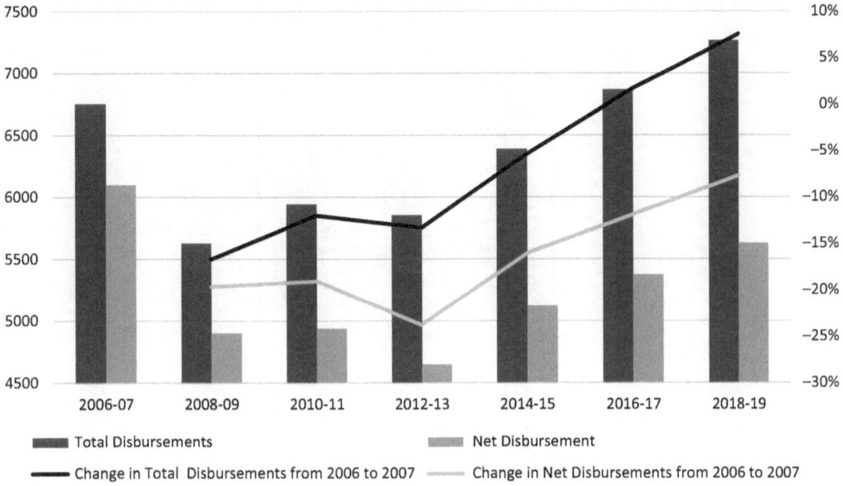

Figure 3.3 Total and Net Disbursements.

notwithstanding a 16-percent drop from 2006–2007 to 2008–2009. Net receipts fell from $6.13 billion in 2006–2007 to $5.75 billion in 2018–2019, or 6 percent. This represented a partial recovery from the steeper loss that occurred between 2006–2007 and 2012–2013, which amounted to 21 percent.

Figure 3.3 shows the unions' aggregated total and net disbursements. These data track aggregated receipts, given that revenue essentially caps what unions can spend. Comparing beginning to end periods, total disbursements rose 8 percent while net disbursements dropped 8 percent. Total receipts fell 17 percent from 2006–2007 to 2008–2009. Net receipts had dipped 24 percent by 2012–2013 compared to 2006–2007.

Breakdowns in Assets, Receipts, and Disbursements

Table 3.1 reports the breakdown of the aggregated 53 unions' assets by reported category. The four largest asset holdings across the seven intervals include investments, fixed assets, US securities, and cash, with the first of these categories consistently comprising more than 50 percent of total assets. Over time, Investments grew from just about 50 percent of all holdings to 60 percent. For the first three time intervals, US treasury securities comprised the second largest set of assets, showing its highest percentage (18.8) in 2006–2007, before falling to under 7 percent by 2012–2013. Holdings in cash climbed from 9.4 percent in 2006–2007 to nearly 14.5 percent in 2018–2019, making it the second largest category of assets in that last interval. Fixed assets as a share of total holdings fell modestly from a peak of 11.7 percent in 2008–2009 to 9.4 percent in 2018–2019.

Table 3.2 breaks down the aggregated unions' revenues from business income (BI) and MBI as a percentage of net receipts over the seven two-year time periods. As reported earlier, the unions' BI fell considerably both in absolute and

Table 3.1 Asset Allocation Percentage

Assets	*2006–2007*	*2008–2009*	*2010–2011*	*2012–2013*	*2014–2015*	*2016–2017*	*2018–2019*
Cash (%)	9.4	11.8	10.7	12.9	13.6	13.6	14.4
Accounts receivable (%)	4.3	4.4	4.1	4.0	3.6	3.4	3.0
Loans receivable (%)	1.6	2.1	2.2	2.8	2.6	2.3	2.5
US treasuries (%)	18.8	15.9	12.1	6.8	6.6	7.3	8.3
Investment assets (%)	50.7	50.8	56.2	60.6	60.9	60.7	59.6
Fixed assets (%)	11.2	11.7	11.5	11.5	10.6	10.6	9.4
Other assets (%)	4.1	3.3	3.1	1.4	2.0	2.0	2.7
Total assets ($ in millions)	6,746.62	6,697.90	6,859.43	7,099.73	7,898.55	8,813.69	10,265.14

Table 3.2 Select Items as a Percentage of Net Receipts

Receipts	*2006–2007*	*2008–2009*	*2010–2011*	*2012–2013*	*2014–2015*	*2016–2017*	*2018–2019*
MBI (%)	47.4	62.6	64.3	69.1	67.7	67.0	67.6
BI (%)	44.9	28.5	27.4	20.3	21.8	21.6	21.7
Other receipts (%)	5.9	7.8	7.2	8.0	7.9	7.8	7.7
Net receipts ($ in millions)	6,129.03	4,956.65	4,965.52	4,813.98	5,131.32	5,459.88	5,747.17

relative terms during the seven time periods examined. BI fell from almost 52 percent as a percentage of net receipts, comparing 2006–207 to 2018–2019, dropping to just 21.7 percent. In contrast, MBI rose about 42.6 percent to over 67 percent as a share of net receipts. The relative decline in BI increased significantly the unions' aggregated dependency on MBI for revenue, meaning a sizable lost opportunity to diversify its recurring income streams. During this period, the unions' "other receipts" as a share of net receipts ranged from a low of 7.7 percent in 2006–2007 to a high of 11.4 percent in 2016–2017 before falling to 10.7 percent in 2018–2019.

Table 3.3 breaks down the unions' aggregated functional expenditures as a share of net disbursements over the same 14-year span. It reports the percentage of net disbursements allocated to the categories of representation, political action, general administration, and general overhead. Over these seven intervals, the most noticeable change in the relative allocation of spending occurred in political action and general overhead, both of which constitute a relatively small share of overall functional spending. General overhead rose from just under 8 to 11.1 percent, or 40 percent. Political spending more than doubled from 3.1 percent of net disbursements in 2006–2007 to a high of 7.2 percent in 2012–2013. Union administration remained relatively flat, fluctuating from 7.7 percent in 2014–2015 to 8.7 percent in the last two intervals. The largest category of spending throughout the period among these specific line items is representation, which ranged from 18.9 percent (2006–2007) to 25.2 percent (2012–2013).

Trends in Operating, Compensation, and Administration Budgets

The unions' MBI and operating budget are covered in Figure 3.4. Each rose more or less steadily over the seven intervals, but MBI rose at a significantly higher rate (34 percent) than the operating budgets (18 percent). At the end of the 14-year span, the nationals' aggregated MBI totaled almost $3.9 billion, compared to operating budgets that totaled $2.9 billion.

The 53 unions' total spending on compensation to officers and employees climbed 15 percent comparing 2006–2007 to 2018–2019, ending the period at about $1.64 billion (see Figure 3.5). Expenditures on administration jumped 18 percent over the entire span, comparing the end to beginning. In 2018–2019, the unions spent a total of almost $1.16 billion on administration.

Trends in Current Assets and Current Liabilities

The data reveal that unions' aggregated current assets vastly exceed current liabilities throughout this 14-year span (Figure 3.6). Comparing end to start periods, the unions' current assets climbed 21 percent while their current liabilities rose 19 percent, which effectively means that the gap between the two widened in comparing these two points in time. To illustrate the huge difference between current assets and current liabilities, the unions held about $2.65 billion in 2018–2019 in

Table 3.3 Select Items as a Percentage of Net Disbursements

Disbursements	*2006–2007*	*2008–2009*	*2010–2011*	*2012–2013*	*2014–2015*	*2016–2017*	*2018–2019*
Representation (%)	18.9	24.9	23.9	25.2	25.1	23.6	22.7
Union administration (%)	8.1	8.1	8.5	8.4	7.7	8.7	8.7
General overhead (%)	7.9	9.7	10.2	11.0	10.7	10.6	11.1
Political (%)	3.1	5.9	5.5	7.2	5.3	5.7	5.3
Other disbursements (%)	0.0	0.0	0.0	0.0	0.0	0.0	0.0
Net disbursements ($ in millions)	6,096.55	4,900.87	4,935.80	4,647.48	5,118.62	5,371.76	5,626.69

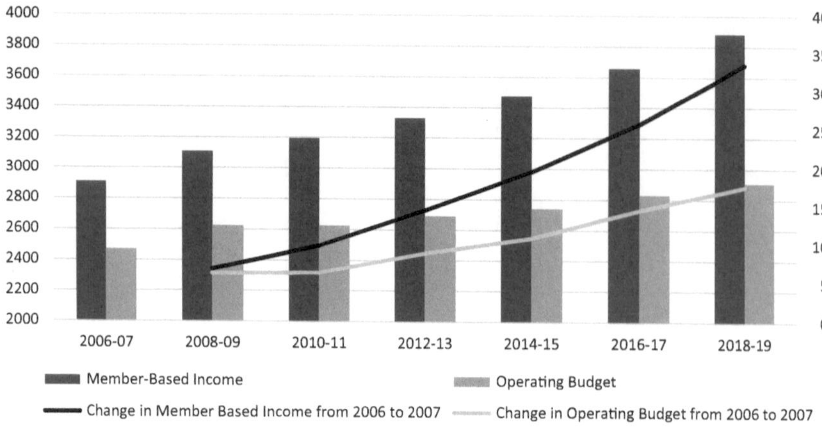

Figure 3.4 Operating Budget and Member-based Income (MBI).

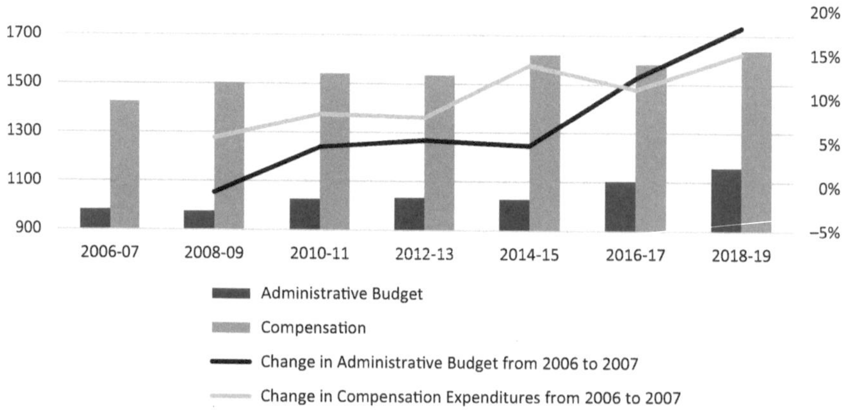

Figure 3.5 National Unions' Administrative Budget and Compensation Expenditures (in Millions).

current assets compared to under $170 million in current liabilities, yielding a 15-fold gap. The net result of the vast and consistent difference between current assets and current liabilities is that "working capital" (current assets minus current liabilities) closely tracks current assets. The unions' aggregated working capital approached nearly $2 billion in 2006–2007 before declining by almost 23 percent in 2012–2013. It rose to about $2.476 billion in 2018–2019, ending the time span 25 percent higher than at the beginning interval.

As shown in Figure 3.7, the unions' operating budgets comprised between 40.5 and 57.9 percent of their net disbursements, with the peak occurring in 2012–2013 and low point in 2006–2007. Compensation comprised between 23 and 33 percent, following a similar pattern in low and peak points. The unions' administrative costs ranged from 16.1 percent (2006–2007) to 22.2 percent (2012–2013).

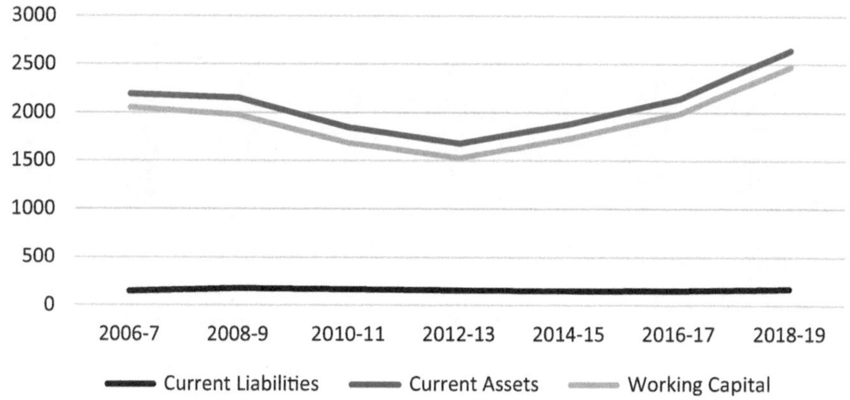

Figure 3.6 Current Assets, Current Liabilities, and Working Capital.

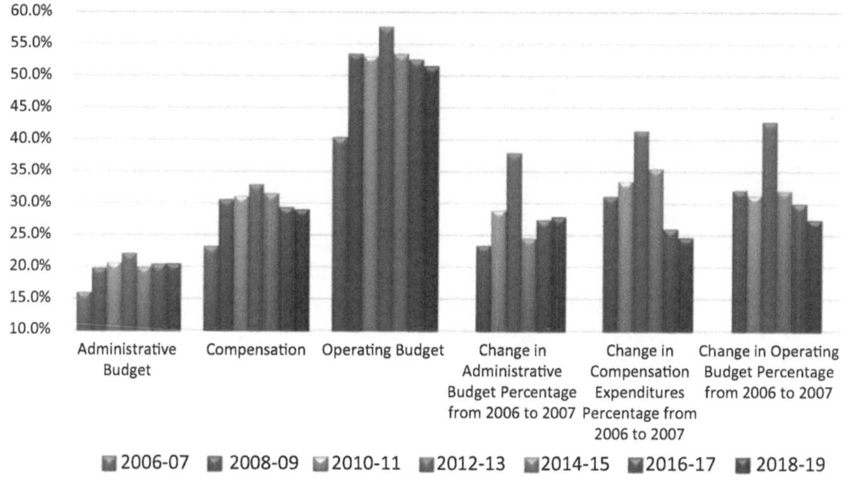

Figure 3.7 National Unions' Compensation Expenditures, Administrative, and Operating Budgets as a Percentage of Net Disbursements.

The relative amount devoted to these sets of expenditures rose during the recession years, which reflected declining levels of net disbursements.

Trends in Per-Member Net Receipts, MBI, Operating Budget, and Administrative Budget

Figure 3.8 reports on the unions' aggregated per-member MBI and net receipts and their spending on administration and operating budgets. Per-member net receipts amounted to slightly above \$333 in 2006–2007 but dropped to \$272.23 in 2008–2009. While it then rose to almost \$306 in 2018–2019, it ended the 14-year span 8.6 percent lower than at the start. The per-member MBI rose by the largest

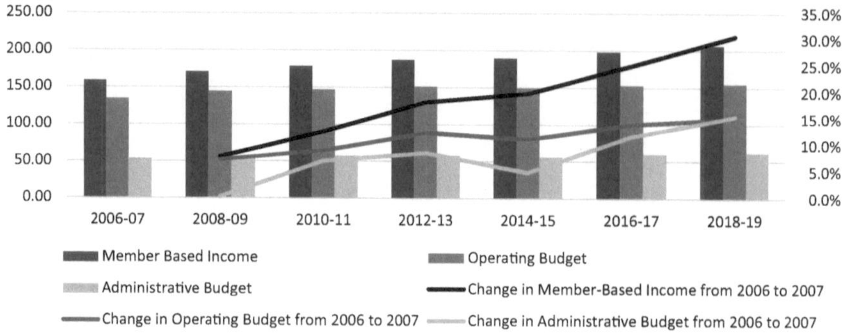

Figure 3.8 National Unions' Member-based Income, Operating, and Administrative Budgets (per Member).

percentage (30.6 percent), comparing end to beginning years, climbing to slightly above \$206 in 2018–2019. Per-member operating budgets increased 15.1 percent from 2006–2007 to 2018–2019, ending at almost \$155. Expenditures on administration jumped 15.5 percent to just under \$62. On a per-member basis, then, the unions, in aggregate, had substantially more MBI than needed to cover operating costs.

Trends in Aggregated Financial Performance

The 53 national unions' aggregated financial performance ratios appear in Figure 3.9. Comparing the end to start two-year averages, the unions' performance ratios improved in each instance. Operating capacity rose from 1.18 to 1.34,

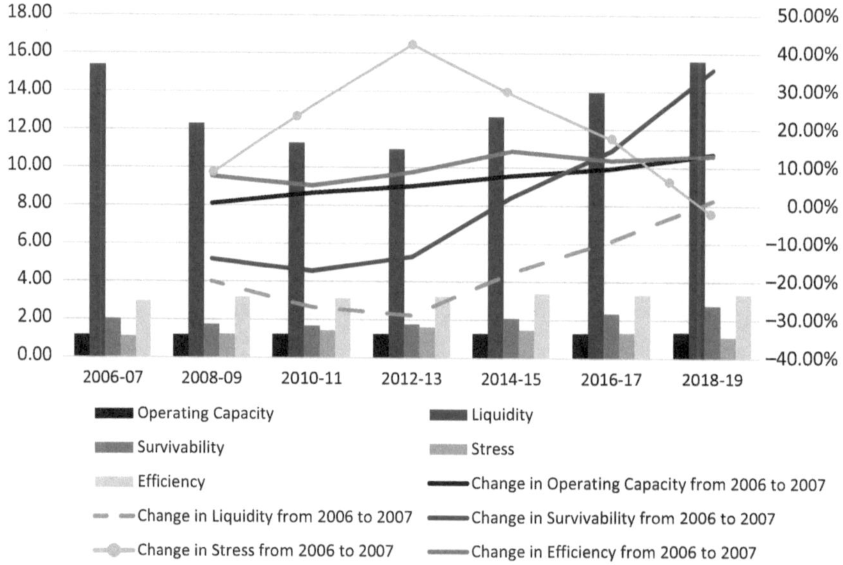

Figure 3.9 National Unions' Financial Ratios.

meaning that for each interval the unions had, aggregated, 18 to 34 percent more in MBI than in operating budget expenses. As suggested in Figure 3.9, the unions' liquidity ratios revealed current assets vastly in excess of current liabilities. In 2006–2007, the ratio approached 15.4, just slightly lower than in 2018–2019, when it was 15.54. The unions' survive ratio stood at 2.03 in 2006–2007, meaning that their net assets exceeded operating budgets by slightly more than two times. In 2018–2019, the ratio was 2.76. Thus, the unions had more than enough in net assets, in aggregate, to cover operating budgets for a considerable period of time beyond the one-year point. The stress ratio also improved comparing the beginning to end periods: 1.13 in 2006–2007 compared to 1.10 in 2018–2019. Keep in mind that a high stress ratio means that operating budgets are relatively high compared to current assets. Reflecting difficult economic times, the unions' aggregated stress ratio rose during the recession years, peaking at 1.60 in 2012–2013. Last, the unions' efficiency showed improvement, particularly comparing the time periods from 2014–2015 to 2018–2019 to the earlier ones. In 2006–2007, the efficiency ratio indicated that the unions had 2.96 times the amount in MBI compared to administration costs. In each of the two-year intervals from 2014–2015 to 2018–2019, the efficiency ratio ranged from 3.39 (2014–2015) to 3.32 (2016–2017). In 2018–2019, the 3.35 ratio indicated that the unions had more than three- and one-third times the amount in MBI than in administrative expenses.

We provide two measures of return on assets: (1) Return on Assets-Net Receipts (ROA-NR), which is the ratio between the unions' aggregated net receipts to their total assets for the relevant time period and (2) RO-A-MBI, which is the ratio between the unions' aggregated MBI to their total assets. Figure 3.10 reports the ROA-NR and ROA-MBI ratios. It shows that the net receipts to total assets ratios deteriorated continually, falling from 0.9 percent to about 0.55 over these

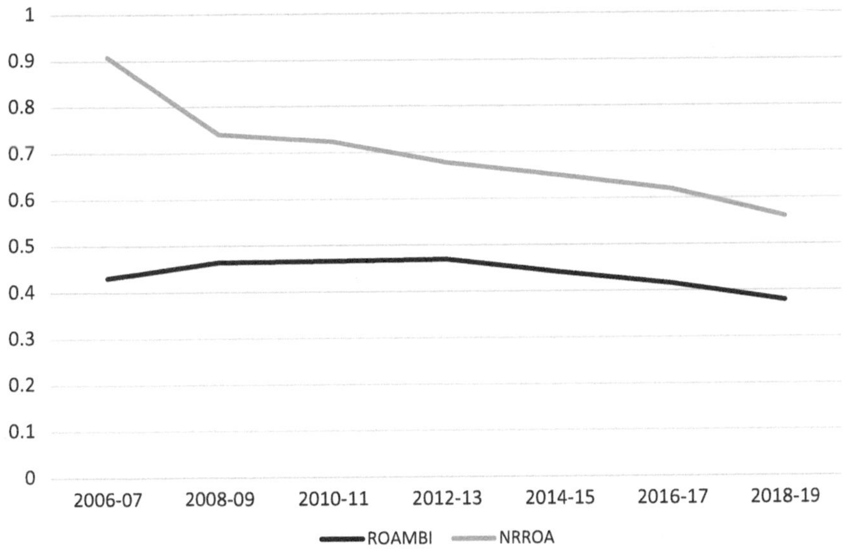

Figure 3.10 Return on Assets: Net Receipts (NRROA) and MBI (ROAMBI).

seven two-year intervals. Thus, at the end of this time frame, the unions, aggregated, had net receipts that approximated 55 percent of their total assets, compared to over 90 percent at the start of the 14 years reviewed. Thus, their combined returns from this financial measure declined significantly.

MBI as a percentage of total assets rose modestly from 43 to nearly 47 percent between 2006–2007 and 2012–2013 but then declined by nearly one-fifth to 37.8 percent in 2018–2019. Thus, to some extent, the unions' position shows a deterioration over the extended time period.

Conclusions

These data reveal several important trends. First, the administrative costs of doing union business continue to rise even during periods in which net revenues may shrink. This suggests that there are some built-in rigidities to operating a union that may be resistant to cuts and that display an innate tendency to rise. Parenthetically, the steady rise in administrative costs lends at least partial support to the theory of "cost disease" espoused by Willman, Bryson, and Froth (2020). Second, notwithstanding declines in net revenues that coincide with the recession and downturn in union membership (aggregated), MBI grew steadily and at a higher rate than operating budgets. Unions retain and actually improve their overall capacity to finance operations from recurring MBI sources. This reflects a financial capacity to offset the negative effects of an economic downturn and attendant loss in union membership. Third, the unions' net-asset positions remain resilient during such economic challenges. Fourth, unions overall indicate that they improve their financial management and hence performance even when they are undergoing stress. While their positions in terms of liquidity and survivability deteriorated when stress rose, the unions recovered as their stress receded. They improved their liquidity even when current liabilities grew. Overall, however, throughout the 14-year span, the unions held their absolute liabilities to modest levels.

4 How Unions Raise Money

Union Dues and Other Member-based Income

This chapter examines how unions raise money from their members. National unions typically derive pertinent revenue from members in two ways: directly from dues paid by members or indirectly from dues paid to locals who pay the national a per capita tax. National unions may also charge other fees, such as initiation fees, to generate revenue. We first review data on the dues rates unions charged to members in 2019 compared to 2006, noting that most had raised their dues. Though dues rates vary widely, they tend to be relatively modest. Thirty-nine of the national unions raise money from either direct dues payments or per capita taxes. On average, unions raised between 32.97 percent of their overall member-based income (MBI) from dues in 2018–2019 compared to 61.65 from per capita taxes. Twelve unions raised between 90 and 100 percent of their net receipts from MBI, and the average percentage rose from 60 to 70.2 percent comparing 2018–2019 to 2006–2007. Reflecting the wide variability in dues rates, unions ranged in per-member MBI from $53.12 in the last two-year interval to over $3427. Five unions raised more than $1,000 in MBI per member.

In this chapter, we provide a detailed discussion on the types of revenues national unions derive from their members in the form of dues, per capita taxes, and fees. National unions vary in terms of how they are financed from members. In some cases, a national organization receives dues payments directly from the membership, which may be a constitutionally fixed portion of the overall dues rate charged. In other cases, unions may collect a per capita tax imposed on local unions, which are the original recipients of the tax. National unions may also charge initiation fees or various other assessments to members to fund operations on an ongoing basis or, in the case of special assessments, in instances of emergency.

To put the matter of national unions' members-based income into perspective, we note that the LMRDA's Bill of Rights clause embedded in the statute gives members at the local and national levels the right to participate in setting dues, fees, and assessments by direct secret-ballot votes or indirect action through duly (secret-ballot) elected delegates. Unions establish the precise mechanisms to comport with these statutory requirements in their constitutions and bylaws. Few issues determined by members or their elected representatives provoke as much controversy as setting dues and other charges for membership.

DOI: 10.4324/9781003335474-5

Funding the National Unions from Member-based Income

National unions raise money from members directly through dues charges paid by eligible rank and file, plus other fees and assessments determined necessary according to constitutional procedures, or through per capita taxes charged to locals and intermediate bodies which essentially "pass-through" the revenue to their respective nationals. As shown in Table 4.1, 39 unions raised revenues from either per capita collections or dues (or both sources). Twenty-seven unions raise revenues only from per capita taxes among these two mechanisms. Fourteen unions do not collect per capita taxes.

Table 4.1 National Unions MBI by Source for FY 2019

Union	*Dues ($)*	*Tax ($)*	*Fees ($)*
ALPA	219,000,000	–	640,422
NATCA	26.578,355	–	–
AMA	1,630,870	–	–
APA	49,347,230	–	–
BRICK	41,857,265	–	347,754
DIRECTOR	24,319,673	–	5,580,310
NALC	36,667,120	–	–
UMW	9,804,058	–	4,483,361
NEA	369,000,000	–	–
USW	298,000,000	–	353,403
TWU	26,373,010	–	–
NTUE	29,528,521	–	649,725
AAUP	7,322,723	–	–
WRITER	34,966,851	–	1,054,278
PLASTER	18,870,206	392,638	227,905
ILA	19,274,120	548,274	–
SIU	–	854,590	675,996
NOVELTY	–	9,34,281	–
INSULATE	–	3,392,492	10,944,216
MUSIC	5,421,127	4,117,404	193,102
IUOE	118,392	4,824,645	89,653
SPFP	–	5,939,993	53,527
JOURNEY	–	6,629,163	32,580
ILWU	–	8,230,259	–
ROOFER	–	8,343,821	394,647
BAKERY	–	9,159,425	89,506
UTILITY	7,603	13,276,541	24,207
OPEIU	–	16,263,226	340,663
BOILER	29,797,315	16,458,746	365,536
CARP	54,831,764	18,861,639	714,035
ELEVATOR	10,000	21,050,230	1,122,472
TU	8,864	29,565,960	92,363
IRON	–	30,363,991	20,600,661
STAGE	–	30,791,066	2,207,560
PAINTER	–	34,135,144	–
APWU	–	44,436,113	11,416,699
NALC	–	44,630,057	–

(*Continued*)

Table 4.1 (Continued)

Union	*Dues ($)*	*Tax ($)*	*Fees ($)*
IAFF	–	52,745,585	257,619
IFPTE	379,332	64,653,130	2,496,299
UNITE	63,982	65,306,598	–
SHEET	–	74,897,066	1,806,416
AFGE	–	79,327,096	–
LIU	–	93,588,796	–
PLUMBER	–	94,959,532	13,623,088
CWA	–	124,000,000	11,970
IBEW	–	144,000,000	2,618,426
IAM	740,861	144,000,000	28,254
AFT	–	179,000,000	–
AFSCME	–	181,000,000	1,135,277
UAW	–	181,000,000	30
IBT	–	189,000,000	5,584,356
UFCW	–	226,000,000	1,799,980
SEIU	–	272,000,000	–

National Unions' Dues Rates, 2019 and 2006

Table 4.2 reports the national unions' dues rates as reported in either their LM-2 forms or constitutions. LM-2 forms include a line item for reporting dues rates and initiation fees. Many unions establish multiple rates for different levels of membership with variations across either occupation or industry. In most cases involving these 53 nationals, the unions report their rates in the forms, either on the specific line or in notes at the end of the disclosures. In some cases, however, it is not possible to find those rates on the online disclosures of the forms.

The data show that unions vary widely in dues rates charges relevant to the national level. Generally speaking, the rates are modest, set as small amounts on a monthly basis. Some nationals set rates based on absolute amounts, requiring payments within specified amounts, which may be tied to members' income levels. In other cases, unions charge a dues payment equivalent to wages earned by workers for a certain number of specified hours, such as two hours of wages earned a month. In yet other unions, dues are tied to a specified percentage of income (e.g. total package or gross earning) earned by the members. As suggested, these dues collections may be made initially by the local unions and then transmitted to the nationals or, alternatively, the collections may be made directly by the national.

Membership-based Income

Table 4.3 provides disaggregated data on the national unions' revenue obtained from dues, per capita taxes, and fees. In 2018–2019, the totals for member-based income (MBI) ranged from a low of $930,000 (NOVELTY) to $371.37 million (NEA). NEA is the only union to raise over $300 million in that interval, with just another four raising more than $200 million. Forty unions had MBI levels below

Table 4.2 National Unions' Dues Rates

Union	*2019*	*2006*
ALPA	1.95% of pay	1.95% of pay
NATCA	1.4% of pay	1.05% of pay
AMA	$26.84–$141.31	$18.7–$71.68
APA	1.5% of pay	1% of pay
UAW	2 hours pay/month	
BAKERY	$12.75/month	$8.75/month
BOILER	$28/month	$20.65/month
BRICK	$.95–$24.35/month	$5.65–$17.9/month
CARP	$15.8/month	$13.75/month
CWA	2.25 hours/month	2.25 hours per month
DIRECTOR	$200–$4550	$200–$4550
IBEW	$10/month	$10/month
ELEVATOR	$64/month	$25/month
IUOE	$18/month	$25/month
EPT	$5.93–$8.72/month	$4.32–$6.35/month
IAFF	$7.29–$14.84/month 9.17–$9.95/month	
UFCW	416.04–$21.05/month	$12.54–$17.90/month
AFGE	$2–$21.96/month	$.50–$16.55/month
INSULATE	$3–$14/month	$2–$14/month
IRON	14–$29.65/month	$10–$21.15/month
JOURNEY	$24 per month	$15–$60/month
LIU	$5–$20/month	$4.5–$13.5/month
NALC	$8.8/biweekly	$6.25/biweekly
NRLCA	$56–$530	$30–$153
ILWU	$7.76–$29.02/month	$6.10–$23.71/month
ILA	.9% of pay	.9% of pay
IAM	$5–$70.3/month	$5–$20.26 month
UMW	$2–$91.91/month	$1.25–$58.05 month
MUSIC	$44–$66/month	$28–$52 month
NEA	.00225 * average pay. 00225	NA
NOVELTY	$15–$82.53 biweekly	$48.7–$108.9
OPEIU	$10.57–$12.92/month	$6.87–$9.37/month
PAINTER	$1–31.7/month	$4.40–$20.10/month
PLASTER	1% gross per month	1% gross per month
PLUMBER	$24–$31/month	$18–$19/month
APWU	$11.11/biweekly	$8.07/biweekly
ROOFER	$21/month	$20/month
SIU	2.5 hours/month	2.25 hours/month
SPFP	2.5 hours/month	2.5 hours/month
SEIU	$12.65/month	$12.65/month
SHEET	$10–$33/month	$5–$26/month
STAGE	$56/quarter	$40–$41/quarter
AFSCME	$18/month	$13.4/month
USW	1.45% of pay/month	1.3% of pay/month
AFT	$19.28/month	$13.2/month
IBT	2.25 times hourly	NA
TU	$2–15.75/month	$2–$9.75/month
TWU	2 hours/month	2 hours/month
NTEU	$35–521/month	$238–498/month
UNITE	$19.15/month	$16.65/month
AAUP	$53–$283/month	$38–$149/month
UTILITY	$24.51/month	$13.05/month
WRITER	1.5% gross earnings	1.5% gross earning

Table 4.3 Member-based Income

Union	*Cycle*							*% Change from 2006–2007 to 2018–2019 (%)*
	2006–2007 ($)	*2008–2009 ($)*	*2010–2011 ($)*	*2012–2013 ($)*	*2014–2015 ($)*	*2016–2017 ($)*	*2018–2019 ($)*	
Air Line Pilots Association	105.77	100.25	107.86	122.60	138.42	185.14	211.83	100.3
Air traffic controllers	19.20	20.09	21.51	23.08	23.43	24.91	26.66	38.9
Aircraft Mechanics Association	2.05	1.07	1.05	1.14	1.24	1.31	1.51	−26.4
Allied Pilots Association	16.27	17.62	17.31	17.23	16.58	28.35	41.08	152.5
Auto workers	180.01	144.42	120.70	115.05	142.56	179.12	180.68	0.4
Bakery, tobacco, and grain	10.02	10.17	10.06	9.96	9.30	8.98	9.02	−10.0
Boilermakers	28.39	38.18	35.57	36.48	38.95	38.55	43.10	51.8
Bricklayers	39.31	37.61	29.57	29.58	32.70	37.70	40.79	3.8
Carpenters	51.19	53.76	52.40	63.12	63.70	66.59	72.79	42.2
Communications workers	139.04	143.22	135.32	127.96	126.36	118.27	124.56	−10.4
Directors Guild of America Inc	17.58	19.68	20.57	21.55	24.80	26.95	29.43	67.4
Electrical Workers IBEW	86.56	93.19	101.22	113.19	127.07	136.74	145.15	67.7
Elevator constructors	8.74	11.26	10.85	10.23	10.95	13.35	21.49	145.9
Engineers, operating	43.38	45.74	49.53	52.53	57.14	60.23	66.54	53.4
Engineers, professional and technical	3.97	4.31	4.73	4.65	4.65	4.98	5.00	25.8
Firefighters	30.56	35.48	38.16	41.32	43.94	46.41	50.99	66.9
Food and commercial workers	187.06	205.40	211.45	210.36	224.27	219.29	226.02	20.8
Government Employees AFGE	41.90	49.44	61.81	66.89	70.29	77.05	80.29	91.6
Insulators	9.36	10.84	11.01	12.24	12.97	12.73	13.82	47.6
Iron workers	33.51	37.94	34.19	39.19	42.17	44.10	49.74	48.4

(Continued)

Table 4.3 (Continued)

Union	*Cycle*							*% Change from 2006–2007 to 2018–2019 (%)*
	2006–2007 ($)	*2008–2009 ($)*	*2010–2011 ($)*	*2012–2013 ($)*	*2014–2015 ($)*	*2016–2017 ($)*	*2018–2019 ($)*	
Journeymen and allied trades	3.71	4.21	4.42	4.06	4.14	4.71	6.35	71.2
Laborers	71.27	76.50	74.17	76.74	79.35	84.00	92.06	29.2
Letter Carriers, National Association	35.64	39.09	40.51	35.76	37.14	40.30	43.94	23.3
Letter carriers, rural	10.29	10.65	10.80	16.49	28.09	30.77	35.13	241.3
Longshore and Warehouse Union	6.91	6.94	6.73	7.14	7.16	7.85	8.13	17.6
Longshoremen's Association	13.16	21.65	18.63	23.73	24.30	24.68	22.77	73.0
Machinists	91.26	98.66	113.60	129.27	135.04	134.62	142.48	56.1
Mine workers, united,	18.76	19.49	20.64	22.16	19.61	14.38	14.77	−21.3
musicians	9.23	9.79	9.07	8.95	9.22	9.43	9.52	3.1
National Education Association	306.41	346.53	366.64	367.38	362.87	368.51	371.37	21.2
Novelty and Production Workers	0.71	0.60	0.58	0.74	0.89	0.90	0.93	30.6
Office and professional employees	11.48	12.14	13.22	13.96	15.02	16.18	16.53	44.0
Painters	24.25	26.31	25.81	25.33	27.03	30.79	32.62	34.5
Plasterers and cement masons	15.59	15.12	11.35	12.13	14.03	16.95	18.70	20.0
plumbers	67.31	74.80	74.41	80.68	86.17	87.08	101.95	51.5
Postal workers, American	53.33	52.56	49.23	50.91	50.81	56.14	57.58	8.0
Roofers	7.18	7.48	7.42	7.21	7.39	8.19	8.71	21.3
Seafarers	1.25	1.11	1.17	1.21	1.24	1.34	1.57	25.0

Security police, fire professionals	4.18	4.25	5.25	5.22	5.18	5.31	5.90	41.1
Service employees	238.74	259.43	291.58	298.75	290.58	279.18	280.67	17.6
Sheet metal, air, rail, and transportation workers	37.93	40.48	42.82	54.41	64.95	69.48	76.43	101.5
Stage and picture operators	16.61	18.51	19.71	21.21	25.03	28.38	32.50	95.6
State, county, and municipal employees	149.96	184.56	189.04	179.37	177.27	184.88	182.12	21.4
Steelworkers	224.87	227.45	248.45	282.73	285.28	275.15	298.23	32.6
Teachers	125.13	146.59	156.97	159.87	164.05	184.86	187.80	50.1
Teamsters	159.08	160.67	161.19	161.54	168.98	178.30	190.27	19.6
Transit Union	17.80	19.82	20.95	21.84	23.59	27.12	29.57	66.2
Transport workers	16.62	17.94	18.64	19.05	20.63	23.12	25.42	53.0
Treasury Employees Union	20.51	27.82	32.57	32.54	33.17	29.86	29.77	45.2
Unite Here	61.51	58.86	47.34	51.34	53.24	56.48	62.56	1.7
University Professors	4.90	5.86	5.66	5.76	6.94	7.38	7.37	50.2
Utility workers	7.88	9.17	9.79	9.68	11.16	11.79	12.95	64.4
Writers Guild West	19.74	20.39	20.99	22.99	25.22	28.10	35.08	77.7
Average	**54.85**	**58.59**	**60.27**	**62.80**	**65.59**	**69.00**	**73.25**	**33.5**

$50 million over the 2018–2019 averaged period, with 11 of these recording less than $10 million. Across these seven two-year intervals, the average union MBI rose 33.5 percent from $54.85 million to $73.25 million between 2006–2007 and 2018–2019. Just four unions (UMW, BAKERY, AMA, and CWA) generated less MBI in 2006–2007 to 2018–2019.

The unions' MBI totals as a percentage of net receipts appear in Table 4.4. The range extended from a high of almost 98 percent (ILWU) to 17.9 percent in 2018–2019. Twelve unions generated more than 90 percent of their net receipts from MBI, while another 29 obtained between 50 and 90 percent. Only seven unions got less than 40 percent from MBI. The average percentage jumped from 60 to 70.2 percent over the seven-year time intervals or 17 percent. Fifteen unions ended up raising less MBI relative to net receipts in 2018–2019 than in 2006–2007.

Dues, Per Capita, and Fees

Table 4.5 shows dues as a percentage of MBI. Parenthetically, as noted earlier, national labor organizations tend to raise the bulk of their MBI from either dues directly or a per capita tax on locals. Thus, 26 unions reported generating no revenue from dues in 2018–2019 (which is generally applicable to the other time intervals). Seven unions got 100 percent from dues, with another 11 generating over 50 percent from dues. The average percentage of MBI from dues grew from 32.29 percent in 2006–2007 to 32.97 percent in 2018–2019, which is a relatively modest 2.1 percent. This trend suggests that unions maintained existing arrangements for generating MBI over this time period, with few exceptions.

The unions' per capita tax as a share of MBI (Table 4.6) ranged from zero to 100 percent, with eight unions drawing all of their MBI in 2018–2019. Fourteen unions received no revenue from a per capita tax. Twenty-six unions raised between 50 and 100 percent from the per capita tax, with 21 of these raising between 90 and 100 percent. The average percentage raised across unions stood at 61.65 percent in 2018–2019 compared to 62.81 percent in 2006–2007. It peaked at 64.81 percent in 2012–2013.

Table 4.7 displays fees as a share of MBI. Only one union (INSULATE) generated more than 50 percent of its MBI from fees in 2018–2019. Five unions generated between 10 and 50 percent. Eighteen unions generated no revenue from fees. Across the unions, the average percentage raised from fees rose from 4.9 percent to 5.38 percent comparing 2006–2007 to 2018–2019.

In Table 4.8, we report the 53 national unions' MBI per member over the seven two-year intervals. Parenthetically, we use per-member MBI as a proxy for the financial burden unions impose on members as a price for joining and maintaining membership. In 2018–2019, the range in per-member MBI extended from a low of $53.12 to almost $3427. Five unions raised more than $1,000 per member in this interval, while six others had levels between $500 and $1,000. Another 38 unions had per-member levels from $100 to $500, with the average being roughly $454.4 in 2018–2019. Over the 14-year span, per-member MBI rose 52.9 percent. Just three unions (SEIU, CWA, and AFT) had a lower per-member MBI in 2018–2029 than 2006–2007.

Table 4.4 Member-based Income as a Percentage of Net Receipts

Union	*Cycle*							*% Change from 2006–2007 to 2018–2019 (%)*
	2006–2007 (%)	*2008–2009 (%)*	*2010–2011 (%)*	*2012–2013 (%)*	*2014–2015 (%)*	*2016–2017 (%)*	*2018–2019 (%)*	
Air Line Pilots Association	45.6	48.3	70.7	68.3	68.5	76.6	70.0	53.5
Air traffic controllers	90.6	85.2	87.0	89.5	90.7	82.7	87.0	−3.9
Aircraft Mechanics Association	25.6	28.3	53.4	46.2	61.6	47.7	48.0	87.0
Allied Pilots Association	36.1	58.0	52.9	61.2	39.8	70.4	83.0	129.8
Auto workers	59.4	50.7	47.5	51.2	59.2	70.8	64.6	8.8
Bakery, tobacco, and grain	36.1	31.1	53.1	52.9	40.6	46.0	75.3	108.5
Boilermakers	79.6	81.4	66.9	61.2	86.2	47.7	51.0	−35.9
Bricklayers	75.4	81.5	80.9	77.0	81.4	83.8	83.3	10.4
Carpenters	26.6	55.0	26.1	53.6	48.1	59.5	47.7	79.4
Communications workers	21.9	27.8	39.9	75.1	84.5	55.3	82.0	274.2
Directors Guild of America Inc.	36.8	39.2	41.5	38.5	44.6	42.2	45.0	22.3
Electrical Workers IBEW	10.4	38.6	40.4	40.2	43.4	39.6	54.4	421.4
Elevator constructors	73.0	69.8	88.6	91.5	83.7	90.6	93.7	28.5
Engineers, operating	52.7	67.8	74.3	75.4	74.4	48.2	32.6	−38.1
Engineers, professional and technical	93.0	95.6	98.2	95.5	91.7	95.8	95.1	2.2
Firefighters	63.5	69.5	73.1	72.9	72.7	69.0	66.2	4.2
Food and commercial workers	82.4	80.8	79.2	76.5	81.6	80.1	77.2	−6.4
Government Employees AFGE	84.3	83.0	73.8	82.3	78.6	83.9	89.3	6.0
Insulators	88.8	92.5	92.6	93.6	89.5	89.7	90.1	1.4
Iron workers	37.8	40.5	37.2	48.4	58.4	48.3	22.2	−41.2

(*Continued*)

Table 4.4 (Continued)

Union	*Cycle*							*% Change from 2006–2007 to 2018–2019 (%)*
	2006–2007 (%)	*2008–2009 (%)*	*2010–2011 (%)*	*2012–2013 (%)*	*2014–2015 (%)*	*2016–2017 (%)*	*2018–2019 (%)*	
Journeymen and allied trades	96.3	99.0	97.8	92.2	88.8	85.1	83.2	−13.7
Laborers	59.0	87.3	82.0	85.5	75.5	78.7	85.0	44.2
Letter Carriers, Natl Association	23.5	31.9	23.4	21.2	18.9	21.1	37.6	60.0
Letter carriers, rural	84.1	81.9	74.0	86.7	88.2	88.7	89.3	6.1
Longshore and Warehouse Union	96.1	97.6	93.6	98.6	98.9	99.1	97.6	1.5
Longshoremen's Association	59.2	78.3	93.9	90.8	82.3	85.3	88.0	48.7
Machinists	74.7	70.7	87.8	86.3	89.5	88.1	87.4	17.0
Mine workers, united,	49.0	57.1	18.7	36.2	25.9	27.0	45.0	−8.1
musicians	70.0	81.0	77.6	76.1	73.5	69.4	68.4	−2.2
National Education Association	88.1	94.2	92.0	94.9	93.8	95.4	95.1	7.9
Novelty and production workers	25.6	21.7	15.8	22.7	21.8	21.7	22.0	−14.0
Office and professional employees	74.1	73.2	78.8	81.5	87.8	92.8	93.2	25.8
Painters	30.5	56.9	53.2	61.7	63.3	67.9	64.3	110.9
Plasterers and cement masons	52.0	46.6	76.2	90.2	93.4	92.9	92.5	77.9
Plumbers	45.7	40.3	42.0	45.0	38.2	34.5	59.2	29.7
Postal workers, American	62.0	64.9	70.7	80.9	85.6	91.2	85.3	37.5
Roofers	80.2	76.0	80.7	80.5	79.9	79.8	84.4	5.2
Seafarers	80.6	79.0	80.3	78.2	78.8	86.9	92.3	14.4
Security police, fire professional	75.3	81.9	87.5	87.6	90.8	92.0	91.4	21.3
Service employees	86.8	79.7	87.5	82.5	90.6	90.6	75.2	−13.3

Sheet metal, air, rail, and transportation workers	37.3	60.4	57.0	82.5	59.6	84.6	71.3	91.4
Stage and picture operators	21.0	22.4	33.4	34.3	37.5	32.7	33.6	60.0
State, county, and municipal employees	91.3	93.4	92.3	90.5	89.9	91.3	92.4	1.2
Steelworkers	32.3	77.7	85.5	86.1	81.3	77.4	76.1	135.5
Teachers	70.7	86.3	84.9	55.4	55.2	63.4	71.3	0.9
Teamsters	87.6	87.4	89.1	91.4	91.1	92.1	91.7	4.7
Transit Union	40.6	61.1	70.7	70.2	18.1	33.2	38.5	−5.1
Transport workers	33.4	35.7	55.3	57.4	64.3	22.3	17.9	−46.5
Treasury Employees Union	71.0	79.4	58.1	67.8	89.2	82.8	77.0	8.4
Unite Here	58.4	55.4	36.0	58.4	61.5	56.8	53.7	−8.1
University Professors	71.5	84.3	88.3	87.4	91.2	81.0	63.7	−11.0
Utility workers	84.7	85.3	63.7	66.5	76.9	78.8	92.5	9.3
Writers Guild West	47.2	34.3	40.3	40.5	44.8	42.9	47.2	−0.1
Average	**60.0**	**65.8**	**66.9**	**70.2**	**69.9**	**69.0**	**70.2**	**17.0**

Table 4.5 Dues as a Percentage of Member-based Income

Union	*Cycle*							*% Change from 2006–2007 to 2018–2019 (%)*
	2006–2007 (%)	*2008–2009 (%)*	*2010–2011 (%)*	*2012–2013 (%)*	*2014–2015 (%)*	*2016–2017 (%)*	*2018–2019 (%)*	
Air Line Pilots Association	99.55	99.20	99.29	99.54	99.60	99.80	99.67	0.1
Air traffic controllers	100.00	100.00	100.00	100.00	100.00	100.00	100.00	0.0
Aircraft Mechanics Association	99.78	99.99	100.00	100.00	99.96	100.00	100.00	0.2
Allied Pilots Association	100.00	100.00	100.00	100.00	100.00	100.00	100.00	0.0
Auto workers	0.00	0.00	0.00	0.00	0.00	0.00	0.00	
Bakery, tobacco, and grain	0.00	0.00	0.00	0.00	0.00	0.00	0.00	
Boilermakers	49.69	55.97	52.76	55.03	57.55	57.41	61.55	23.9
Bricklayers	98.53	98.80	99.23	98.99	99.20	99.28	99.06	0.5
Carpenters	0.00	0.00	0.00	0.00	0.00	0.00	37.66	
Communications workers	99.92	0.00	0.00	0.00	0.00	0.00	0.00	−100.0
Directors Guild of America Inc	84.29	85.25	83.69	83.58	82.43	80.27	81.91	−2.8
Electrical Workers IBEW	0.00	0.00	0.00	0.00	0.00	0.00	0.00	
Elevator constructors	0.00	0.00	0.00	0.00	0.00	0.00	0.02	
Engineers, operating	0.77	2.01	1.87	2.04	1.90	1.76	1.09	41.8
Engineers, professional and technical	5.10	5.52	4.67	4.72	4.94	5.00	3.55	−30.5
Firefighters	0.00	0.00	0.00	0.00	0.00	0.00	0.00	
Food and commercial workers	0.00	0.00	0.00	0.00	0.00	0.00	0.00	
Government Employees AFGE	0.00	0.00	0.00	0.00	0.00	0.00	0.00	
Insulators	0.00	0.00	0.00	0.00	0.00	0.00	0.00	
Iron workers	0.00	0.00	0.00	0.00	0.00	0.00	0.00	
Journeymen and Allied Trades	0.02	0.00	0.00	0.00	0.00	0.00	0.00	−100.0

Laborers	0.00	0.00	0.00	0.00	0.00	0.00	0.00	
Letter Carriers, Natl Association	0.00	0.00	0.00	0.00	0.00	0.00	0.00	
Letter carriers, rural	88.97	94.57	94.69	93.68	100.00	100.00	100.00	12.4
Longshore and Warehouse Union	0.00	0.00	0.00	0.00	0.00	0.00	49.36	
Longshoremen's Association	96.70	96.04	98.98	98.54	98.48	98.01	97.98	1.3
Machinists	0.91	0.78	0.59	0.54	0.54	0.22	0.42	−53.3
Mine workers, united	59.46	59.90	58.91	60.99	63.97	70.19	68.27	14.8
Musicians	49.44	51.66	50.82	53.06	53.22	54.14	55.48	12.2
National Education Association	100.00	100.00	100.00	100.00	100.00	100.00	100.00	0.0
Novelty and production workers	0.00	0.00	0.00	0.00	0.00	0.00	0.00	
Office and professional employees	0.00	0.00	0.00	0.00	0.00	0.00	0.00	
Painters	0.00	0.00	48.71	0.00	0.00	0.00	0.00	
Plasterers and cement masons	97.32	98.57	98.73	98.54	98.37	97.17	96.24	−1.1
Plumbers	0.00	0.00	0.00	0.00	0.00	0.00	0.00	
Postal workers, American	0.00	0.00	0.00	0.00	0.00	0.00	0.00	
Roofers	0.00	0.00	0.00	0.00	0.00	0.00	0.00	
Seafarers	0.00	0.00	0.00	0.00	0.00	0.00	0.00	
Security police, fire professionals	0.00	0.00	0.00	0.00	0.00	0.00	0.00	
Service employees	0.02	0.00	0.00	0.00	0.00	0.00	0.00	−100.0

(*Continued*)

Table 4.5 (Continued)

Union	*Cycle*							*% Change from 2006–2007 to 2018–2019 (%)*
	2006–2007 (%)	*2008–2009 (%)*	*2010–2011 (%)*	*2012–2013 (%)*	*2014–2015 (%)*	*2016–2017 (%)*	*2018–2019 (%)*	
Sheet metal, air, rail, and transportation workers	0.00	0.22	0.00	0.00	0.00	0.00	0.00	
Stage and picture operators	0.00	0.00	0.00	0.00	0.00	0.00	0.00	
State, county, and municipal employees	0.00	0.00	0.00	0.01	0.00	0.00	0.00	
Steelworkers	99.89	99.92	99.91	99.90	99.87	99.89	99.88	0.0
Teachers	0.00	0.00	0.00	0.00	48.37	0.00	0.00	
Teamsters	0.00	0.00	0.00	0.00	0.00	0.00	0.00	
Transit Union	0.05	0.07	0.06	0.04	0.03	0.04	0.03	−46.5
Transport workers	100.00	100.00	100.00	100.00	100.00	100.00	100.00	0.0
Treasury Employees Union	95.99	96.42	97.05	96.30	97.41	93.52	98.05	2.1
Unite Here	0.00	0.00	0.39	0.12	0.00	0.00	0.09	
University Professors	91.66	92.77	92.43	95.70	100.00	100.00	100.00	9.1
Utility Workers	0.00	0.00	0.00	0.00	0.00	0.00	0.03	
Writers Guild West	93.14	92.72	92.77	93.67	94.93	96.08	96.98	4.1
Average	**32.29**	**30.76**	**31.61**	**30.85**	**32.09**	**31.18**	**32.97**	**2.1**

Table 4.6 Taxes as a Percentage of Member-based Income

Union	*Cycle*							*% Change from 2006–2007 to 2018–2019 (%)*
	2006–2007 (%)	*2008–2009 (%)*	*2010–2011 (%)*	*2012–2013 (%)*	*2014–2015 (%)*	*2016–2017 (%)*	*2018–2019 (%)*	
Air Line Pilots Association	0.00	0.00	0.00	0.00	0.00	0.00	0.00	
Air Traffic Controllers	0.00	0.00	0.00	0.00	0.00	0.00	0.00	
Aircraft Mechanics Association	0.00	0.00	0.00	0.00	0.00	0.00	0.00	
Allied Pilots Association	0.00	0.00	0.00	0.00	0.00	0.00	0.00	
Auto workers	99.97	99.98	99.99	100.00	100.00	100.00	100.00	0.0
Bakery, tobacco, and grain	99.09	99.20	99.32	99.25	99.15	99.05	99.00	−0.1
Boilermakers	48.98	42.72	46.13	44.02	41.61	41.78	37.67	−23.1
Bricklayers	0.00	0.00	0.00	0.00	0.00	0.00	0.00	
Carpenters	97.42	98.33	98.79	98.77	98.67	98.81	61.34	−37.0
Communications workers	0.00	99.90	99.94	100.00	100.00	99.88	99.98	
Directors Guild of America Inc	0.00	0.00	0.00	0.00	0.00	0.00	0.00	
Electrical Workers IBEW	96.11	97.20	97.87	98.31	98.74	98.49	98.51	2.5
Elevator constructors	94.94	93.75	95.08	95.07	94.69	94.00	94.79	−0.2
Engineers, Operating	92.28	93.79	95.46	95.16	94.93	95.15	95.28	3.3
Engineers, professional and technical	94.63	94.46	95.30	93.40	93.10	93.17	94.67	0.0
Firefighters	99.38	99.44	99.68	99.66	99.63	99.58	99.48	0.1
Food and commercial workers	98.80	99.04	99.28	99.21	99.16	99.11	99.19	0.4
Government Employees AFGE	100.00	100.00	100.00	100.00	100.00	100.00	100.00	0.0
Insulators	24.19	23.21	20.66	19.71	19.48	23.04	23.17	−4.2
Iron workers	72.90	73.34	75.23	71.71	67.68	66.01	59.96	−17.7

(*Continued*)

Table 4.6 (Continued)

Union	*Cycle*							*% Change from 2006–2007 to 2018–2019 (%)*
	2006–2007 (%)	*2008–2009 (%)*	*2010–2011 (%)*	*2012–2013 (%)*	*2014–2015 (%)*	*2016–2017 (%)*	*2018–2019 (%)*	
Journeymen and allied trades	99.98	100.00	100.00	100.00	100.00	100.00	99.74	−0.2
Laborers	93.84	94.56	97.65	100.00	100.00	100.00	100.00	6.6
Letter Carriers, National Association	100.00	100.00	100.00	100.00	100.00	100.00	100.00	0.0
Letter carriers, rural	0.00	0.00	0.00	0.00	0.00	0.00	0.00	
Longshore and Warehouse Union	100.00	100.00	100.00	100.00	100.00	100.00	50.64	−49.4
Longshoremen's Association	3.30	3.96	1.02	1.46	1.52	1.99	2.02	−38.8
Machinists	99.08	99.18	99.39	99.45	99.41	99.76	99.54	0.5
Mine workers, united	0.00	0.00	0.00	0.00	0.00	0.00	0.00	
Musicians	44.09	45.13	47.01	45.08	45.20	44.14	42.57	−3.4
National Education Association	0.00	0.00	0.00	0.00	0.00	0.00	0.00	
Novelty and production workers	100.00	100.00	100.00	100.00	100.00	100.00	100.00	0.0
Office and professional employees	98.29	98.32	98.35	98.04	98.17	97.95	97.93	−0.4
Painters	97.13	97.75	50.37	100.00	100.00	100.00	100.00	3.0
Plasterers and cement masons	0.00	0.00	0.00	0.77	0.00	1.54	2.62	
Plumbers	98.42	98.36	98.68	94.06	94.66	96.47	91.71	−6.8
Postal workers, American	90.38	90.76	87.43	82.98	81.43	79.17	79.97	−11.5
Roofers	96.81	94.70	95.93	95.90	95.71	95.62	95.56	−1.3
Seafarers	90.56	89.43	84.34	78.00	70.18	65.07	55.84	−38.3
Security police, fire professionals	99.02	98.94	99.31	99.37	99.17	99.24	99.08	0.1

Service employees	99.98	100.00	100.00	100.00	100.00	100.00	100.00	0.0
Sheet metal, air, rail, and transportation workers	95.91	95.68	97.66	97.41	98.17	98.01	97.97	2.2
Stage and picture operators	100.00	100.00	100.00	100.00	93.48	92.97	93.35	−6.7
State, county, and municipal employees	99.59	99.60	99.59	99.54	99.57	99.41	99.38	−0.2
Steelworkers	0.05	0.00	0.00	0.00	0.00	0.00	0.00	−100.0
Teachers	100.00	100.00	100.00	100.00	51.63	100.00	100.00	0.0
Teamsters	96.95	97.83	98.24	97.98	97.47	97.26	97.07	0.1
Transit Union	99.39	99.13	99.09	99.40	99.47	99.29	99.66	0.3
Transport workers	0.00	0.00	0.00	0.00	0.00	0.00	0.00	
Treasury Employees Union	0.00	0.00	0.00	0.00	0.00	0.00	0.00	
Unite Here	99.78	99.87	99.49	99.79	99.92	99.90	99.91	0.1
University professors	8.34	7.23	7.57	4.30	0.00	0.00	0.00	−100.0
Utility workers	99.47	99.58	99.76	99.68	99.61	99.59	99.70	0.2
Writers Guild West	0.00	0.00	0.00	0.00	0.00	0.00	0.00	
Average	**62.81**	**64.61**	**63.84**	**64.29**	**62.86**	**63.69**	**61.65**	**−1.9**

Table 4.7 Fees as a Percentage of Member-based Income

Union	*Cycles*							*% Change from 2006–2007 to 2018–2019 (%)*
	2006–2007 (%)	*2008–2009 (%)*	*2010–2011 (%)*	*2012–2013 (%)*	*2014–2015 (%)*	*2016–2017 (%)*	*2018–2019 (%)*	
Air Line Pilots Association	0.45	0.80	0.71	0.46	0.40	0.20	0.33	−27.2
Air traffic controllers	0.00	0.00	0.00	0.00	0.00	0.00	0.00	
Aircraft Mechanics Association	0.22	0.01	0.00	0.00	0.04	0.00	0.00	−100.0
Allied Pilots Association	0.00	0.00	0.00	0.00	0.00	0.00	0.00	
Auto workers	0.03	0.02	0.01	0.00	0.00	0.00	0.00	−99.9
Bakery, tobacco, and grain	0.91	0.80	0.68	0.75	0.85	0.95	1.00	10.4
Boilermakers	1.33	1.31	1.10	0.96	0.84	0.81	0.78	−41.1
Bricklayers	1.47	1.20	0.77	1.01	0.80	0.72	0.94	−35.8
Carpenters	2.58	1.67	1.21	1.23	1.33	1.19	0.99	−61.5
Communications workers	0.08	0.10	0.06	0.00	0.00	0.12	0.02	−77.5
Directors Guild of America Inc	15.71	14.75	16.31	16.42	17.57	19.73	18.09	15.2
Electrical Workers IBEW	3.89	2.80	2.13	1.69	1.26	1.51	1.49	−61.8
Elevator constructors	5.06	6.25	4.92	4.93	5.31	6.00	5.18	2.5
Engineers, operating	6.95	4.20	2.68	2.80	3.17	3.09	3.62	−47.9
Engineers, professional and technical	0.27	0.02	0.04	1.88	1.96	1.83	1.78	563.5
Firefighters	0.62	0.56	0.32	0.34	0.37	0.42	0.52	−16.3
Food and commercial workers	1.20	0.96	0.72	0.79	0.84	0.89	0.81	−32.9
Government Employees AFGE	0.00	0.00	0.00	0.00	0.00	0.00	0.00	
Insulators	75.81	76.79	79.34	80.29	80.52	76.96	76.83	1.3
Iron workers	27.10	26.66	24.77	28.29	32.32	33.99	40.04	47.7

Journeymen and allied trades	0.00	0.00	0.00	0.00	0.00	0.00	0.26	
Laborers	6.16	5.44	2.35	0.00	0.00	0.00	0.00	−100.0
Letter Carriers, Natl Association	0.00	0.00	0.00	0.00	0.00	0.00	0.00	
Letter carriers, rural	11.03	5.43	5.31	6.32	0.00	0.00	0.00	−100.0
Longshore and Warehouse Union	0.00	0.00	0.00	0.00	0.00	0.00	0.00	
Longshoremen's Association	0.00	0.00	0.00	0.00	0.00	0.00	0.00	
Machinists	0.02	0.04	0.02	0.01	0.04	0.01	0.03	109.8
Mine workers, united	40.54	40.10	41.09	39.01	36.03	29.81	31.73	−21.7
Musicians	6.47	3.22	2.17	1.86	1.58	1.72	1.95	−69.8
National Education Association	0.00	0.00	0.00	0.00	0.00	0.00	0.00	
Novelty and production workers	0.00	0.00	0.00	0.00	0.00	0.00	0.00	
Office and professional employees	1.71	1.68	1.65	1.96	1.83	2.05	2.07	21.1
Painters	2.87	2.25	0.93	0.00	0.00	0.00	0.00	−100.0
Plasterers and cement masons	2.68	1.43	1.27	0.69	1.63	1.29	1.14	−57.5
Plumbers	1.58	1.64	1.32	5.94	5.34	3.53	8.29	423.5
Postal workers, American	9.62	9.24	12.57	17.02	18.57	20.83	20.03	108.1
Roofers	3.19	5.30	4.07	4.10	4.29	4.38	4.44	39.1
Seafarers	9.44	10.57	15.66	22.00	29.82	34.93	44.16	367.8
Security police, fire professionals	0.98	1.06	0.69	0.63	0.83	0.76	0.92	−5.5
Service employees	0.00	0.00	0.00	0.00	0.00	0.00	0.00	
Sheet metal, air, rail, and transportation workers	4.09	4.10	2.34	2.59	1.83	1.99	2.03	−50.4
Stage and picture operators	0.00	0.00	0.00	0.00	6.52	7.03	6.65	

(*Continued*)

Table 4.7 (Continued)

Union	*Cycles*							*% Change from 2006–2007 to 2018–2019 (%)*
	2006–2007 (%)	*2008–2009 (%)*	*2010–2011 (%)*	*2012–2013 (%)*	*2014–2015 (%)*	*2016–2017 (%)*	*2018–2019 (%)*	
State, county, and municipal employees	0.41	0.40	0.41	0.45	0.43	0.59	0.62	49.9
Steelworkers	0.06	0.08	0.09	0.10	0.13	0.11	0.12	115.5
Teachers	0.00	0.00	0.00	0.00	0.00	0.00	0.00	−100.0
Teamsters	3.05	2.17	1.76	2.02	2.53	2.74	2.93	−4.0
Transit Union	0.56	0.80	0.85	0.56	0.50	0.68	0.32	−43.9
Transport workers	0.00	0.00	0.00	0.00	0.00	0.00	0.00	
Treasury employees union	4.01	3.58	2.95	3.70	2.59	6.48	1.95	−51.3
Unite Here	0.22	0.13	0.13	0.09	0.08	0.10	0.00	−100.0
University professors	0.00	0.00	0.00	0.00	0.00	0.00	0.00	
Utility workers	0.53	0.42	0.24	0.32	0.39	0.41	0.27	−49.3
Writers Guild West	6.86	7.28	7.23	6.33	5.07	3.92	3.02	−55.9
Average	**4.90**	**4.63**	**4.54**	**4.86**	**5.05**	**5.13**	**5.38**	**9.9**

Table 4.8 Member-based Income per Member

Union	*Cycle*							*% Change from 2006–2007 to 2018–2019 (%)*
	2006–2007	*2008–2009*	*2010–2011*	*2012–2013*	*2014–2015*	*2016–2017*	*2018–2019*	
Air Line Pilots Association	1,726.23	1,798.54	1,810.09	2,502.13	2,723.03	3,295.03	3,426.97	98.5
Air Traffic Controllers	1,314.47	1,325.31	1,332.91	1,425.22	1,423.00	1,443.73	1,441.69	9.7
Aircraft Mechanics Association	200.44	290.45	374.52	361.48	385.98	388.45	425.98	112.5
Allied Pilots Association	1,473.92	1,851.76	1,850.33	1,777.74	1,347.95	1,955.83	2,866.45	94.5
Auto workers	358.81	367.37	318.74	297.32	351.09	423.04	454.80	26.8
Bakery, tobacco, and grain	107.39	115.31	120.53	129.48	130.07	133.47	139.21	29.6
Boilermakers	442.78	596.87	591.57	646.79	711.60	739.25	874.79	97.6
Bricklayers	413.26	401.92	353.24	383.85	448.45	512.30	555.17	34.3
Carpenters	97.80	109.17	119.78	152.68	148.14	152.95	166.65	70.4
Communications workers	217.32	274.75	278.36	271.64	201.95	183.40	193.27	−11.1
Directors Guild of America Inc	1,297.24	1,367.48	1,396.38	1,412.80	1,546.65	1,581.88	1,635.90	26.1
Electrical Workers IBEW	123.93	131.90	150.94	171.47	192.38	204.44	214.99	73.5
Elevator constructors	330.87	386.26	389.22	402.61	434.95	493.28	748.62	126.3
Engineers, operating	108.29	112.92	128.09	138.19	152.00	158.95	167.09	54.3
Engineers, professional and technical	65.66	67.61	69.73	75.09	77.02	83.76	85.40	30.1
Firefighters	108.87	120.33	129.21	140.37	147.53	151.56	160.94	47.8
Food and commercial workers	143.06	156.17	164.10	165.22	176.39	174.58	182.39	27.5
Government Employees AFGE	180.26	192.38	217.15	222.67	224.72	234.15	244.68	35.7
Insulators	450.12	488.34	523.94	558.81	583.85	570.52	616.99	37.1
Iron workers	256.45	274.49	273.94	321.74	334.43	344.08	385.01	50.1

(*Continued*)

Table 4.8 (Continued)

Union	*Cycle*							*% Change from 2006–2007 to 2018–2019 (%)*
	2006–2007	*2008–2009*	*2010–2011*	*2012–2013*	*2014–2015*	*2016–2017*	*2018–2019*	
Journeymen and allied trades	74.37	73.73	78.54	73.45	71.33	72.13	81.97	10.2
Laborers	110.93	117.55	124.55	135.93	144.97	145.09	160.67	44.8
Letter Carriers, National Association	123.72	135.34	143.82	133.74	135.42	138.75	151.99	22.9
Letter carriers, rural	93.82	94.25	99.88	159.39	271.09	277.20	303.49	223.5
Longshore and Warehouse Union	179.64	166.87	149.65	191.92	206.30	220.93	224.77	25.1
Longshoremen's Association	302.51	497.65	856.41	545.57	620.93	680.29	708.40	134.2
Machinists	140.91	157.17	192.91	225.34	237.29	238.64	247.15	75.4
Mine workers, united	225.77	250.49	264.18	299.98	269.98	220.15	246.97	9.4
Musicians	102.98	110.15	102.28	112.42	119.62	126.46	130.76	27.0
National Education Association	103.25	107.43	115.08	121.00	122.67	123.75	124.24	20.3
Novelty and production workers	41.08	41.66	40.48	45.36	46.49	49.77	54.89	33.6
Office and professional employees	110.45	114.84	131.65	139.24	145.25	148.80	174.47	58.0
Painters	185.71	203.75	229.78	242.28	256.80	280.19	291.28	56.9
Plasterers and cement masons	366.30	352.34	285.02	317.43	366.92	406.13	422.46	15.3
Plumbers	204.22	216.89	220.29	244.47	260.91	256.92	289.58	41.8
Postal workers, American	190.67	203.68	198.06	210.12	209.06	227.83	250.81	31.5
Roofers	306.99	321.97	335.35	340.17	355.70	380.10	388.02	26.4
Seafarers	33.92	32.81	36.34	39.51	42.03	45.71	53.12	56.6

Security police, fire professionals	210.53	162.71	207.37	295.40	304.16	312.47	326.69	55.2
Service employees	146.13	141.58	151.93	159.57	153.68	146.15	144.63	−1.0
Sheet metal, air, rail, and transportation workers	252.94	272.24	311.02	322.62	316.23	341.70	372.89	47.4
Stage and picture operators	155.43	165.85	175.23	183.83	207.77	218.01	228.26	46.9
State, county, and municipal employees	103.29	124.35	130.87	129.73	134.18	139.72	136.57	32.2
Steelworkers	309.43	341.60	410.02	465.99	483.02	486.68	515.52	66.6
Teachers	151.25	167.96	178.27	132.36	102.19	117.89	111.71	−26.1
Teamsters	112.76	116.13	122.27	128.42	130.75	139.65	140.22	24.3
Transit Union	97.53	104.74	109.75	114.19	122.14	136.62	147.27	51.0
Transport workers	142.74	147.60	157.77	164.83	177.16	182.13	185.26	29.8
Treasury Employees Union	263.90	342.93	380.46	396.03	422.15	373.92	372.59	41.2
Unite Here	133.76	193.94	204.32	199.76	201.59	204.14	205.21	53.4
University professors	119.32	142.38	142.89	153.13	179.81	180.21	166.25	39.3
Utility workers	157.53	183.41	195.74	193.65	223.23	259.71	289.41	83.7
Writers Guild West	1,080.23	1,066.60	1,051.13	1,096.81	1,164.12	1,223.51	1,454.11	34.6
Average	**297.19**	**326.45**	**342.00**	**363.60**	**376.34**	**409.92**	**454.50**	**52.9**

Table 4.9 Nationals' Membership by Category

Category	*Count*	*Percentage*
Active	78,93,126	41.7%
Agency	1,20,036	0.6%
Apprentice	1,29,334	0.7%
Associate	1,18,496	0.6%
Members	5,52,912	2.9%
Regular	37,36,042	19.7%
Retired	16,39,230	8.7%
Full time	18,01,072	9.5%
Total	1,89,33,277	
Voting	5,52,912	2.9%
Non-voting	1,83,80,365	97.1%

National Unions' Membership Status, 2019

As noted, unions may differentiate dues rates across members' membership status. Several different types of membership (or dues payers) exist, with rates varying across status. Table 4.9 shows that a sizable number of union members are neither active nor full-dues paying members. Specifically, based on data reported in the union's LM-2 disclosures for 2019, 42 percent of the members across all 53 nationals are classified as "active." Another 19.7 percent fall into the category of "regular" members, with an additional 9.5 percent designated as "full time." Just about 9 percent are "retired" members. Less than 1 percent of the total membership of over 18.9 million falls into each of the classifications of agency payers, apprentices, or associate members.

5 The Unions' Balance Sheets

This chapter presents disaggregated data on the 53 unions' balance sheets. It finds that, on average, the unions total assets' rose 52 percent comparing end to beginning periods, with net assets rising 60 percent. Two unions had more than $1 billion in total assets in the last interval, while three had more than $500 million. On average, the unions' working capital (current assets minus current liabilities) rose 21 percent comparing 2018–2019 to 2006–2007. Seven unions had working capital in excess of $100 million in this last two-year period. Across the unions, the average fixed assets rose from just above $14 million to over $18 million or 27 percent. Over the seven time periods, more than one-third of the total assets are held in working capital. On average, non-fixed assets amounted to between 43 and 46 percent of total assets over the 14 years. In 2018–2019, only three unions held more than one-third of their total in fixed assets. Thirty-four unions had less than 10 percent in the fixed category in 2018–2019. Nearly 83 percent of the unions' liabilities, on average, are held in the umbrella "other" category. Sixty percent of the total other liabilities are comprised of post-retirement healthcare and pension obligations.

We inspect the 53 unions' balance sheets on a disaggregated basis in this chapter. Our data cover the unions' total and net assets, working capital (current assets minus current liabilities), non-fixed investments, and fixed assets. Also, we report the unions' assets, by major category, as a share of total assets and then examine the unions' liabilities.

Total and Net Assets

Table 5.1 reports the national unions' total assets for each of the seven two-year (averaged) periods. It reveals that the average total assets of the unions ranged from a low of just slightly above $126 million (2008–2009) to just under $194 million in 2018–2019. Comparing the end to beginning periods, the average total assets

DOI: 10.4324/9781003335474-6

Table 5.1 Total Assets

Union	*Cycle*							*% Change from 2006–2007 to 2018–2019 (%)*
	2006–2007 ($)	*2008–2009 ($)*	*2010–2011 ($)*	*2012–2013 ($)*	*2014–2015 ($)*	*2016–2017 ($)*	*2018–2019 ($)*	
Air Line Pilots Association	188.76	145.56	123.26	112.63	116.62	200.03	317.64	68.3
Air traffic controllers	23.13	21.14	18.13	16.77	16.50	19.25	18.18	−21.4
Aircraft Mechanics Association	1.81	1.20	1.37	1.38	1.74	2.09	2.55	40.7
Allied Pilots Association	41.62	37.60	42.96	42.22	47.17	46.77	59.21	42.3
Auto workers	1,259.62	1,164.88	1,060.50	996.95	961.54	1,033.35	1,111.15	−11.8
Bakery, tobacco, and grain	39.70	33.80	32.01	31.31	31.45	33.33	33.83	−14.8
Boilermakers	60.70	73.96	73.74	64.40	58.71	59.92	58.77	−3.2
Bricklayers	62.53	60.76	53.79	59.92	65.60	79.51	97.95	56.6
Carpenters	383.05	520.71	556.38	616.98	656.05	684.22	743.69	94.2
Communications workers	543.16	535.29	561.74	514.37	574.31	529.44	554.96	2.2
Directors Guild of America Inc	69.58	77.65	76.78	78.99	77.97	81.93	91.42	31.4
Electrical Workers IBEW	595.16	486.90	491.28	494.64	546.49	546.80	587.02	−1.4
Elevator constructors	16.28	18.97	22.34	20.09	18.28	19.12	29.76	82.8
Engineers, operating	295.50	281.95	312.81	340.58	371.25	462.33	527.51	78.5
Engineers, professional, and technical	1.40	1.67	1.85	2.61	3.28	3.61	4.02	187.7
Firefighters	29.55	26.54	29.27	30.35	31.09	32.55	30.75	4.1
Food and commercial workers	155.89	161.70	178.85	196.84	202.75	274.97	370.47	137.7
Government Employees AFGE	44.62	41.07	46.58	52.76	46.47	45.41	45.68	2.4
Insulators	16.90	18.46	19.95	18.12	21.96	23.67	27.05	60.1
Iron workers	101.20	96.97	97.63	95.06	109.37	108.51	118.87	17.5

Journeymen and allied trades	1.21	1.60	1.22	1.00	1.38	1.77	3.15	161.0
Laborers	119.16	124.88	141.97	166.45	189.35	216.12	267.47	124.5
Letter Carriers, National Association	226.83	291.29	316.51	290.66	325.21	337.90	352.85	55.6
Letter carriers, rural	17.14	17.11	17.22	15.82	16.13	16.56	19.72	15.0
Longshore and Warehouse Union	2.33	2.87	3.38	4.33	6.45	8.09	8.25	253.8
Longshoremen's Association	29.03	16.97	12.84	27.21	42.77	54.11	63.79	119.7
Machinists	225.47	151.36	154.99	155.19	173.69	193.12	233.15	3.4
Mine workers, united	162.51	167.71	175.07	177.78	172.54	163.06	153.31	−5.7
Musicians	12.04	13.44	12.11	14.02	16.20	20.99	27.14	125.5
National Education Association	187.48	201.56	220.18	274.38	349.97	373.41	409.05	118.2
Novelty and production workers	4.66	4.34	4.17	4.52	5.67	6.17	7.09	52.2
Office and professional employees	10.73	13.25	14.96	14.11	13.51	17.21	23.75	121.3
Painters	61.87	82.33	78.46	78.53	76.39	85.40	86.70	40.1
Plasterers and cement masons	20.79	19.55	14.76	15.00	18.32	30.84	40.34	94.0
Plumbers	125.93	195.41	213.02	216.31	259.48	251.56	292.25	132.1
Postal workers, American	38.34	46.37	55.01	58.75	67.69	87.97	121.20	216.1
Roofers	28.30	29.82	31.16	32.69	32.96	36.06	39.53	39.7
Seafarers	1.01	0.82	0.65	0.58	0.99	0.86	1.46	44.3
Security police, fire professionals	3.95	3.40	5.56	8.33	10.72	12.31	17.01	330.3
Service employees	179.43	188.72	227.57	245.60	288.70	328.39	425.73	137.3
Sheet metal, air, rail, and transportation workers	79.51	77.66	85.27	113.48	148.82	170.32	201.83	153.8
Stage and picture operators	43.35	54.28	60.39	66.16	66.09	72.60	78.22	80.4

(Continued)

Table 5.1 (Continued)

Union	*Cycle*							*% Change from 2006–2007 to 2018–2019 (%)*
	2006–2007 ($)	*2008–2009 ($)*	*2010–2011 ($)*	*2012–2013 ($)*	*2014–2015 ($)*	*2016–2017 ($)*	*2018–2019 ($)*	
State, county, and municipal employees	67.90	87.85	102.01	109.37	125.24	180.75	264.15	289.0
Steelworkers	343.09	290.69	368.33	538.73	710.89	884.51	1,197.34	249.0
Teachers	98.71	105.91	104.25	101.57	94.93	104.39	132.19	33.9
Teamsters	192.73	168.94	204.58	230.96	263.88	304.86	372.93	93.5
Transit Union	131.79	124.27	109.93	104.56	152.56	165.26	178.64	35.6
Transport workers	50.27	41.27	29.10	24.82	61.66	112.60	65.47	30.2
Treasury Employees Union	24.62	20.19	29.93	39.94	40.62	42.21	44.33	80.1
Unite Here	259.27	275.28	188.11	107.46	119.45	143.39	177.64	−31.5
University Professors	3.77	3.69	4.23	3.53	3.18	4.98	8.72	131.5
Utility workers	5.02	8.40	8.35	7.84	10.71	14.79	19.34	285.4
Writers Guild West	58.22	59.91	62.89	63.05	73.81	84.34	100.95	73.4
Average	**127.29**	**126.38**	**129.42**	**133.96**	**149.03**	**166.30**	**193.68**	**52.2**

held by the unions rose 52 percent, though a noticeable drop occurred in 2008–2009. Two unions had total assets greater than $1 billion in 2018–2019, with another four reporting more than $500 million. Eighteen unions had an average of more than $100 million in total assets in 2018–2019. Twenty-one unions reported under $50 million in this two-year interval, with seven having less than $10 million. Only seven unions ended the 14-year span with less in total assets than at the start.

Trends in net assets appear in Table 5.2. On average, the unions' net assets rose from about $95 million in 2006–2007 to slightly above $151 million in 2018–2019, or nearly 60 percent. Between 2006–2007 and 2010–2011, the average held in net assets across the 53 unions dropped to $83.35, or about 12 percent. Only three unions had net assets exceeding $500 million in 2018–2019. Nineteen unions reported net assets between $100 million and $500 million in this period. Twenty-three unions had net assets below $50 million, with one reporting a negative number for this dimension (AFGE). Ten unions reported having less net assets on average in 2018–2019 than in 2006–2007.

Working Capital

In Table 5.3, we show the unions' current assets in excess of current liabilities, which captures their "working capital." This measures their relative capacities to fund ongoing operations after paying immediately due bills, without liquidating assets. The unions' average working capital rose about 21 percent from nearly $38.7 million to $46.7 million between 2006–207 and 2018–2019. This increase occurred notwithstanding a fall of 26 percent between 2006–2007 and 2012–2013, when the average stood at $28.8 million. In 2018–2019, seven unions had working capital in excess of $100 million for the two-year averaged period, while 14 reported less than $10 million. The overall range in 2018–2019 extended with just slightly above $1 million to over $255 million, with the average being about $46.7 million. Twelve unions reported lower amounts of working capital in 2018–2019 than in 2006–2007.

Asset Allocations

The unions' total investments in securities and other non-fixed assets appear in Table 5.4. Comparing the end to beginning periods, the average in investments climbed almost 80 percent to $115.5 million, after falling slightly from 2006–2007 to 2008–2009. Two unions showed more than $500 million in non-fixed assets, with another 15 reporting from $100 to $500 million. Sixteen unions reported less than $10 million in this asset category in 2018–2019. Ten unions reported a lower amount of non-fixed assets in 2018–2019 than in 2006–2007.

In Table 5.5, we cover the unions' fixed assets. It shows that, on average, the unions' fixed assets rose from $14.2 million in 2006–2007 to more than

Table 5.2 Net Assets

Union	*Cycle*							*% Change from 2006–2007 to 2018–2019 (%)*
	2006–2007 ($)	*2008–2009 ($)*	*2010–2011 ($)*	*2012–2013 ($)*	*2014–2015 ($)*	*2016–2017 ($)*	*2018–2019 ($)*	
Air Line Pilots Association	138.97	88.00	60.81	36.47	35.02	100.11	206.67	48.7
Air traffic controllers	16.73	15.10	12.97	12.58	12.81	10.36	8.74	−47.7
Aircraft Mechanics Association	0.60	0.12	1.01	1.07	1.45	1.76	2.08	249.9
Allied Pilots Association	30.77	28.45	31.37	36.51	41.84	41.50	48.77	58.5
Auto workers	1,239.12	1,159.19	1,054.64	989.41	953.57	904.45	999.51	−19.3
Bakery, tobacco, and grain	34.42	18.10	17.23	20.68	20.08	26.01	27.44	−20.3
Boilermakers	59.59	73.14	65.02	55.54	57.60	56.33	54.20	−9.1
Bricklayers	58.49	57.95	49.29	56.04	63.44	77.35	95.54	63.3
Carpenters	375.90	515.25	551.28	611.90	650.60	676.73	736.05	95.8
Communications workers	365.55	335.52	279.33	193.14	276.70	254.05	313.09	−14.4
Directors Guild of America Inc	44.33	49.54	51.22	52.99	55.55	58.24	64.71	46.0
Electrical Workers IBEW	385.24	241.66	223.13	185.94	295.76	388.04	420.67	9.2
Elevator constructors	16.03	18.45	21.84	17.69	17.47	12.96	23.57	47.0
Engineers, operating	273.17	232.53	258.83	298.99	330.26	335.65	337.95	23.7
Engineers, professional, and technical	1.18	1.43	1.61	0.99	1.99	2.56	3.19	170.4
Firefighters	21.54	9.90	1.54	−2.69	−1.84	−31.11	24.32	12.9
Food and Commercial Workers	151.53	155.99	174.18	191.76	197.42	269.08	364.46	140.5
Government Employees AFGE	−1.25	−27.26	−26.09	−25.90	−27.01	−38.23	−43.72	3392.3
Insulators	13.88	13.79	14.10	13.64	16.86	19.57	22.66	63.2
Iron workers	97.46	94.32	96.51	94.34	108.44	107.20	117.06	20.1
Journeymen and allied trades	1.04	1.26	0.86	0.78	1.20	1.59	2.93	181.4
Laborers	114.49	122.97	139.57	163.14	184.79	214.63	264.60	131.1
Letter Carriers, National Association	177.98	195.43	235.23	247.70	285.55	300.86	316.50	77.8
Letter carriers, rural	10.07	10.06	8.39	7.51	7.39	6.79	7.90	−21.6
Longshore and Warehouse Union	1.81	2.30	2.77	3.46	5.77	7.36	6.06	234.0
Longshoremen's Association	29.03	16.93	12.81	22.75	36.34	47.25	56.82	95.7

Machinists	217.13	142.08	145.78	148.52	169.89	189.70	230.88	6.3
Mine workers, united	161.57	166.40	173.94	177.29	172.12	160.83	141.41	−12.5
Musicians	8.85	9.33	8.61	10.81	12.81	15.52	20.35	129.9
National Education Association	119.38	143.28	162.25	215.30	294.90	317.77	355.80	198.0
Novelty and production workers	0.67	0.62	0.02	0.03	1.03	1.19	1.99	198.1
Office and professional employees	10.12	12.17	14.42	13.39	12.88	16.73	23.35	130.7
Painters	53.06	78.71	74.46	74.24	72.81	82.26	83.26	56.9
Plasterers and cement masons	20.60	19.39	14.71	14.98	18.30	30.27	39.26	90.6
Plumbers	92.76	143.41	173.04	187.41	233.04	226.96	271.23	192.4
Postal workers, American	33.92	40.13	48.79	54.07	63.51	83.81	115.41	240.2
Roofers	26.92	28.64	29.96	31.29	31.19	34.12	37.41	39.0
Seafarers	0.38	0.17	0.02	−0.17	−0.08	−0.11	0.69	84.2
Security police, fire professionals	2.90	1.57	3.35	5.12	6.69	7.51	10.28	254.9
Service employees	63.98	50.24	108.61	122.38	157.89	222.65	346.73	441.9
Sheet metal, air, rail, and transportation workers	49.54	25.66	27.60	21.02	88.03	99.44	137.57	177.7
Stage and picture operators	35.62	41.40	40.35	37.67	42.90	48.96	50.14	40.8
State, county, and municipal employees	16.27	24.31	25.42	19.82	30.03	78.29	167.70	930.5
Steelworkers	−154.21	−319.17	−448.49	−177.38	36.80	309.37	578.34	−475.0
Teachers	58.97	59.10	43.16	47.78	30.08	13.02	39.70	−32.7
Teamsters	108.27	76.05	123.18	163.95	214.60	284.12	344.20	217.9
Transit Union	124.72	117.02	103.23	97.93	145.74	158.21	170.69	36.9
Transport workers	50.25	41.24	28.93	24.45	24.18	112.52	65.40	30.1
Treasury Employees Union	21.76	16.58	15.84	23.43	26.23	31.00	35.78	64.4
Unite Here	200.89	198.32	122.46	91.40	118.33	141.55	174.02	−13.4
University Professors	0.88	0.82	1.07	0.60	−0.25	1.05	4.77	443.0
Utility workers	3.54	5.38	6.22	5.88	8.51	12.24	16.47	365.6
Writers Guild West	31.48	28.98	31.30	36.06	47.18	56.16	72.46	130.2
Average	**94.68**	**86.45**	**83.35**	**89.31**	**107.33**	**124.27**	**151.27**	**59.8**

Table 5.3 Working Capital

Union	*Cycle*							*% Change from 2006–2007 to 2018–2019 (%)*
	2006–2007 ($)	*2008–2009 ($)*	*2010–2011 ($)*	*2012–2013 ($)*	*2014–2015 ($)*	*2016–2017 ($)*	*2018–2019 ($)*	
Air Line Pilots Association	−0.53	10.28	1.18	−6.60	6.18	17.26	15.91	−3089.4
Air traffic controllers	7.25	6.95	5.77	6.36	4.92	2.53	2.06	−71.6
Aircraft Mechanics Association	0.97	0.36	0.40	0.50	0.73	0.70	1.06	9.9
Allied Pilots Association	15.47	9.86	10.94	7.69	11.61	8.67	15.59	0.8
Auto workers	798.11	659.04	332.07	79.13	82.75	161.67	214.63	−73.1
Bakery, tobacco, and grain	10.26	14.60	12.90	14.74	16.03	19.00	19.92	94.1
Boilermakers	15.76	13.93	3.67	4.73	6.23	8.28	8.51	−46.0
Bricklayers	31.89	26.69	14.57	19.60	21.75	32.40	47.90	50.2
Carpenters	27.18	41.91	96.11	50.32	44.77	74.44	90.29	232.2
Communications workers	106.57	107.29	132.60	150.18	116.62	26.65	35.65	−66.5
Directors Guild of America Inc	27.04	33.58	30.04	29.85	27.62	31.19	35.19	30.2
Electrical Workers IBEW	47.14	30.96	42.85	44.92	50.89	56.69	81.58	73.0
Elevator constructors	3.84	9.22	17.23	14.16	11.60	15.17	21.54	461.4
Engineers, operating	127.43	79.34	24.77	11.19	10.81	31.98	15.33	−88.0
Engineers, professional, and technical	0.88	1.14	1.35	1.82	1.75	1.70	1.67	89.4
Firefighters	10.57	13.40	13.64	13.91	12.85	14.80	14.18	34.2
Food and Commercial Workers	64.46	108.21	92.80	80.28	72.30	105.25	138.09	114.2
Government Employees AFGE	7.70	5.85	9.87	12.31	8.08	10.84	15.71	104.0
Insulators	12.41	13.85	15.72	14.52	11.50	7.74	10.97	−11.6
Iron workers	26.24	32.26	29.49	24.70	27.64	27.72	34.39	31.1
Journeymen and allied trades	0.85	1.19	0.81	0.71	1.11	1.46	2.77	226.4
Laborers	19.37	17.24	23.61	30.65	32.66	35.80	48.80	151.9
Letter Carriers, National Association	84.28	109.35	83.03	44.21	64.39	67.15	43.84	−48.0
Letter carriers, rural	9.45	8.81	8.27	6.44	7.05	7.85	11.83	25.1
Longshore and Warehouse Union	1.84	2.26	2.80	3.66	5.91	7.43	7.61	313.5
Longshoremen's Association	26.69	14.67	9.69	19.80	27.02	33.69	30.90	15.8

Machinists	30.20	32.27	32.32	38.33	39.59	31.53	26.00	−13.9
Mine workers, united	73.30	21.54	8.82	11.76	6.31	9.70	4.98	−93.2
Musicians	10.65	12.37	11.19	13.38	15.75	20.37	25.63	140.7
National Education Association	67.07	79.77	68.20	115.06	184.65	190.95	207.92	210.0
Novelty and production workers	0.67	0.44	0.30	0.68	0.74	0.68	1.61	140.6
Office and professional employees	7.32	10.13	12.64	11.53	11.60	15.87	22.45	206.8
Painters	20.73	15.06	16.11	24.58	23.78	15.80	17.15	−17.3
Plasterers and cement masons	4.44	6.82	3.03	4.17	5.08	12.86	12.89	190.5
Plumbers	53.24	74.01	67.50	62.94	77.88	82.32	110.69	107.9
Postal workers, American	12.06	12.49	10.64	10.24	11.74	12.12	18.52	53.5
Roofers	1.95	3.59	7.81	9.08	8.03	7.37	6.29	223.5
Seafarers	1.14	0.86	0.69	0.62	1.02	0.86	1.44	25.9
Security police, fire professionals	0.80	1.19	3.87	7.49	9.90	11.56	16.36	1946.0
Service employees	40.41	53.73	106.63	88.63	114.93	143.08	232.78	476.0
Sheet metal, air, rail, and transportation workers	10.87	7.51	4.30	19.93	36.95	28.15	34.91	221.3
Stage and picture operators	19.75	22.73	29.70	29.56	20.35	21.84	25.18	27.5
State, county, and municipal employees	47.69	70.39	86.62	97.19	114.29	169.82	255.27	435.3
Steelworkers	56.21	45.59	88.98	156.88	212.39	191.18	234.81	317.7
Teachers	27.62	32.50	17.72	25.06	25.68	42.27	48.53	75.7
Teamsters	26.45	22.67	18.96	39.32	38.79	43.22	32.16	21.6
Transit Union	9.91	22.56	3.91	3.99	8.21	22.58	7.16	−27.8
Transport workers	12.88	6.27	3.88	3.16	6.56	11.52	41.55	222.6
Treasury Employees Union	2.52	1.96	6.71	6.46	5.01	5.23	5.32	111.0
Unite Here	7.70	11.91	18.78	28.78	25.31	29.91	48.58	530.9
University Professors	1.76	1.74	2.23	2.36	2.76	4.55	8.30	372.6
Utility workers	1.63	3.31	1.34	1.59	2.28	5.75	7.24	343.7
Writers Guild West	18.64	29.84	34.52	33.21	39.72	49.24	56.39	202.5
Average	**38.69**	**37.27**	**31.77**	**28.79**	**32.72**	**37.52**	**46.72**	**20.7**

Table 5.4 Securities and Non-Fixed Assets

Union	*Cycle*							*% Change from 2006–2007 to 2018–2019 (%)*
	2006–2007 ($)	*2008–2009 ($)*	*2010–2011 ($)*	*2012–2013 ($)*	*2014–2015 ($)*	*2016–2017 ($)*	*2018–2019 ($)*	
Air Line Pilots Association	149.15	97.89	87.06	77.83	68.47	139.50	230.87	54.8
Air traffic controllers	4.55	2.92	1.77	0.66	1.80	6.39	5.31	16.6
Aircraft Mechanics Association	0.00	0.57	0.74	0.67	0.83	1.16	1.22	
Allied Pilots Association	16.01	18.82	22.16	26.53	25.30	24.93	31.07	94.0
Auto workers	304.90	335.41	544.88	719.88	684.23	668.58	685.20	124.7
Bakery, tobacco, and grain	24.79	13.86	14.84	12.56	11.23	10.16	10.33	−58.4
Boilermakers	37.32	50.45	57.50	47.04	41.79	40.95	37.88	1.5
Bricklayers	21.02	26.08	32.91	35.45	38.65	42.95	45.33	115.7
Carpenters	238.22	373.88	360.64	421.70	425.06	434.77	493.28	107.1
Communications workers	345.40	356.14	362.91	303.58	401.81	439.50	469.35	35.9
Directors Guild of America Inc	10.07	15.17	20.06	23.12	24.79	29.16	32.30	220.9
Electrical Workers IBEW	438.01	357.66	345.63	419.59	471.37	464.37	486.81	11.1
Elevator constructors	6.02	5.56	0.00	1.98	2.45	0.00	2.42	−59.8
Engineers, operating	143.78	178.20	263.22	307.66	340.07	343.19	342.74	138.4
Engineers, professional, and technical	0.36	0.31	0.29	0.65	1.35	1.79	2.23	511.8
Firefighters	7.86	5.68	8.88	10.85	11.16	11.07	9.25	17.8
Food and Commercial Workers	72.02	35.86	70.84	101.11	115.17	152.94	213.76	196.8
Government Employees AFGE	18.74	15.21	16.27	16.56	12.33	7.02	6.67	−64.4
Insulators	1.22	1.35	1.17	0.92	7.79	13.54	14.12	1054.3
Iron workers	70.04	60.49	63.98	65.52	76.87	75.59	78.79	12.5
Journeymen and allied trades	0.00	0.00	0.00	0.00	0.00	0.00	0.00	
Laborers	77.51	88.28	95.33	103.51	104.91	82.22	113.84	46.9
Letter Carriers, National Association	102.92	105.07	176.32	231.97	249.44	249.06	281.10	173.1
Letter carriers, rural	0.00	0.00	0.00	0.00	0.00	0.00	0.00	
Longshore and Warehouse Union	0.12	0.13	0.06	0.00	0.00	0.00	0.00	−100.0
Longshoremen's Association	1.54	1.95	2.77	3.69	11.86	11.94	24.91	1522.2

Machinists	155.76	81.85	86.90	84.08	99.79	136.32	185.03	18.8
Mine workers, united	86.55	143.87	164.33	157.12	164.23	152.03	146.69	69.5
Musicians	0.04	0.04	0.04	0.04	0.05	0.05	0.05	20.8
National Education Association	39.87	44.08	65.40	57.55	77.01	96.40	132.82	233.1
Novelty and production workers	3.89	3.76	3.76	3.75	4.84	5.38	5.38	38.2
Office and professional employees	1.93	1.59	0.40	0.38	0.38	0.37	0.36	−81.4
Painters	27.05	49.23	30.14	25.58	24.59	44.68	47.09	74.1
Plasterers and cement masons	15.35	11.74	11.03	10.34	12.83	13.93	19.15	24.8
Plumbers	31.85	42.68	63.42	71.94	98.89	118.83	136.43	328.4
Postal workers, American	21.62	29.34	30.13	24.81	33.67	52.50	79.35	267.0
Roofers	24.63	24.69	21.95	21.90	22.94	26.59	30.24	22.8
Seafarers	0.00	0.00	0.00	0.00	0.00	0.00	0.00	
Security police, fire professionals	2.68	1.70	1.27	0.11	0.00	0.00	0.00	−100.0
Service employees	17.34	3.26	7.30	37.42	54.38	67.79	80.72	365.4
Sheet metal, air, rail, and transportation workers	63.94	65.12	74.36	86.27	106.56	136.86	162.61	154.3
Stage and picture operators	18.55	26.59	25.55	22.50	24.26	30.23	24.37	31.4
State, county, and municipal employees	0.13	0.13	0.13	0.13	0.23	0.23	0.23	86.6
Steelworkers	247.05	210.01	254.16	355.76	470.05	641.54	836.95	238.8
Teachers	49.53	53.44	54.75	59.61	54.80	29.56	39.87	−19.5
Teamsters	80.23	69.14	115.96	125.73	158.95	211.45	266.93	232.7
Transit Union	115.85	95.03	98.35	93.52	124.37	98.05	121.79	5.1
Transport workers	33.72	25.66	14.88	11.60	15.29	93.71	22.60	−33.0
Treasury Employees Union	19.10	15.35	20.92	31.15	32.78	34.12	35.42	85.4
Unite Here	235.25	229.41	133.96	57.73	67.87	75.92	81.47	−65.4
University Professors	1.24	1.23	1.53	0.79	0.00	0.00	0.00	−100.0
Utility workers	2.81	4.66	6.04	5.69	7.31	8.47	11.67	314.7
Writers Guild West	31.34	20.21	20.57	22.41	27.00	27.81	34.72	10.8
Average	**64.51**	**64.17**	**72.78**	**81.15**	**90.79**	**101.01**	**115.49**	**79.0**

Table 5.5 Fixed Assets

Union	*Cycle*							*% Change from 2006–2007 to 2018–2019 (%)*
	2006–2007 ($)	*2008–2009 ($)*	*2010–2011 ($)*	*2012–2013 ($)*	*2014–2015 ($)*	*2016–2017 ($)*	*2018–2019 ($)*	
Air Line Pilots Association	16.68	15.50	13.49	15.66	16.03	14.14	25.28	51.6
Air traffic controllers	10.27	9.63	9.34	8.93	8.46	8.88	8.76	−14.7
Aircraft Mechanics Association	0.10	0.04	0.01	0.00	0.01	0.02	0.01	−93.1
Allied Pilots Association	5.55	5.51	4.43	3.73	4.88	6.55	7.31	31.6
Auto workers	103.58	105.61	108.48	109.50	97.10	97.29	100.74	−2.7
Bakery, tobacco, and grain	4.31	4.22	4.02	3.70	3.95	3.68	3.21	−25.4
Boilermakers	6.97	9.34	11.98	11.47	9.95	10.01	11.82	69.4
Bricklayers	4.90	4.86	4.07	3.57	3.02	2.72	2.91	−40.6
Carpenters	110.98	100.65	95.95	125.05	158.24	145.69	138.66	24.9
Communications workers	49.85	46.66	43.86	41.04	38.05	36.30	38.66	−22.4
Directors Guild of America Inc	28.60	26.07	23.82	22.90	22.62	18.97	20.01	−30.0
Electrical Workers IBEW	32.56	31.24	26.55	23.10	18.59	14.90	11.84	−63.6
Elevator constructors	3.87	3.75	3.79	3.59	3.44	3.21	4.38	13.1
Engineers, operating	14.54	21.21	21.06	17.69	15.95	82.03	86.93	497.9
Engineers, professional, and technical	0.08	0.10	0.12	0.09	0.10	0.09	0.10	32.4
Firefighters	1.37	2.73	2.69	2.97	4.57	4.20	4.34	215.7
Food and Commercial Workers	12.00	9.37	8.72	8.68	8.33	9.47	11.04	−8.0
Government Employees AFGE	13.97	16.62	18.06	21.42	23.75	23.48	20.42	46.2
Insulators	2.85	2.96	2.86	2.60	2.58	2.26	1.88	−33.9
Iron workers	4.30	3.54	3.64	3.83	3.64	3.55	3.64	−15.5
Journeymen and allied trades	0.16	0.06	0.00	0.01	0.01	0.01	0.00	−97.6
Laborers	15.42	15.93	15.50	14.36	23.99	62.75	60.84	294.5
Letter Carriers, National Association	2.53	2.21	1.71	2.85	3.94	14.10	20.21	697.5
Letter carriers, rural	5.99	6.95	7.25	7.42	6.26	5.69	5.18	−13.4
Longshore and Warehouse Union	0.15	0.10	0.04	0.01	0.02	0.03	0.02	−87.0
Longshoremen's Association	0.02	0.00	0.05	0.07	0.34	0.69	0.48	3027.4

Machinists	35.32	33.32	32.36	28.52	25.18	22.30	18.73	−47.0
Mine workers, united	2.18	1.82	1.74	1.59	1.29	1.20	1.45	−33.6
Musicians	0.57	0.31	0.25	0.14	0.07	0.18	1.09	90.3
National Education Association	53.23	48.87	47.11	55.42	45.51	38.66	27.32	−48.7
Novelty and production workers	0.00	0.00	0.00	0.00	0.00	0.00	0.00	0.0
Office and professional employees	0.09	0.04	0.33	0.68	0.56	0.34	0.17	82.6
Painters	12.42	14.67	29.29	25.62	23.77	20.92	17.67	42.3
Plasterers and cement masons	0.65	0.58	0.36	0.22	0.16	3.58	7.62	1073.7
Plumbers	10.42	43.76	46.81	45.26	45.69	43.32	42.03	303.3
Postal workers, American	4.35	3.68	13.37	22.97	21.48	22.47	22.63	420.1
Roofers	0.12	0.06	0.10	0.14	0.10	0.06	0.75	510.5
Seafarers	0.00	0.00	0.00	0.00	0.00	0.00	0.00	0.0
Security police, fire professionals	0.38	0.33	0.32	0.53	0.51	0.54	0.55	45.1
Service employees	92.28	88.28	83.19	80.06	80.31	80.24	75.86	−17.8
Sheet metal, air, rail, and transportation workers	0.47	0.39	0.29	0.85	1.00	0.71	0.59	26.0
Stage and picture operators	3.71	3.90	4.06	12.12	20.56	19.79	27.71	647.5
State, county, and municipal employees	9.05	6.92	5.49	3.58	2.74	3.23	3.44	−62.0
Steelworkers	15.91	13.31	10.93	11.66	13.78	17.82	16.44	3.3
Teachers	4.31	4.50	4.65	3.22	2.45	12.27	19.83	360.3
Teamsters	38.15	46.12	43.88	40.90	36.87	33.75	36.84	−3.4
Transit Union	5.26	5.67	6.89	6.17	5.87	2.76	0.53	−89.9
Transport workers	2.13	5.64	8.11	7.39	1.41	0.75	0.73	−65.7
Treasury Employees Union	1.74	1.26	0.87	0.53	0.44	0.48	0.68	−61.1
Unite Here	1.45	9.73	14.49	12.86	25.10	35.65	43.53	2903.6
University Professors	0.24	0.25	0.29	0.28	0.12	0.11	0.06	−74.5
Utility workers	0.04	0.05	0.06	0.04	0.04	0.16	0.07	65.9
Writers Guild West	6.73	5.94	5.33	5.05	5.22	5.37	7.25	7.8
Average	**14.20**	**14.80**	**14.95**	**15.47**	**15.81**	**17.69**	**18.15**	**27.8**

$18 million in 2018–2019, or roughly 27 percent. Five unions' fixed assets exceeded $50 million in this last two-year period. Thirty unions show fixed assets totaling less than $10 million in 2018–2019. Twenty-four had less held in this category at this end interval compared to the start of the 14-year span.

Working capital as a share of total assets appears in Table 5.6. This percentage reveals the relative amount of discretionary liquid assets possessed. Across these seven two-year intervals, the unions consistently held more than one-third of their total assets in working capital. The range in average working capital extended from 36.3 percent to just above 39 percent. Seven unions maintained an average of more than 90 percent of their total assets in working capital in 2018–2019, with another eight possessing between 50 and 90 percent in available reserves. Only six unions reported having less than 10 percent of total assets in working capital in this last two-year period. Overall, the unions' average percentage holdings rose a modest seven percent comparing 2018–2019 to 2006–2007. Twenty-three unions held a lower percentage in working capital at the end of the period than at the start.

In Table 5.7, we report the unions' non-fixed assets as a percentage of their total assets. On average, the unions' held 43.2 to 45.7 percent of their assets in this category. Eleven unions held more than 70 percent in non-fixed assets, while another ten had less than 10 percent. As suggested, the percentages held relatively steady over these seven intervals. Twenty-two unions held less in non-fixed assets in 2018–2019 than in 2006–2007.

In 2018–2019, only three unions held more than one-third of their total assets in fixed assets (Table 5.8). Just another six put more than 20 percent in this category. Thirty-four unions, however, allocated less than 10 percent to fixed assets. On average, the unions ended the period with roughly 11 percent less of the share of their total assets held as fixed. Thirty-one unions had a lower percentage of fixed assets relative to total assets in 2018–2019 than in 2006–2007.

Liabilities

Total

Table 5.9 reports the unions' total liabilities over the seven intervals. On average, the unions' liabilities ranged from a low of $32.62 million to over $46 million (2010–2011). The average liabilities rose by 30 percent comparing 2018–2019 to 2006–2007. Only six unions reported more than $100 million in total liabilities in 2018–2019. Thirty−three unions reported less than $10 million in total liabilities in this last two-year period. Thirty-six unions ended the period with higher total liabilities than at the start. Among these, 16 unions had liabilities more than 100 percent higher in 2018–2019 than in 2006–2007.

Table 5.6 Working Capital as a Percentage of Total Assets

Union	*Cycle*							*% Change from 2006–2007 to 2018–2019 (%)*
	2006–2007 (%)	*2008–2009 (%)*	*2010–2011 (%)*	*2012–2013 (%)*	*2014–2015 (%)*	*2016–2017 (%)*	*2018–2019 (%)*	
Air Line Pilots Association	−0.3	7.1	1.0	−5.9	5.3	8.6	5.0	1876.4
Air traffic controllers	31.4	32.9	31.8	37.9	29.8	13.1	11.3	−63.8
Aircraft Mechanics Association	53.5	29.7	28.8	36.5	42.3	33.5	41.7	−21.9
Allied Pilots Association	37.2	26.2	25.5	18.2	24.6	18.5	26.3	−29.2
Auto workers	63.4	56.6	31.3	7.9	8.6	15.6	19.3	−69.5
Bakery, tobacco, and grain	25.8	43.2	40.3	47.1	51.0	57.0	58.9	127.8
Boilermakers	26.0	18.8	5.0	7.4	10.6	13.8	14.5	−44.2
Bricklayers	51.0	43.9	27.1	32.7	33.2	40.8	48.9	−4.1
Carpenters	7.1	8.0	17.3	8.2	6.8	10.9	12.1	71.1
Communications workers	19.6	20.0	23.6	29.2	20.3	5.0	6.4	−67.3
Directors Guild of America Inc	38.9	43.2	39.1	37.8	35.4	38.1	38.5	−0.9
Electrical Workers IBEW	7.9	6.4	8.7	9.1	9.3	10.4	13.9	75.4
Elevator constructors	23.6	48.6	77.1	70.5	63.5	79.4	72.4	207.2
Engineers, operating	43.1	28.1	7.9	3.3	2.9	6.9	2.9	−93.3
Engineers, professional, and technical	63.2	68.1	73.3	69.7	53.3	47.0	41.6	−34.1
Firefighters	35.8	50.5	46.6	45.8	41.3	45.5	46.1	28.9
Food and Commercial Workers	41.3	66.9	51.9	40.8	35.7	38.3	37.3	−9.9
Government Employees AFGE	17.3	14.2	21.2	23.3	17.4	23.9	34.4	99.3
Insulators	73.4	75.1	78.8	80.1	52.4	32.7	40.6	−44.8

(*Continued*)

Table 5.6 (Continued)

Union	*Cycle*							*% Change from 2006–2007 to 2018–2019 (%)*
	2006–2007 (%)	*2008–2009 (%)*	*2010–2011 (%)*	*2012–2013 (%)*	*2014–2015 (%)*	*2016–2017 (%)*	*2018–2019 (%)*	
Iron workers	25.9	33.3	30.2	26.0	25.3	25.5	28.9	11.6
Journeymen and allied trades	70.2	74.5	66.5	70.3	80.7	82.8	87.8	25.0
Laborers	16.3	13.8	16.6	18.4	17.3	16.6	18.2	12.2
Letter Carriers, National Association	37.2	37.5	26.2	15.2	19.8	19.9	12.4	−66.6
Letter carriers, rural	55.1	51.5	48.0	40.7	43.7	47.4	60.0	8.8
Longshore and Warehouse Union	79.0	78.7	82.8	84.5	91.6	91.8	92.3	16.9
Longshoremen's Association	91.9	86.4	75.5	72.8	63.2	62.3	48.4	−47.3
Machinists	13.4	21.3	20.9	24.7	22.8	16.3	11.2	−16.7
Mine workers, united	45.1	12.8	5.0	6.6	3.7	5.9	3.2	−92.8
Musicians	88.5	92.0	92.4	95.4	97.2	97.1	94.4	6.8
National Education Association	35.8	39.6	31.0	41.9	52.8	51.1	50.8	42.1
Novelty and production workers	14.4	10.0	7.1	15.1	13.1	11.1	22.7	58.1
Office and professional employees	68.2	76.4	84.5	81.7	85.9	92.2	94.5	38.6
Painters	33.5	18.3	20.5	31.3	31.1	18.5	19.8	−41.0
Plasterers and cement masons	21.3	34.9	20.5	27.8	27.7	41.7	32.0	49.8
Plumbers	42.3	37.9	31.7	29.1	30.0	32.7	37.9	−10.4
Postal workers, American	31.5	26.9	19.3	17.4	17.3	13.8	15.3	−51.4
Roofers	6.9	12.0	25.1	27.8	24.4	20.4	15.9	131.5
Seafarers	112.7	105.1	106.0	106.8	102.7	99.7	98.3	−12.8

Security police, fire professionals	20.2	34.9	69.7	90.0	92.3	93.9	96.2	375.4
Service employees	22.5	28.5	46.9	36.1	39.8	43.6	54.7	142.8
Sheet metal, air, rail, and transportation workers	13.7	9.7	5.0	17.6	24.8	16.5	17.3	26.6
Stage and picture operators	45.5	41.9	49.2	44.7	30.8	30.1	32.2	−29.3
State, county, and municipal employees	70.2	80.1	84.9	88.9	91.3	94.0	96.6	37.6
Steelworkers	16.4	15.7	24.2	29.1	29.9	21.6	19.6	19.7
Teachers	28.0	30.7	17.0	24.7	27.1	40.5	36.7	31.2
Teamsters	13.7	13.4	9.3	17.0	14.7	14.2	8.6	−37.2
Transit Union	7.5	18.2	3.6	3.8	5.4	13.7	4.0	−46.7
Transport workers	25.6	15.2	13.3	12.7	10.6	10.2	63.5	147.7
Treasury Employees Union	10.2	9.7	22.4	16.2	12.3	12.4	12.0	17.2
Unite Here	3.0	4.3	10.0	26.8	21.2	20.9	27.3	820.8
University Professors	46.7	47.0	52.8	66.8	86.7	91.2	95.2	104.1
Utility workers	32.5	39.4	16.1	20.4	21.3	38.9	37.5	15.1
Writers Guild West	32.0	49.8	54.9	52.7	53.8	58.4	55.9	74.4
Average	**36.5**	**37.5**	**36.3**	**37.4**	**36.9**	**37.5**	**39.1**	**7.1**

Table 5.7 Investments as a Percentage of Total Assets

Union	*Cycle*							*Change from 2006–2007 to 2018–2019 (%)*
	2006–2007 (%)	*2008–2009 (%)*	*2010–2011 (%)*	*2012–2013 (%)*	*2014–2015 (%)*	*2016–2017 (%)*	*2018–2019 (%)*	
Air Line Pilots Association	79.0	67.3	70.6	69.1	58.7	69.7	72.7	−8.0
Air traffic controllers	19.7	13.8	9.7	3.9	10.9	33.2	29.2	48.4
Aircraft Mechanics Association	0.0	47.7	53.8	48.5	47.7	55.7	47.9	
Allied Pilots Association	38.5	50.0	51.6	62.8	53.6	53.3	52.5	36.4
Auto workers	24.2	28.8	51.4	72.2	71.2	64.7	61.7	154.8
Bakery, tobacco, and grain	62.4	41.0	46.4	40.1	35.7	30.5	30.5	−51.1
Boilermakers	61.5	68.2	78.0	73.0	71.2	68.3	64.5	4.9
Bricklayers	33.6	42.9	61.2	59.2	58.9	54.0	46.3	37.7
Carpenters	62.2	71.8	64.8	68.3	64.8	63.5	66.3	6.7
Communications workers	63.6	66.5	64.6	59.0	70.0	83.0	84.6	33.0
Directors Guild of America Inc	14.5	19.5	26.1	29.3	31.8	35.6	35.3	144.2
Electrical Workers IBEW	73.6	73.5	70.4	84.8	86.3	84.9	82.9	12.7
Elevator constructors	37.0	29.3	0.0	9.9	13.4	0.0	8.1	−78.0
Engineers, operating	48.7	63.2	84.1	90.3	91.6	74.2	65.0	33.5
Engineers, professional, and technical	26.0	18.5	15.9	25.1	41.0	49.6	55.4	112.7
Firefighters	26.6	21.4	30.3	35.7	35.9	34.0	30.1	13.2
Food and Commercial Workers	46.2	22.2	39.6	51.4	56.8	55.6	57.7	24.9
Government Employees AFGE	42.0	37.0	34.9	31.4	26.5	15.4	14.6	−65.2
Insulators	7.2	7.3	5.8	5.1	35.5	57.2	52.2	621.1
Iron workers	69.2	62.4	65.5	68.9	70.3	69.7	66.3	−4.2
Journeymen and allied trades	0.0	0.0	0.0	0.0	0.0	0.0	0.0	

Laborers	65.1	70.7	67.2	62.2	55.4	38.0	42.6	−34.6
Letter Carriers, National Association	45.4	36.1	55.7	79.8	76.7	73.7	79.7	75.6
Letter carriers, rural	0.0	0.0	0.0	0.0	0.0	0.0	0.0	
Longshore and Warehouse Union	5.0	4.4	1.9	0.0	0.0	0.0	0.0	−100.0
Longshoremen's Association	5.3	11.5	21.5	13.5	27.7	22.1	39.1	638.3
Machinists	69.1	54.1	56.1	54.2	57.5	70.6	79.4	14.9
Mine workers, united	53.3	85.8	93.9	88.4	95.2	93.2	95.7	79.7
Musicians	0.3	0.3	0.4	0.3	0.3	0.2	0.2	−46.4
National Education Association	21.3	21.9	29.7	21.0	22.0	25.8	32.5	52.7
Novelty and production workers	83.5	86.5	90.3	83.1	85.4	87.3	75.8	−9.2
Office and professional employees	18.0	12.0	2.7	2.7	2.8	2.1	1.5	−91.6
Painters	43.7	59.8	38.4	32.6	32.2	52.3	54.3	24.3
Plasterers and cement masons	73.8	60.1	74.8	68.9	70.0	45.2	47.5	−35.7
Plumbers	25.3	21.8	29.8	33.3	38.1	47.2	46.7	84.6
Postal workers, American	56.4	63.3	54.8	42.2	49.7	59.7	65.5	16.1
Roofers	87.0	82.8	70.4	67.0	69.6	73.7	76.5	−12.1
Seafarers	0.0	0.0	0.0	0.0	0.0	0.0	0.0	
Security police, fire professionals	67.8	49.9	22.8	1.4	0.0	0.0	0.0	−100.0
Service employees	9.7	1.7	3.2	15.2	18.8	20.6	19.0	96.2
Sheet metal, air, rail, and transportation workers	80.4	83.9	87.2	76.0	71.6	80.4	80.6	0.2

(Continued)

Table 5.7 (Continued)

Union	*Cycle*							*Change from 2006–2007 to 2018–2019 (%)*
	2006–2007 (%)	*2008–2009 (%)*	*2010–2011 (%)*	*2012–2013 (%)*	*2014–2015 (%)*	*2016–2017 (%)*	*2018–2019 (%)*	
Stage and picture operators	42.8	49.0	42.3	34.0	36.7	41.6	31.2	−27.2
State, county, and municipal employees	0.2	0.1	0.1	0.1	0.2	0.1	0.1	−52.0
Steelworkers	72.0	72.2	69.0	66.0	66.1	72.5	69.9	−2.9
Teachers	50.2	50.5	52.5	58.7	57.7	28.3	30.2	−39.9
Teamsters	41.6	40.9	56.7	54.4	60.2	69.4	71.6	71.9
Transit Union	87.9	76.5	89.5	89.4	81.5	59.3	68.2	−22.4
Transport workers	67.1	62.2	51.1	46.7	24.8	83.2	34.5	−48.5
Treasury Employees Union	77.6	76.0	69.9	78.0	80.7	80.8	79.9	3.0
Unite Here	90.7	83.3	71.2	53.7	56.8	52.9	45.9	−49.5
University Professors	33.1	33.3	36.1	22.3	0.0	0.0	0.0	−100.0
Utility workers	56.1	55.5	72.3	72.6	68.3	57.2	60.3	7.6
Writers Guild West	53.8	33.7	32.7	35.5	36.6	33.0	34.4	−36.1
Average	**43.8**	**43.2**	**44.7**	**44.2**	**44.8**	**45.7**	**45.0**	**2.9**

Table 5.8 Fixed Assets as a Percentage of Total Assets

Union	*Cycle*							*% Change from 2006–2007 to 2018–2019 (%)*
	2006–2007 (%)	*2008–2009 (%)*	*2010–2011 (%)*	*2012–2013 (%)*	*2014–2015 (%)*	*2016–2017 (%)*	*2018–2019 (%)*	
Air Line Pilots Association	8.8	10.6	10.9	13.9	13.7	7.1	8.0	−9.9
Air traffic controllers	44.4	45.6	51.5	53.3	51.3	46.2	48.2	8.5
Aircraft Mechanics Association	5.5	3.6	0.9	0.3	0.4	0.7	0.3	−95.1
Allied Pilots Association	13.3	14.7	10.3	8.8	10.3	14.0	12.3	−7.5
Auto workers	8.2	9.1	10.2	11.0	10.1	9.4	9.1	10.3
Bakery, tobacco, and grain	10.8	12.5	12.5	11.8	12.6	11.1	9.5	−12.4
Boilermakers	11.5	12.6	16.2	17.8	16.9	16.7	20.1	75.0
Bricklayers	7.8	8.0	7.6	6.0	4.6	3.4	3.0	−62.1
Carpenters	29.0	19.3	17.2	20.3	24.1	21.3	18.6	−35.6
Communications workers	9.2	8.7	7.8	8.0	6.6	6.9	7.0	−24.1
Directors Guild of America Inc	41.1	33.6	31.0	29.0	29.0	23.2	21.9	−46.8
Electrical Workers IBEW	5.5	6.4	5.4	4.7	3.4	2.7	2.0	−63.1
Elevator constructors	23.8	19.8	16.9	17.9	18.8	16.8	14.7	−38.1
Engineers, operating	4.9	7.5	6.7	5.2	4.3	17.7	16.5	234.9
Engineers, professional, and technical	5.4	6.1	6.3	3.5	3.0	2.6	2.5	−54.0
Firefighters	4.6	10.3	9.2	9.8	14.7	12.9	14.1	203.4
Food and Commercial Workers	7.7	5.8	4.9	4.4	4.1	3.4	3.0	−61.3
Government Employees AFGE	31.3	40.5	38.8	40.6	51.1	51.7	44.7	42.8
Insulators	16.9	16.0	14.4	14.3	11.7	9.6	7.0	−58.7

(Continued)

Table 5.8 (Continued)

Union	*Cycle*							*% Change from 2006–2007 to 2018–2019 (%)*
	2006–2007 (%)	*2008–2009 (%)*	*2010–2011 (%)*	*2012–2013 (%)*	*2014–2015 (%)*	*2016–2017 (%)*	*2018–2019 (%)*	
Iron workers	4.3	3.6	3.7	4.0	3.3	3.3	3.1	−28.1
Journeymen and allied trades	13.1	3.6	0.3	1.1	1.0	0.7	0.1	−99.1
Laborers	12.9	12.8	10.9	8.6	12.7	29.0	22.7	75.8
Letter Carriers, National Association	1.1	0.8	0.5	1.0	1.2	4.2	5.7	412.7
Letter carriers, rural	34.9	40.6	42.1	46.9	38.8	34.4	26.3	−24.7
Longshore and Warehouse Union	6.4	3.3	1.1	0.3	0.3	0.3	0.2	−96.3
Longshoremen's Association	0.1	0.0	0.4	0.2	0.8	1.3	0.7	1323.3
Machinists	15.7	22.0	20.9	18.4	14.5	11.5	8.0	−48.7
Mine workers, united	1.3	1.1	1.0	0.9	0.7	0.7	0.9	−29.6
Musicians	4.7	2.3	2.1	1.0	0.4	0.9	4.0	−15.6
National Education Association	28.4	24.2	21.4	20.2	13.0	10.4	6.7	−76.5
Novelty and production workers	0.0	0.0	0.0	0.0	0.0	0.0	0.0	
Office and professional employees	0.9	0.3	2.2	4.8	4.1	2.0	0.7	−17.5
Painters	20.1	17.8	37.3	32.6	31.1	24.5	20.4	1.6
Plasterers and cement masons	3.1	3.0	2.5	1.5	0.9	11.6	18.9	504.9
Plumbers	8.3	22.4	22.0	20.9	17.6	17.2	14.4	73.8
Postal workers, American	11.3	7.9	24.3	39.1	31.7	25.5	18.7	64.5
Roofers	0.4	0.2	0.3	0.4	0.3	0.2	1.9	337.0
Seafarers	0.1	0.1	0.1	0.2	0.1	0.1	0.1	−30.7
Security police, fire professionals	9.5	9.8	5.7	6.4	4.8	4.4	3.2	−66.3

Service employees	51.4	46.8	36.6	32.6	27.8	24.4	17.8	−65.4
Sheet metal, air, rail, and transportation workers	0.6	0.5	0.3	0.7	0.7	0.4	0.3	−50.4
Stage and picture operators	8.6	7.2	6.7	18.3	31.1	27.3	35.4	314.3
State, county, and municipal employees	13.3	7.9	5.4	3.3	2.2	1.8	1.3	−90.2
Steelworkers	4.6	4.6	3.0	2.2	1.9	2.0	1.4	−70.4
Teachers	4.4	4.3	4.5	3.2	2.6	11.7	15.0	243.7
Teamsters	19.8	27.3	21.5	17.7	14.0	11.1	9.9	−50.1
Transit Union	4.0	4.6	6.3	5.9	3.8	1.7	0.3	−92.6
Transport workers	4.2	13.7	27.9	29.8	2.3	0.7	1.1	−73.7
Treasury Employees Union	7.1	6.3	2.9	1.3	1.1	1.1	1.5	−78.4
Unite Here	0.6	3.5	7.7	12.0	21.0	24.9	24.5	4284.0
University Professors	6.3	6.7	6.7	7.9	3.7	2.2	0.7	−89.0
Utility workers	0.9	0.6	0.7	0.5	0.3	1.1	0.4	−56.9
Writers Guild West	11.6	9.9	8.5	8.0	7.1	6.4	7.2	−37.9
Average	**11.4**	**11.5**	**11.6**	**11.9**	**11.1**	**10.9**	**10.1**	**−11.2**

Table 5.9 Total Liabilities

Union	*Cycle*							*% Change from 2006–2007 to 2018–2019 (%)*
	2006–2007 ($)	*2008–2009 ($)*	*2010–2011 ($)*	*2012–2013 ($)*	*2014–2015 ($)*	*2016–2017 ($)*	*2018–2019 ($)*	
Air Line Pilots Association	49.79	57.56	62.45	76.16	81.61	99.92	110.97	122.9
Air traffic controllers	6.40	6.04	5.17	4.19	3.69	8.89	9.44	47.4
Aircraft Mechanics Association	1.22	1.08	0.37	0.31	0.28	0.33	0.46	−61.9
Allied Pilots Association	10.85	9.15	11.59	5.71	5.33	5.27	10.45	−3.7
Auto workers	20.50	5.69	5.86	7.54	7.97	128.90	111.64	444.6
Bakery, tobacco, and grain	5.29	15.70	14.79	10.63	11.36	7.31	6.39	20.8
Boilermakers	1.11	0.83	8.72	8.87	1.11	3.59	4.57	312.7
Bricklayers	4.05	2.81	4.50	3.88	2.15	2.16	2.41	−40.4
Carpenters	7.14	5.46	5.10	5.09	5.45	7.48	7.64	7.0
Communications workers	177.61	199.76	282.41	321.23	297.61	275.38	241.87	36.2
Directors Guild of America Inc	25.25	28.11	25.56	25.99	22.42	23.69	26.71	5.8
Electrical Workers IBEW	209.92	245.24	268.15	308.70	250.73	158.76	166.34	−20.8
Elevator constructors	0.25	0.52	0.51	2.40	0.81	6.16	6.18	2389.8
Engineers, operating	22.34	49.41	53.98	41.59	40.98	126.68	189.56	748.7
Engineers, professional, and technical	0.22	0.24	0.24	1.62	1.29	1.05	0.83	281.2
Firefighters	8.01	16.64	27.73	33.04	32.92	63.66	6.43	−19.7
Food and Commercial Workers	4.35	5.71	4.67	5.08	5.33	5.88	6.00	37.9
Government Employees AFGE	45.88	68.33	72.68	78.66	73.48	83.64	89.40	94.9
Insulators	3.01	4.66	5.85	4.47	5.10	4.10	4.39	45.6
Iron workers	3.74	2.65	1.12	0.73	0.93	1.31	1.81	−51.6
Journeymen and allied trades	0.17	0.34	0.36	0.22	0.17	0.18	0.22	32.8

Laborers	4.67	1.91	2.40	3.31	4.56	1.49	2.87	−38.5
Letter Carriers, National Association	48.85	95.86	81.28	42.96	39.66	37.04	36.35	−25.6
Letter carriers, rural	7.08	7.05	8.83	8.30	8.74	9.77	11.82	67.0
Longshore and Warehouse Union	0.52	0.57	0.61	0.88	0.68	0.73	2.19	323.2
Longshoremen's Association	0.00	0.03	0.03	4.46	6.43	6.86	6.97	
Machinists	8.34	9.27	9.21	6.67	3.80	3.42	2.27	−72.8
Mine workers, united	0.94	1.31	1.13	0.49	0.42	2.23	11.91	1169.1
Musicians	3.19	4.12	3.50	3.21	3.39	5.47	6.79	113.1
National Education Association	68.09	58.28	57.93	59.08	55.07	55.64	53.25	−21.8
Novelty and production workers	3.99	3.72	4.15	4.49	4.64	4.98	5.10	27.8
Office and professional employees	0.61	1.07	0.55	0.73	0.63	0.48	0.40	−34.2
Painters	8.81	3.62	4.01	4.29	3.58	3.14	3.44	−61.0
Plasterers and cement masons	0.19	0.16	0.05	0.02	0.02	0.57	1.08	456.7
Plumbers	33.17	52.00	39.98	28.91	26.44	24.60	21.02	−36.6
Postal workers, American	4.42	6.24	6.23	4.68	4.18	4.17	5.79	31.0
Roofers	1.38	1.18	1.21	1.40	1.77	1.94	2.12	54.2
Seafarers	0.64	0.64	0.63	0.75	1.07	0.97	0.77	20.8
Security police, fire professionals	1.06	1.83	2.21	3.21	4.03	4.81	6.73	537.2
Service employees	115.45	138.48	118.96	123.22	130.81	105.74	79.00	−31.6
Sheet metal, air, rail, and transportation workers	29.98	52.00	57.67	92.47	60.79	70.88	64.25	114.3
Stage and picture operators	7.73	12.89	20.04	28.49	23.20	23.64	28.07	263.1

(*Continued*)

Table 5.9 (Continued)

Union	*Cycle*							*% Change from 2006–2007 to 2018–2019 (%)*
	2006–2007 ($)	*2008–2009 ($)*	*2010–2011 ($)*	*2012–2013 ($)*	*2014–2015 ($)*	*2016–2017 ($)*	*2018–2019 ($)*	
State, county, and municipal employees	51.63	63.54	76.59	89.55	95.21	102.46	96.46	86.8
Steelworkers	497.30	609.85	816.82	716.11	674.09	575.14	619.00	24.5
Teachers	39.74	46.81	61.09	53.79	64.85	91.38	92.49	132.7
Teamsters	84.45	92.90	81.40	67.01	49.28	20.74	28.73	−66.0
Transit Union	7.07	7.25	6.70	6.63	6.82	7.05	7.95	12.5
Transport workers	0.02	0.03	0.17	0.37	37.48	0.08	0.07	319.8
Treasury Employees Union	2.85	3.61	14.10	16.51	14.39	11.21	8.55	199.8
Unite Here	58.38	76.97	65.66	16.07	1.11	1.84	3.61	−93.8
University Professors	2.89	2.87	3.17	2.94	3.43	3.94	3.94	36.6
Utility workers	1.48	3.02	2.13	1.96	2.20	2.55	2.87	93.6
Writers Guild West	26.74	30.93	31.59	26.99	26.63	28.19	28.49	6.5
Average	**32.62**	**39.92**	**46.07**	**44.64**	**41.70**	**42.03**	**42.42**	**30.0**

Table 5.10 Other Liabilities for 2019

Union	*Total Liabilities ($)*	*Other Liabilities ($)*	*Other Liabilities as a Percentage of Total Liabilities (%)*
Air Line Pilots Association	1,24,091.73	95,436.02	76.9
Air traffic controllers	8,672.91	2,199.47	25.4
Aircraft Mechanics Association	622.29	313.30	50.3
Allied Pilots Association	15,544.70	13,652.07	87.8
Auto workers	1,07,355.24	1,05,131.96	97.9
Bakery, tobacco, and grain	4,039.88	3,907.35	96.7
Boilermakers	5,164.94	476.14	9.2
Bricklayers	2,314.92	1,716.26	74.1
Carpenters	6,586.09	5,768.68	87.6
Communications workers	2,33,318.73	2,27,043.68	97.3
Directors Guild of America Inc	28,618.10	25,541.48	89.2
Electrical Workers IBEW	1,89,558.41	1,86,531.78	98.4
Elevator constructors	5,347.44	4,996.14	93.4
Engineers, operating	1,80,749.86	56,515.70	31.3
Engineers, professional, and technical	776.33	331.23	42.7
Firefighters	5,910.05	4,884.47	82.6
Food and Commercial Workers	6,168.14	589.79	9.6
Government Employees AFGE	97,906.74	95,712.86	97.8
Insulators	4,176.51	4,176.51	100.0
Iron workers	2,097.62	323.21	15.4
Journeymen and allied trades	192.48	15.93	8.3
Laborers	2,284.67	1,152.71	50.5
Letter Carriers, National Association	33,881.71	32,033.66	94.5
Letter carriers, rural	12,195.90	11,417.78	93.6
Longshore and Warehouse Union	2,516.72	2,267.42	90.1
Longshoremen's Association	7,288.84	—	0.0
Machinists	1,143.08	484.13	42.4
Mine workers, united	11,860.29	858.25	7.2
Musicians	6,974.03	6,824.04	97.8
National Education Association	45,904.96	26,909.83	58.6
Novelty and production workers	5,329.69	5,269.83	98.9
Office and professional employees	376.10	3.97	1.1
Painters	3,542.28	1,779.40	50.2
Plasterers and cement masons	1,120.08	868.92	77.6
Plumbers	18,070.07	148.53	0.8
Postal workers, American	5,518.82	4,957.32	89.8
Roofers	2,168.22	2,081.86	96.0
Seafarers	721.65	24.72	3.4
Security police, fire professionals	7,132.42	7,126.03	99.9
Service employees	64,533.94	23,310.14	36.1
Sheet metal, air, rail, and transportation workers	57,650.00	56,454.53	97.9
Stage and picture operators	31,086.59	30,511.91	98.2
State, county, and municipal employees	98,889.94	94,311.17	95.4
Steelworkers	6,53,989.14	6,41,691.65	98.1
Teachers	91,362.44	55,479.03	60.7
Teamsters	30,601.38	976.77	3.2

(*Continued*)

Table 5.10 (Continued)

Union	*Total Liabilities ($)*	*Other Liabilities ($)*	*Other Liabilities as a Percentage of Total Liabilities (%)*
Transit Union	8,578.39	7,357.11	85.8
Transport workers	51.03	51.03	100.0
Treasury Employees Union	8,115.95	6,979.52	86.0
Unite Here	2,751.71	768.23	27.9
University Professors	3,470.21	3,257.36	93.9
Utility workers	3,015.86	2,814.47	93.3
Writers Guild West	28,058.43	26,130.11	93.1
Total	**22,79,397.63**	**18,89,565.42**	**82.9**

Other

Most of the unions' aggregated liabilities fall into the miscellaneous "other" category. In 2019, for example, about 83 percent of the nearly $2.8 billion of these 53 nationals' liabilities lie in this classification (Table 5.10). On a disaggregated basis, union liabilities vary from roughly $51,000 (TWU) to just under $654 million (USW). Six unions show liabilities greater than $100 million. The "other" category constitutes between 31 and 98.4 percent of totals among this set. A significant share of the "other" liabilities includes the unions' post-retirement healthcare and pension benefits, either to their own employees or retirees among rank and file where a contractual obligation exists.

Post-Retirement

We inspect the "other" liabilities in order to garner a better understanding of their contents. In reviewing the raw LM-2 forms for each of the unions filed for 2019, we discover from the itemization of these liabilities that many unions included their accrued post-retirement healthcare and pension liabilities for their employees and officers, while others do not report them. Unions report their finances generally on a cash-accounting basis, which does not account for longer-term liabilities owed to promises made to pay for retiree healthcare and pensions. Some unions, however, do report such liabilities. In the case of the UAW, its "other liabilities" include payments the union itself owes to a Voluntary Employee Beneficial Association (VEBA) set up to provide for the healthcare of their own employees upon retirement. (These differences between unions in accounting practices with respect to liabilities raise a question about how to make comparisons on reported data. If some unions include accrued post-retirement liabilities while others do not, then straightforward comparisons in their total liabilities are of the apples-to-oranges variety. We address this issue in the forthcoming chapter on reforms.)

Table 5.11 reports the unions' post-retirement liabilities for healthcare and pensions in 2019. Thirty unions report no liabilities. However, this does not necessarily mean they have no post-retirement debts. Rather, the unions may just choose

Table 5.11 Retirement Liabilities for 2019

Union	*Accrued Post-retirement ($)*	*Accrued Post-retirement Benefit ($)*	*Accrued Post-retirement Benefit Costs ($)*	*Accrued Post-retirement Benefits ($)*	*Accrued Post-retirement Healthcare ($)*	*Accumulated Post-retirement Medical Benefit ($)*	*Post-retirement Benefits ($)*	*Total Post-retirement ($)*
Air Line Pilots Association	—	—	—	24,473.91	—	—	—	24,473.91
Air traffic controllers	—	—	—	—	—	—	—	—
Aircraft Mechanics Association	—	—	—	—	—	—	—	—
Allied Pilots Association	—	—	—	—	—	—	—	—
Auto workers	—	—	—	—	—	—	—	—
Bakery, tobacco, and grain	—	—	—	—	—	—	—	—
Boilermakers	—	—	—	—	—	—	—	—
Bricklayers	—	—	—	—	—	—	—	—
Carpenters	—	—	—	—	—	—	—	—
Communications workers	—	—	—	—	—	—	—	—
Directors Guild of America Inc	—	—	—	—	—	—	—	—
Electrical Workers IBEW	—	—	73,216.01	—	—	—	—	73,216.01
Elevator constructors	—	—	—	—	—	—	—	—
Engineers, operating	—	—	—	—	—	—	—	—
Engineers, professional, and technical	—	—	—	—	—	—	—	—
Firefighters	—	—	—	—	—	—	—	—
Food and Commercial Workers	—	—	—	—	—	—	—	—
Government Employees AFGE	—	—	—	—	—	—	—	—
Insulators	—	—	—	—	—	—	—	—
Iron workers	—	—	—	—	—	—	—	—
Journeymen and allied trades	—	—	—	—	—	—	—	—
Laborers	—	—	—	—	—	—	—	—

(*Continued*)

Table 5.11 (Continued)

Union	*Accrued Post-retirement ($)*	*Accrued Post-retirement Benefit ($)*	*Accrued Post-retirement Benefit Costs ($)*	*Accrued Post-retirement Benefits ($)*	*Accrued Post-retirement Healthcare ($)*	*Accumulated Post-retirement Medical Benefit ($)*	*Post-retirement Benefits ($)*	*Total Post-retirement ($)*
Letter Carriers, National Association	—	—	—	—	—	—	24,262.63	24,262.63
Letter carriers, rural	—	—	—	—	—	—	2,802.00	2,802.00
Longshore and Warehouse Union	—	—	—	—	—	—	—	—
Longshoremen's Association	—	—	—	—	—	—	—	—
Machinists	—	—	—	—	—	—	—	—
Mine workers, united	—	—	—	—	—	—	—	—
Musicians	—	—	—	—	—	—	—	—
National Education Association	—	—	—	—	—	—	—	—
Novelty and production workers	—	—	—	—	—	—	—	—
Office and professional employees	—	—	—	—	—	—	—	—
Painters	1,544.40	—	—	—	—	—	—	1,544.40
Plasterers and cement masons	—	—	—	—	—	—	—	—
Plumbers	—	—	—	—	—	—	—	—
Postal workers, American	—	—	—	—	—	—	—	—
Roofers	—	—	—	—	—	—	—	—
Seafarers	—	—	—	—	—	—	—	—
Security police, fire professionals	—	—	—	—	—	—	—	—
Service employees	—	—	—	—	—	—	—	—
Sheet metal, air, rail, and transportation workers	—	—	—	—	12,658.04	—	—	12,658.04
Stage and picture operators	—	—	—	—	—	—	—	—

State, county, and municipal employees	—	68,833.00	—	—	—	—	—	68,833.00
Steelworkers	—	—	—	—	—	—	—	—
Teachers	—	—	—	36,053.68	—	—	—	36,053.68
Teamsters	—	—	—	884.97	—	—	—	884.97
Transit Union	—	—	—	—	—	—	—	—
Transport workers	—	—	—	—	—	—	—	—
Treasury Employees Union	—	—	—	—	—	—	—	—
Unite Here	—	—	—	—	—	—	—	—
University Professors	—	—	—	—	—	2,451.85	—	2,451.85
Utility workers	—	—	—	—	—	—	—	—
Writers Guild West	—	—	—	—	—	—	—	—
Total	1,544.40	68,833.00	73,216.01	61,412.56	12,658.04	2,451.85	27,064.63	2,47,180.48

not to include their accrued liabilities in this regard. As shown in Table 5.11, four unions (USW, CWA, IBEW, and UAW) report post-retirement liabilities of more than $100 million in 2019, with the USW indicating the largest debt by an order of magnitude to the second ranking (the CWA with around $196 million). Altogether, the 53 nationals report post-retirement liabilities of roughly $1.41 billion or slightly more than 60 percent of their total reported debt.

6 The Income Statement

Revenues

This chapter examines the revenue side of the income statement with disaggregated data. The average amount of total revenues across the 53 unions rose 8.7 percent comparing end to beginning points to $139 million. Only two unions had total receipts above $500 million in 2018–2019, with seven less than $10 million. Twelve unions ended the period with lower total receipts than they had at the start. The unions' average net receipts fell 6.2 percent. Only four unions had net receipts greater than $300 million in 2018–2019. Ten unions had less than $10 million and 14 ended the period with lower net receipts. Four unions had member-based income (MBI) greater than $200 million in 2018–2019, with 11 less than $10 million. On average, MBI rose 33.5 percent over the seven two-year intervals. Only four unions ended the period with less MBI than at the start. In contrast, business income (BI) fell 55 percent over the seven intervals and 34 unions ended the period with less BI. Only three unions generated more than $100 million in BI in 2018–2019 compared to 14 with less than $1 million. Over time, the unions, on average, became more dependent on MBI and less dependent on BI as a share of net receipts.

We examine the receipts of the national unions over the 2006–2019 period, with data reported by two-year averages. The analysis focuses on the unions' total receipts and net revenues, which exclude intra-union transmittals. It then breaks down the revenues by two major sources: member-based and business income (MBI and BI). We report the absolute amount of these revenues (in millions), with the unions ranked from highest-to-lowest amounts for 2018–2019. MBI and BI as a percentage of net receipts follow, reported again from highest-to-lowest amounts for 2018–2019. On each of these dimensions, we show the average amounts and percentages across unions for each two-year period and the percentage change comparing 2018–2019 to 2006–2007.

Total and Net Receipts

Table 6.1 reveals the unions' total receipts. In 2018–2019, only one union (IBEW) had over $1 billion in total receipts, with just one other union (USW) reporting more than $500 million. Another four unions took in more than $300 million, while an additional seven had between $200 and $300 million. Twenty-one nationals reported total income under $50 million, with seven of these having less

DOI: 10.4324/9781003335474-7

Table 6.1 Total Receipts

Union	*Cycles*							*% Change from 2006–2007 to 2018–2019 (%)*
	2006–2007 ($)	*2008–2009 ($)*	*2010–2011 ($)*	*2012–2013 ($)*	*2014–2015 ($)*	*2016–2017 ($)*	*2018–2019 ($)*	
Air Line Pilots Association	247.36	226.78	183.94	197.96	222.84	261.01	325.13	31.4
Air traffic controllers	21.22	23.59	24.71	25.79	25.83	30.12	30.64	44.4
Aircraft Mechanics Association	11.35	5.46	2.99	3.69	3.41	4.22	4.79	−57.8
Allied Pilots Association	45.28	30.41	32.70	28.17	41.63	40.28	49.50	9.3
Auto workers	315.73	296.59	265.91	237.58	254.46	267.41	293.59	−7.0
Bakery, tobacco, and grain	27.78	32.69	18.97	18.83	22.88	19.53	12.00	−56.8
Boilermakers	36.74	49.11	59.19	63.97	50.34	84.42	88.01	139.6
Bricklayers	54.66	46.85	36.97	38.87	40.64	45.60	49.66	−9.1
Carpenters	192.46	97.73	200.81	117.80	132.50	111.95	152.56	−20.7
Communications workers	771.58	656.12	468.77	292.37	274.59	444.29	275.78	−64.3
Directors Guild of America Inc	47.76	50.24	49.63	56.01	55.56	63.88	65.38	36.9
Electrical Workers IBEW	875.11	337.24	608.79	788.75	835.42	1,010.53	1,098.21	25.5
Elevator constructors	12.11	16.12	12.24	11.45	13.36	14.98	24.17	99.6
Engineers, operating	82.31	67.45	66.61	69.70	79.10	125.90	206.06	150.4
Engineers, professional, and technical	4.37	4.80	5.14	5.19	5.37	5.46	5.33	21.9
Firefighters	48.10	51.04	52.22	56.68	60.43	67.29	76.98	60.1
Food and Commercial Workers	231.37	259.29	271.67	280.12	280.33	280.14	299.12	29.3
Government Employees AFGE	65.43	81.92	113.95	118.44	132.61	140.35	141.56	116.4
Insulators	10.54	11.72	11.89	13.08	14.48	14.19	15.34	45.5
Iron workers	88.60	93.73	91.80	80.94	72.27	91.35	224.01	152.8
Journeymen and allied trades	3.86	4.28	4.53	4.40	4.66	5.54	7.63	97.9

Laborers	120.92	87.66	90.42	89.80	105.06	106.72	108.32	−10.4
Letter Carriers, National Association	216.01	199.90	233.06	241.37	267.17	264.21	200.95	−7.0
Letter carriers, rural	29.20	31.82	35.31	37.33	42.84	46.01	51.69	77.0
Longshore and Warehouse Union	7.19	7.11	7.22	7.24	7.24	7.92	8.33	15.8
Longshoremen's Association	27.41	27.65	24.53	33.89	39.50	38.99	36.75	34.1
Machinists	122.71	143.06	142.16	169.85	177.24	179.63	194.60	58.6
Mine workers, united	45.16	54.37	130.68	81.05	94.92	69.43	50.31	11.4
Musicians	15.79	16.14	14.47	14.17	15.76	21.00	26.00	64.7
National Education Association	348.07	368.09	398.55	387.25	386.94	386.37	390.93	12.3
Novelty and production workers	2.77	2.77	3.69	3.29	4.10	4.12	4.21	51.8
Office and professional employees	15.57	17.06	17.66	18.03	18.01	18.35	18.57	19.3
Painters	79.47	47.22	48.55	41.04	42.73	45.31	50.69	−36.2
Plasterers and cement masons	29.98	32.44	14.96	13.44	15.03	18.25	20.22	−32.6
Plumbers	147.31	185.71	177.34	179.26	225.64	252.75	172.10	16.8
Postal workers, American	161.44	150.14	131.21	119.90	114.82	121.48	130.10	−19.4
Roofers	8.98	9.86	9.20	8.95	9.26	10.26	10.36	15.3
Seafarers	1.56	1.41	1.46	1.55	1.57	1.54	1.70	9.1
Security police, fire professionals	6.95	6.68	8.44	7.24	7.72	9.03	10.49	51.0
Service employees	275.19	325.70	333.55	362.40	321.50	309.46	373.25	35.6
Sheet metal, air, rail, and transportation workers	101.81	67.03	75.08	91.21	177.48	147.48	177.28	74.1
Stage and picture operators	79.08	82.72	58.98	61.75	66.94	86.98	96.83	22.5
State, county, and municipal employees	165.39	197.90	205.13	198.25	197.35	202.74	197.30	19.3

(Continued)

Table 6.1 (Continued)

Union	*Cycles*							*% Change from 2006–2007 to 2018–2019 (%)*
	2006–2007 ($)	*2008–2009 ($)*	*2010–2011 ($)*	*2012–2013 ($)*	*2014–2015 ($)*	*2016–2017 ($)*	*2018–2019 ($)*	
Steelworkers	844.92	449.33	452.75	507.88	530.22	526.64	574.96	−32.0
Teachers	207.96	201.68	217.73	323.38	336.15	329.89	304.83	46.6
Teamsters	182.07	183.89	181.67	178.28	187.01	195.06	209.01	14.8
Transit Union	43.89	32.46	29.67	31.13	130.60	81.58	76.79	75.0
Transport workers	65.88	65.12	49.34	46.72	45.46	118.49	158.61	140.7
Treasury Employees Union	32.33	35.12	56.19	48.07	37.29	41.44	44.03	36.2
Unite Here	143.58	120.85	142.71	90.54	90.58	106.51	123.61	−13.9
University Professors	7.00	7.04	6.49	6.59	7.60	9.11	11.57	65.2
Utility workers	9.82	11.26	15.98	14.80	14.90	15.24	14.28	45.3
Writers Guild West	41.82	59.40	52.04	56.71	56.31	65.52	74.36	77.8
Average	**127.94**	**107.01**	**112.26**	**112.87**	**120.71**	**131.43**	**139.03**	**8.7**

than $10 million in 2018–2019. Comparing the end to the beginning of these reporting intervals, 12 unions had less income.

The average amount of total receipts across unions fell from almost $128 million in 2006–2007 to just barely above $107 million during the subsequent two years. It rose continually to above $139 million in 2018–2019. Thus, after dropping roughly 16 percent in 2008–2009 compared to 2006–2007, the average total receipts ended the 14-year span 8.7 percent higher than at the beginning.

Table 6.2 reports the nationals' net receipts. In 2018–2019, only four unions had net receipts in excess of $300 million, with another seven having between $200 and $300 million. Fourteen unions had less than $20 million, with ten of these under $10 million in averaged annual net receipts for these two years. Overall, the average in net receipts fell 6.2 percent comparing the end to beginning points in time. However, net receipts, on average, dropped from $115.64 million to $90.83 million, or more than 21 percent, between 2006–2007 and 2012–2013. Fourteen unions had lower levels of net receipts in 2018–2019 than in 2006–2007.

MBI and BI

The unions' MBI totals appear in Table 6.3. Four unions generated an average of more than $200 million in MBI in 2018–2019. Eight received between $100 and $200 million. Sixteen unions derived less than $20 million, on average, for these two years, 11 of which claimed less than $10 million. The average amount of receipts rose continually over this time period, climbing 33.5 percent from $54.85 million in 2006–2007 to $73.25 million in 2018–2019. Only four unions ended the period with a two-year average in MBI less than at the beginning.

Table 6.4 reports the unions' BI over the seven two-year intervals. It includes the revenues generated from the sale of supplies, rents, dividends, and interest. The data show that, in 2018–2019, BI ranged from a negligible amount of under $500 (SIU) to more than $161 million (IRON). Three unions reported BI greater than $100 million, on average, in this last two-year interval. Thirty-four unions, in contrast, reported less than $10 million, with 14 unions having received less than $1 million from these business-related transactions.

The average amount of BI dropped significantly from 2006–2007 to 2012–2013, falling from roughly $52 million or 65 percent to less than $19 million. Comparing the beginning to end intervals, average BI fell 55 percent. Thirty-four unions ended the period with lower levels of BI than at the start in 2006–2007.

MBI and BI as a Percentage of Net Receipts

The data show that, on average, unions raised somewhere from 60 to 72 percent of their net receipts from MBI over these seven intervals (Table 6.5). The increase comparing the end to beginning intervals stood at 17 percent. Fifteen unions did, however, end the period with a smaller percentage of net receipts from MBI than in 2006–2007. The range in MBI as a share of net receipts extended from 17.9 percent to 97.6 percent in 2018–2019. Twelve unions generated more than 90 percent of their net receipts from MBI in this last interval, with 17 more recording between 70 and 90 percent. Only 12 unions reported getting less than 50 percent of net receipts from MBI.

Table 6.6 reports BI as a share of net receipts across the 53 national unions. On average, the unions' BI shrank by almost 55 percent during 2006–2007 through

Table 6.2 Net Receipts

Union	*Cycles*							*% Change from 2006–2007 to 2018–2019 (%)*
	2006–2007 ($)	*2008–2009 ($)*	*2010–2011 ($)*	*2012–2013 ($)*	*2014–2015 ($)*	*2016–2017 ($)*	*2018–2019 ($)*	
Air Line Pilots Association	232.03	207.78	152.50	179.59	202.12	241.54	302.72	30.5
Air traffic controllers	21.21	23.59	24.71	25.79	25.83	30.12	30.64	44.5
Aircraft Mechanics Association	8.00	3.78	1.97	2.46	2.02	2.75	3.15	−60.6
Allied Pilots Association	45.06	30.41	32.70	28.16	41.62	40.28	49.50	9.9
Auto workers	303.12	285.10	254.28	224.86	240.90	253.11	279.74	−7.7
Bakery, tobacco, and grain	27.77	32.65	18.96	18.83	22.88	19.52	11.98	−56.9
Boilermakers	35.67	46.91	53.20	59.62	45.17	80.87	84.45	136.8
Bricklayers	52.10	46.17	36.56	38.42	40.15	45.01	48.99	−6.0
Carpenters	192.46	97.73	200.81	117.80	132.50	111.95	152.56	−20.7
Communications workers	634.42	514.94	339.29	170.45	149.45	213.85	151.89	−76.1
Directors Guild of America Inc	47.76	50.24	49.63	56.01	55.56	63.88	65.38	36.9
Electrical Workers IBEW	830.16	241.58	250.42	281.36	292.55	345.52	267.02	−67.8
Elevator constructors	11.98	16.12	12.24	11.18	13.09	14.73	22.93	91.4
Engineers, operating	82.31	67.45	66.61	69.70	76.79	124.96	203.82	147.6
Engineers, professional, and technical	4.27	4.51	4.82	4.87	5.07	5.20	5.26	23.0
Firefighters	48.10	51.04	52.22	56.68	60.43	67.29	76.98	60.1
Food and Commercial Workers	226.90	254.29	266.98	275.10	274.79	273.88	292.88	29.1
Government Employees AFGE	49.73	59.60	83.72	81.25	89.42	91.80	89.89	80.8
Insulators	10.54	11.72	11.89	13.08	14.48	14.19	15.34	45.5
Iron workers	88.60	93.73	91.80	80.94	72.27	91.35	223.70	152.5
Journeymen and allied trades	3.85	4.25	4.52	4.40	4.66	5.54	7.63	98.3

Laborers	120.90	87.65	90.42	89.80	105.06	106.72	108.32	−10.4
Letter Carriers, National Association	151.68	122.39	172.87	168.48	196.83	191.19	116.88	−22.9
Letter carriers, rural	12.24	13.00	14.59	19.02	31.84	34.68	39.35	221.6
Longshore and Warehouse Union	7.19	7.11	7.19	7.24	7.24	7.92	8.33	15.8
Longshoremen's Association	22.23	27.65	19.84	26.14	29.54	28.94	25.87	16.4
Machinists	122.14	139.59	129.37	149.74	150.89	152.72	163.05	33.5
Mine workers, united	38.26	34.16	110.19	61.15	75.75	53.17	32.80	−14.3
Musicians	13.20	12.09	11.69	11.76	12.55	13.59	13.91	5.4
National Education Association	347.99	367.97	398.47	387.18	386.78	386.25	390.70	12.3
Novelty and production workers	2.77	2.77	3.69	3.29	4.10	4.12	4.21	51.8
Office and professional employees	15.50	16.58	16.77	17.13	17.11	17.44	17.73	14.4
Painters	79.47	46.22	48.55	41.04	42.73	45.31	50.69	−36.2
Plasterers and cement masons	29.98	32.43	14.89	13.44	15.02	18.25	20.22	−32.6
Plumbers	147.31	185.71	177.34	179.26	225.64	252.75	172.10	16.8
Postal workers, American	86.01	81.04	69.58	62.91	59.36	61.59	67.52	−21.5
Roofers	8.96	9.85	9.20	8.95	9.25	10.25	10.33	15.3
Seafarers	1.55	1.41	1.46	1.55	1.57	1.54	1.70	9.2
Security police, fire professionals	5.55	5.19	6.00	5.96	5.70	5.78	6.46	16.4
Service employees	275.03	325.49	333.39	362.25	320.85	308.03	372.99	35.6
Sheet metal, air, rail, and transportation workers	101.81	67.03	75.08	65.92	109.05	82.15	107.19	5.3
Stage and picture operators	79.08	82.72	58.98	61.75	66.70	86.82	96.69	22.3

(Continued)

Table 6.2 (Continued)

Union	*Cycles*							*% Change from 2006–2007 to 2018–2019 (%)*
	2006–2007 ($)	*2008–2009 ($)*	*2010–2011 ($)*	*2012–2013 ($)*	*2014–2015 ($)*	*2016–2017 ($)*	*2018–2019 ($)*	
State, county, and municipal employees	164.22	197.57	204.85	198.20	197.13	202.48	197.01	20.0
Steelworkers	695.65	292.63	290.67	328.21	351.05	355.30	391.73	−43.7
Teachers	177.03	169.93	184.98	288.33	297.42	291.63	263.44	48.8
Teamsters	181.63	183.89	180.95	176.66	185.54	193.68	207.53	14.3
Transit Union	43.86	32.45	29.63	31.10	130.60	81.58	76.79	75.1
Transport workers	49.68	50.21	33.69	33.16	32.09	103.60	142.04	185.9
Treasury Employees Union	28.87	35.03	56.10	48.00	37.18	36.07	38.68	34.0
Unite Here	105.26	106.18	131.45	87.97	86.53	99.39	116.54	10.7
University Professors	6.86	6.95	6.41	6.59	7.60	9.11	11.57	68.7
Utility workers	9.30	10.75	15.37	14.56	14.52	14.97	13.99	50.4
Writers Guild West	41.82	59.40	52.04	56.71	56.31	65.52	74.36	77.8
Average	**115.64**	**93.52**	**93.69**	**90.83**	**96.82**	**103.02**	**108.44**	**−6.2**

Table 6.3 Member-based Income

Union	*Cycles*							*% Change from 2006–2007 to 2018–2019 (%)*
	2006–2007 ($)	*2008–2009 ($)*	*2010–2011 ($)*	*2012–2013 ($)*	*2014–2015 ($)*	*2016–2017 ($)*	*2018–2019 ($)*	
Air Line Pilots Association	105.77	100.25	107.86	122.60	138.42	185.14	211.83	100.3
Air traffic controllers	19.20	20.09	21.51	23.08	23.43	24.91	26.66	38.9
Aircraft Mechanics Association	2.05	1.07	1.05	1.14	1.24	1.31	1.51	−26.4
Allied Pilots Association	16.27	17.62	17.31	17.23	16.58	28.35	41.08	152.5
Auto workers	180.01	144.42	120.70	115.05	142.56	179.12	180.68	0.4
Bakery, tobacco, and grain	10.02	10.17	10.06	9.96	9.30	8.98	9.02	−10.0
Boilermakers	28.39	38.18	35.57	36.48	38.95	38.55	43.10	51.8
Bricklayers	39.31	37.61	29.57	29.58	32.70	37.70	40.79	3.8
Carpenters	51.19	53.76	52.40	63.12	63.70	66.59	72.79	42.2
Communications workers	139.04	143.22	135.32	127.96	126.36	118.27	124.56	−10.4
Directors Guild of America Inc	17.58	19.68	20.57	21.55	24.80	26.95	29.43	67.4
Electrical Workers IBEW	86.56	93.19	101.22	113.19	127.07	136.74	145.15	67.7
Elevator constructors	8.74	11.26	10.85	10.23	10.95	13.35	21.49	145.9
Engineers, operating	43.38	45.74	49.53	52.53	57.14	60.23	66.54	53.4
Engineers, professional, and technical	3.97	4.31	4.73	4.65	4.65	4.98	5.00	25.8
Firefighters	30.56	35.48	38.16	41.32	43.94	46.41	50.99	66.9
Food and Commercial Workers	187.06	205.40	211.45	210.36	224.27	219.29	226.02	20.8
Government Employees AFGE	41.90	49.44	61.81	66.89	70.29	77.05	80.29	91.6
Insulators	9.36	10.84	11.01	12.24	12.97	12.73	13.82	47.6

(*Continued*)

Table 6.3 (Continued)

Union	*Cycles*							*% Change from 2006–2007 to 2018–2019 (%)*
	2006–2007 ($)	*2008–2009 ($)*	*2010–2011 ($)*	*2012–2013 ($)*	*2014–2015 ($)*	*2016–2017 ($)*	*2018–2019 ($)*	
Iron workers	33.51	37.94	34.19	39.19	42.17	44.10	49.74	48.4
Journeymen and allied trades	3.71	4.21	4.42	4.06	4.14	4.71	6.35	71.2
Laborers	71.27	76.50	74.17	76.74	79.35	84.00	92.06	29.2
Letter Carriers, National Association	35.64	39.09	40.51	35.76	37.14	40.30	43.94	23.3
Letter carriers, rural	10.29	10.65	10.80	16.49	28.09	30.77	35.13	241.3
Longshore and Warehouse Union	6.91	6.94	6.73	7.14	7.16	7.85	8.13	17.6
Longshoremen's Association	13.16	21.65	18.63	23.73	24.30	24.68	22.77	73.0
Machinists	91.26	98.66	113.60	129.27	135.04	134.62	142.48	56.1
Mine workers, united	18.76	19.49	20.64	22.16	19.61	14.38	14.77	−21.3
Musicians	9.23	9.79	9.07	8.95	9.22	9.43	9.52	3.1
National Education Association	306.41	346.53	366.64	367.38	362.87	368.51	371.37	21.2
Novelty and production workers	0.71	0.60	0.58	0.74	0.89	0.90	0.93	30.6
Office and professional employees	11.48	12.14	13.22	13.96	15.02	16.18	16.53	44.0
Painters	24.25	26.31	25.81	25.33	27.03	30.79	32.62	34.5
Plasterers and cement masons	15.59	15.12	11.35	12.13	14.03	16.95	18.70	20.0
Plumbers	67.31	74.80	74.41	80.68	86.17	87.08	101.95	51.5
Postal workers, American	53.33	52.56	49.23	50.91	50.81	56.14	57.58	8.0
Roofers	7.18	7.48	7.42	7.21	7.39	8.19	8.71	21.3
Seafarers	1.25	1.11	1.17	1.21	1.24	1.34	1.57	25.0
Security police, fire professionals	4.18	4.25	5.25	5.22	5.18	5.31	5.90	41.1

Service employees	238.74	259.43	291.58	298.75	290.58	279.18	280.67	17.6
Sheet metal, air, rail, and transportation workers	37.93	40.48	42.82	54.41	64.95	69.48	76.43	101.5
Stage and picture operators	16.61	18.51	19.71	21.21	25.03	28.38	32.50	95.6
State, county, and municipal employees	149.96	184.56	189.04	179.37	177.27	184.88	182.12	21.4
Steelworkers	224.87	227.45	248.45	282.73	285.28	275.15	298.23	32.6
Teachers	125.13	146.59	156.97	159.87	164.05	184.86	187.80	50.1
Teamsters	159.08	160.67	161.19	161.54	168.98	178.30	190.27	19.6
Transit Union	17.80	19.82	20.95	21.84	23.59	27.12	29.57	66.2
Transport workers	16.62	17.94	18.64	19.05	20.63	23.12	25.42	53.0
Treasury Employees Union	20.51	27.82	32.57	32.54	33.17	29.86	29.77	45.2
Unite Here	61.51	58.86	47.34	51.34	53.24	56.48	62.56	1.7
University Professors	4.90	5.86	5.66	5.76	6.94	7.38	7.37	50.2
Utility workers	7.88	9.17	9.79	9.68	11.16	11.79	12.95	64.4
Writers Guild West	19.74	20.39	20.99	22.99	25.22	28.10	35.08	77.7
Average	**54.85**	**58.59**	**60.27**	**62.80**	**65.59**	**69.00**	**73.25**	**33.5**

Table 6.4 Business Income

Union	*Cycles*							*% Change from 2006–2007 to 2018–2019 (%)*
	2006–2007 ($)	*2008–2009 ($)*	*2010–2011 ($)*	*2012–2013 ($)*	*2014–2015 ($)*	*2016–2017 ($)*	*2018–2019 ($)*	
Air Line Pilots Association	102.08	87.70	25.45	34.57	22.78	39.46	68.04	−33.3
Air traffic controllers	1.73	2.94	2.33	1.99	0.76	0.89	2.27	30.8
Aircraft Mechanics Association	0.04	0.42	0.43	0.49	0.39	0.83	0.79	1731.5
Allied Pilots Association	25.77	12.09	14.92	10.24	15.20	9.18	8.01	−68.9
Auto workers	78.20	103.69	101.99	71.51	59.97	29.52	68.51	−12.4
Bakery, tobacco, and grain	16.43	21.60	8.31	8.07	13.12	9.95	2.49	−84.8
Boilermakers	5.39	3.59	4.94	17.58	3.64	6.18	5.75	6.8
Bricklayers	4.85	0.91	0.15	2.04	0.64	0.16	0.34	−93.0
Carpenters	128.63	26.05	134.72	39.90	46.28	22.14	43.37	−66.3
Communications workers	464.38	355.56	190.54	29.84	16.95	57.26	16.13	−96.5
Directors Guild of America Inc	7.66	7.09	6.53	7.00	7.06	6.78	8.42	10.0
Electrical Workers IBEW	734.23	139.32	138.63	155.61	155.03	196.58	107.66	−85.3
Elevator constructors	3.06	4.69	1.07	0.26	1.81	0.76	0.47	−84.6
Engineers, operating	34.53	18.32	13.91	14.12	15.53	12.96	82.64	139.3
Engineers, professional, and technical	0.04	0.03	0.02	0.04	0.04	0.03	0.05	28.0
Firefighters	5.45	0.67	0.49	0.52	0.47	0.70	1.75	−67.9
Food and Commercial Workers	13.08	24.14	31.25	43.93	31.25	31.57	44.30	238.6
Government Employees AFGE	4.13	4.82	10.84	8.08	13.15	7.27	2.52	−39.0
Insulators	0.60	0.28	0.26	0.12	1.08	0.79	1.10	85.6
Iron workers	47.81	47.38	47.99	31.05	20.25	35.79	161.61	238.0
Journeymen and allied trades	0.02	0.01	0.00	0.00	0.00	0.00	0.03	23.4

Laborers	39.35	4.80	9.04	4.52	17.13	12.82	7.89	−80.0
Letter Carriers, National Association	114.07	81.42	130.05	130.18	157.41	147.98	70.83	−37.9
Letter carriers, rural	0.48	0.23	0.34	0.02	0.02	0.03	0.31	−35.0
Longshore and Warehouse Union	0.02	0.03	0.08	0.00	0.00	0.00	0.01	−72.6
Longshoremen's Association	8.23	5.10	0.18	0.53	2.85	3.03	0.86	−89.5
Machinists	17.83	28.62	4.75	6.52	3.55	4.84	6.52	−63.5
Mine workers, united	18.13	14.06	89.11	38.62	48.58	34.64	12.08	−33.4
Musicians	1.95	0.22	0.02	0.06	0.08	0.13	0.35	−82.0
National Education Association	2.44	1.42	0.21	2.17	2.27	1.34	5.20	112.7
Novelty and production workers	2.04	2.17	3.10	2.53	3.19	3.18	3.28	61.2
Office and professional employees	1.77	1.36	0.61	0.12	0.10	0.23	0.17	−90.4
Painters	44.03	9.11	12.04	5.26	5.73	4.10	6.80	−84.6
Plasterers and cement masons	13.65	16.78	2.38	0.65	0.41	0.87	1.12	−91.8
Plumbers	78.16	91.46	99.76	95.27	134.30	154.96	65.68	−16.0
Postal workers, American	30.82	25.12	17.88	9.94	7.15	4.64	9.11	−70.4
Roofers	1.56	2.11	1.53	1.52	1.56	1.84	1.25	−20.3
Seafarers	0.01	0.01	0.00	0.00	0.00	0.00	0.00	−97.2
Security police, fire professionals	0.93	0.45	0.34	0.46	0.07	0.05	0.17	−82.0
Service employees	6.71	11.14	15.21	42.17	5.25	7.23	55.55	728.5
Sheet metal, air, rail, and transportation workers	61.54	23.48	29.47	5.32	37.12	6.50	25.99	−57.8
Stage and picture operators	60.16	62.02	37.05	37.91	40.00	56.81	62.30	3.6

(Continued)

Table 6.4 (Continued)

Union	*Cycles*							*% Change from 2006–2007 to 2018–2019 (%)*
	2006–2007 ($)	*2008–2009 ($)*	*2010–2011 ($)*	*2012–2013 ($)*	*2014–2015 ($)*	*2016–2017 ($)*	*2018–2019 ($)*	
State, county, and municipal employees	2.96	1.37	4.52	6.31	8.80	5.45	3.69	24.8
Steelworkers	457.16	51.45	30.03	24.62	48.64	59.15	57.41	−87.4
Teachers	14.21	11.68	15.53	14.91	11.94	21.92	13.31	−6.3
Teamsters	4.05	13.32	8.23	5.38	7.12	7.20	9.73	140.4
Transit Union	25.21	11.84	7.94	8.43	106.10	53.81	46.67	85.1
Transport workers	31.72	29.53	13.77	9.01	10.04	79.38	111.60	251.8
Treasury Employees Union	6.52	5.42	22.01	14.76	3.49	5.24	5.65	−13.4
Unite Here	23.41	33.74	65.66	28.74	27.11	28.81	37.54	60.3
University Professors	1.00	0.41	0.14	0.07	0.05	0.01	0.07	−93.2
Utility workers	0.99	1.14	3.11	3.03	2.25	2.56	0.42	−57.9
Writers Guild West	3.49	10.62	2.23	1.41	1.31	1.53	2.10	−39.9
Average	**51.94**	**26.66**	**25.68**	**18.44**	**21.11**	**22.25**	**23.58**	**−54.6**

Table 6.5 Member-based Income as a Percentage of Net Receipts

Union	*Cycles*							*% Change from 2006–2007 to 2018–2019 (%)*
	2006–2007 (%)	*2008–2009 (%)*	*2010–2011 (%)*	*2012–2013 (%)*	*2014–2015 (%)*	*2016–2017 (%)*	*2018–2019 (%)*	
Air Line Pilots Association	45.6	48.3	70.7	68.3	68.5	76.6	70.0	53.5
Air traffic controllers	90.6	85.2	87.0	89.5	90.7	82.7	87.0	−3.9
Aircraft Mechanics Association	25.6	28.3	53.4	46.2	61.6	47.7	48.0	87.0
Allied Pilots Association	36.1	58.0	52.9	61.2	39.8	70.4	83.0	129.8
Auto workers	59.4	50.7	47.5	51.2	59.2	70.8	64.6	8.8
Bakery, tobacco, and grain	36.1	31.1	53.1	52.9	40.6	46.0	75.3	108.5
Boilermakers	79.6	81.4	66.9	61.2	86.2	47.7	51.0	−35.9
Bricklayers	75.4	81.5	80.9	77.0	81.4	83.8	83.3	10.4
Carpenters	26.6	55.0	26.1	53.6	48.1	59.5	47.7	79.4
Communications workers	21.9	27.8	39.9	75.1	84.5	55.3	82.0	274.2
Directors Guild of America Inc	36.8	39.2	41.5	38.5	44.6	42.2	45.0	22.3
Electrical Workers IBEW	10.4	38.6	40.4	40.2	43.4	39.6	54.4	421.4
Elevator constructors	73.0	69.8	88.6	91.5	83.7	90.6	93.7	28.5
Engineers, operating	52.7	67.8	74.3	75.4	74.4	48.2	32.6	−38.1
Engineers, professional, and technical	93.0	95.6	98.2	95.5	91.7	95.8	95.1	2.2
Firefighters	63.5	69.5	73.1	72.9	72.7	69.0	66.2	4.2
Food and Commercial Workers	82.4	80.8	79.2	76.5	81.6	80.1	77.2	−6.4
Government Employees AFGE	84.3	83.0	73.8	82.3	78.6	83.9	89.3	6.0
Insulators	88.8	92.5	92.6	93.6	89.5	89.7	90.1	1.4

(*Continued*)

Table 6.5 (Continued)

Union	*Cycles*							*% Change from 2006–2007 to 2018–2019 (%)*
	2006–2007 (%)	*2008–2009 (%)*	*2010–2011 (%)*	*2012–2013 (%)*	*2014–2015 (%)*	*2016–2017 (%)*	*2018–2019 (%)*	
Iron workers	37.8	40.5	37.2	48.4	58.4	48.3	22.2	−41.2
Journeymen and allied trades	96.3	99.0	97.8	92.2	88.8	85.1	83.2	−13.7
Laborers	59.0	87.3	82.0	85.5	75.5	78.7	85.0	44.2
Letter Carriers, National Association	23.5	31.9	23.4	21.2	18.9	21.1	37.6	60.0
Letter carriers, rural	84.1	81.9	74.0	86.7	88.2	88.7	89.3	6.1
Longshore and Warehouse Union	96.1	97.6	93.6	98.6	98.9	99.1	97.6	1.5
Longshoremen's Association	59.2	78.3	93.9	90.8	82.3	85.3	88.0	48.7
Machinists	74.7	70.7	87.8	86.3	89.5	88.1	87.4	17.0
Mine workers, united	49.0	57.1	18.7	36.2	25.9	27.0	45.0	−8.1
Musicians	70.0	81.0	77.6	76.1	73.5	69.4	68.4	−2.2
National Education Association	88.1	94.2	92.0	94.9	93.8	95.4	95.1	7.9
Novelty and production workers	25.6	21.7	15.8	22.7	21.8	21.7	22.0	−14.0
Office and professional employees	74.1	73.2	78.8	81.5	87.8	92.8	93.2	25.8
Painters	30.5	56.9	53.2	61.7	63.3	67.9	64.3	110.9
Plasterers and cement masons	52.0	46.6	76.2	90.2	93.4	92.9	92.5	77.9
Plumbers	45.7	40.3	42.0	45.0	38.2	34.5	59.2	29.7
Postal workers, American	62.0	64.9	70.7	80.9	85.6	91.2	85.3	37.5
Roofers	80.2	76.0	80.7	80.5	79.9	79.8	84.4	5.2
Seafarers	80.6	79.0	80.3	78.2	78.8	86.9	92.3	14.4
Security police, fire professionals	75.3	81.9	87.5	87.6	90.8	92.0	91.4	21.3

Service employees	86.8	79.7	87.5	82.5	90.6	90.6	75.2	−13.3
Sheet metal, air, rail, and transportation workers	37.3	60.4	57.0	82.5	59.6	84.6	71.3	91.4
Stage and picture operators	21.0	22.4	33.4	34.3	37.5	32.7	33.6	60.0
State, county, and municipal employees	91.3	93.4	92.3	90.5	89.9	91.3	92.4	1.2
Steelworkers	32.3	77.7	85.5	86.1	81.3	77.4	76.1	135.5
Teachers	70.7	86.3	84.9	55.4	55.2	63.4	71.3	0.9
Teamsters	87.6	87.4	89.1	91.4	91.1	92.1	91.7	4.7
Transit Union	40.6	61.1	70.7	70.2	18.1	33.2	38.5	−5.1
Transport workers	33.4	35.7	55.3	57.4	64.3	22.3	17.9	−46.5
Treasury Employees Union	71.0	79.4	58.1	67.8	89.2	82.8	77.0	8.4
Unite Here	58.4	55.4	36.0	58.4	61.5	56.8	53.7	−8.1
University Professors	71.5	84.3	88.3	87.4	91.2	81.0	63.7	−11.0
Utility workers	84.7	85.3	63.7	66.5	76.9	78.8	92.5	9.3
Writers Guild West	47.2	34.3	40.3	40.5	44.8	42.9	47.2	−0.1
Average	**60.0**	**65.8**	**66.9**	**70.2**	**69.9**	**69.0**	**70.2**	**17.0**

Table 6.6 Business Income as a Percentage of Net Receipts

Union	*Cycles*							*% Change from 2006–2007 to 2018–2019 (%)*
	2006–2007 (%)	*2008–2009 (%)*	*2010–2011 (%)*	*2012–2013 (%)*	*2014–2015 (%)*	*2016–2017 (%)*	*2018–2019 (%)*	
Air Line Pilots Association	44.0	42.2	16.7	19.2	11.3	16.3	22.5	−48.9
Air traffic controllers	8.2	12.5	9.4	7.7	3.0	3.0	7.4	−9.5
Aircraft Mechanics Association	0.5	11.2	21.7	19.8	19.3	30.3	25.0	4554.1
Allied Pilots Association	57.2	39.8	45.6	36.4	36.5	22.8	16.2	−71.7
Auto workers	25.8	36.4	40.1	31.8	24.9	11.7	24.5	−5.1
Bakery, tobacco, and grain	59.2	66.1	43.8	42.9	57.4	51.0	20.8	−64.9
Boilermakers	15.1	7.6	9.3	29.5	8.1	7.6	6.8	−54.9
Bricklayers	9.3	2.0	0.4	5.3	1.6	0.3	0.7	−92.6
Carpenters	66.8	26.7	67.1	33.9	34.9	19.8	28.4	−57.5
Communications workers	73.2	69.0	56.2	17.5	11.3	26.8	10.6	−85.5
Directors Guild of America Inc	16.0	14.1	13.2	12.5	12.7	10.6	12.9	−19.6
Electrical Workers IBEW	88.4	57.7	55.4	55.3	53.0	56.9	40.3	−54.4
Elevator constructors	25.6	29.1	8.7	2.3	13.8	5.2	2.1	−92.0
Engineers, operating	41.9	27.2	20.9	20.3	20.2	10.4	40.5	−3.3
Engineers, professional, and technical	0.9	0.7	0.5	0.8	0.9	0.6	1.0	4.1
Firefighters	11.3	1.3	0.9	0.9	0.8	1.0	2.3	−79.9
Food and Commercial Workers	5.8	9.5	11.7	16.0	11.4	11.5	15.1	162.3
Government Employees AFGE	8.3	8.1	13.0	9.9	14.7	7.9	2.8	−66.3
Insulators	5.6	2.4	2.2	0.9	7.5	5.6	7.2	27.5
Iron workers	54.0	50.6	52.3	38.4	28.0	39.2	72.2	33.9
Journeymen and allied trades	0.6	0.1	0.0	0.0	0.0	0.0	0.4	−37.8

Laborers	32.6	5.5	10.0	5.0	16.3	12.0	7.3	−77.6
Letter Carriers, National Association	75.2	66.5	75.2	77.3	80.0	77.4	60.6	−19.4
Letter carriers, rural	3.9	1.8	2.3	0.1	0.0	0.1	0.8	−79.8
Longshore and Warehouse Union	0.3	0.5	1.1	0.0	0.1	0.0	0.1	−76.4
Longshoremen's Association	37.0	18.4	0.9	2.0	9.6	10.5	3.3	−91.0
Machinists	14.6	20.5	3.7	4.4	2.4	3.2	4.0	−72.6
Mine workers, united	47.4	41.2	80.9	63.2	64.1	65.1	36.8	−22.3
Musicians	14.8	1.8	0.2	0.5	0.7	1.0	2.5	−82.9
National Education Association	0.7	0.4	0.1	0.6	0.6	0.3	1.3	89.5
Novelty and production workers	73.4	78.2	83.9	77.0	77.7	77.2	77.9	6.2
Office and professional employees	11.4	8.2	3.7	0.7	0.6	1.3	1.0	−91.6
Painters	55.4	19.7	24.8	12.8	13.4	9.1	13.4	−75.8
Plasterers and cement masons	45.5	51.7	16.0	4.8	2.7	4.8	5.5	−87.8
Plumbers	53.1	49.2	56.3	53.1	59.5	61.3	38.2	−28.1
Postal workers, American	35.8	31.0	25.7	15.8	12.0	7.5	13.5	−62.4
Roofers	17.5	21.4	16.7	16.9	16.9	18.0	12.1	−30.8
Seafarers	0.9	0.6	0.1	0.0	0.0	0.0	0.0	−97.4
Security police, fire professionals	16.8	8.6	5.7	7.6	1.3	0.8	2.6	−84.5
Service employees	2.4	3.4	4.6	11.6	1.6	2.3	14.9	510.9
Sheet metal, air, rail, and transportation workers	60.4	35.0	39.2	8.1	34.0	7.9	24.2	−59.9
Stage and picture operators	76.1	75.0	62.8	61.4	60.0	65.4	64.4	−15.3
State, county, and municipal employees	1.8	0.7	2.2	3.2	4.5	2.7	1.9	4.0

(Continued)

Table 6.6 (Continued)

Union	*Cycles*							*% Change from 2006–2007 to 2018–2019 (%)*
	2006–2007 (%)	*2008–2009 (%)*	*2010–2011 (%)*	*2012–2013 (%)*	*2014–2015 (%)*	*2016–2017 (%)*	*2018–2019 (%)*	
Steelworkers	65.7	17.6	10.3	7.5	13.9	16.6	14.7	−77.7
Teachers	8.0	6.9	8.4	5.2	4.0	7.5	5.1	−37.0
Teamsters	2.2	7.2	4.5	3.0	3.8	3.7	4.7	110.4
Transit Union	57.5	36.5	26.8	27.1	81.2	66.0	60.8	5.7
Transport workers	63.9	58.8	40.9	27.2	31.3	76.6	78.6	23.1
Treasury Employees Union	22.6	15.5	39.2	30.7	9.4	14.5	14.6	−35.4
Unite Here	22.2	31.8	50.0	32.7	31.3	29.0	32.2	44.8
University Professors	14.5	6.0	2.1	1.0	0.7	0.1	0.6	−95.9
Utility workers	10.7	10.6	20.3	20.8	15.5	17.1	3.0	−72.0
Writers Guild West	8.3	17.9	4.3	2.5	2.3	2.3	2.8	−66.2
Average	**29.6**	**23.8**	**22.9**	**18.6**	**19.3**	**18.9**	**18.2**	**−38.7**

2018–2019, falling from $51.94 to $23.58. It had dropped to a low of $18.44 in 2012–2013 before rising modestly thereafter. In 2018–2019, only three unions generated more than $100 million in BI, but 14 raised less than $1 million. Thirty-six unions ended the 14-year span with less BI than at the beginning.

Overall, unions ended the seven two-year intervals with slightly less net receipts, which nonetheless reflected a significant recovery from the loss experienced during the Great Recession, when these revenues declined from $115.64 million to just above $90 million (a nearly 21.5 percent drop). This aggregate situation, however, masks considerable variation, as ten unions experienced a drop (comparing between to end periods) of more than 20 percent in net receipts. Over this time period, unions became more dependent, in aggregate, on MBI, which climbed as an average of net receipts across unions from 60 percent to 70.2 percent. Only four unions ended the period with less MBI than at the beginning, with the overall increase reaching 33.5 percent. Twenty-one unions saw their MBI jump by more than 50 percent comparing beginning to end intervals. While growing more dependent on MBI as a source of revenue, the unions experienced a sizable drop in BI. They had nearly 55 percent less BI in 2018–2019 than in 2006–2007, with this source of revenue dropping to a low of $18.4 million in total from $51.94 at the beginning, or 64.5 percent. The drop in BI constrains the unions' overall capacity to raise additional income, as union membership has remained stagnant or dropped for many unions. Internal union politics limit the ability of unions to raise dues and fees to offset membership losses or reductions in BI.

7 Disbursements

This chapter covers the disbursements side of the income statement. Over the seven intervals, the unions' average total disbursements rose 7.5 percent. Net disbursements, in contrast, fell 23.5 percent. Only three unions had net disbursements above $300 million in 2018–2019. The unions' administrative expenditures rose 14 percent, on average, over the seven intervals, while the compensation budget rose 15 percent. Average operating budgets climbed 18 percent comparing end to beginning periods. On average, the unions ended the 14-year time period spending relatively more on administration, compensation, and overall operations.

We report on the nationals' disbursements based on seven two-year averages covering the years between 2006 and 2019. In addition to total and net assets, the chapter shows the unions' spending on administration and compensation as well as their operating budgets. Administration includes expenditures on general overhead, union administration, and supplies. Compensation encompasses the gross salaries paid to officers and employees and their benefits. A union's operating budget incorporates administrative disbursements plus expenditures on representation and politics. As will become evident, the national unions' disbursements, in aggregate, pattern trends in overall receipts. In short, a union's receipts impose the principal constraint on how much they can spend.

Total and Net Disbursements

Table 7.1 reports the unions' total disbursements over the seven two-year periods. It reveals that only two unions spent more than $500 million in 2018–2019, including transmittals, with just one having expenditures exceeding $1 billion. Thirteen unions spent between $200 and $300 million, six of which disbursed totals from $200 to $300 million. In contrast, another 13 unions spent less than $20 million on average for the 2018–2019 interval. Eight of these unions had total expenditures less than $10 million.

Comparing the end to beginning periods, the average two-year total disbursements rose 7.5 percent from $127.4 million to $137 million. However, as was the case with total receipts, the average in total disbursements fell 16.7 percent to

DOI: 10.4324/9781003335474-8

Table 7.1 Total Disbursements

Union	*Cycle*							*% Change from 2006–2007 to 2018–2019 (%)*
	2006–2007 ($)	*2008–2009 ($)*	*2010–2011 ($)*	*2012–2013 ($)*	*2014–2015 ($)*	*2016–2017 ($)*	*2018–2019 ($)*	
Air Line Pilots Association	242.07	217.71	192.72	200.95	216.11	260.00	327.68	35.4
Air traffic controllers	21.21	23.56	24.77	24.85	27.11	30.45	30.10	41.9
Aircraft Mechanics Association	11.26	5.62	3.03	3.52	3.40	4.26	4.52	−59.9
Allied Pilots Association	42.49	32.95	30.39	31.01	40.73	38.00	44.58	4.9
Auto workers	317.63	294.80	266.59	237.10	253.41	267.60	293.70	−7.5
Bakery, tobacco, and grain	27.82	33.04	19.14	18.01	23.35	19.27	12.13	−56.4
Boilermakers	36.82	47.57	64.54	62.60	49.96	85.27	85.58	132.4
Bricklayers	50.53	51.45	39.93	37.00	40.77	37.74	42.37	−16.2
Carpenters	190.29	89.10	197.39	112.80	141.93	103.79	152.82	−19.7
Communications workers	778.23	640.80	486.34	279.83	279.16	442.90	270.09	−65.3
Directors Guild of America Inc	45.32	47.54	52.58	56.05	56.36	60.53	65.05	43.6
Electrical Workers IBEW	889.50	334.43	605.50	787.97	838.00	1,002.51	1,074.13	20.8
Elevator constructors	11.69	11.47	10.12	14.68	12.67	13.54	24.29	107.8
Engineers, operating	54.01	96.75	68.91	68.48	79.55	125.81	206.09	281.6
Engineers, professional, and technical	4.32	4.59	5.02	5.10	5.53	5.69	5.17	19.6
Firefighters	49.49	50.42	52.77	55.93	61.00	66.41	77.24	56.1
Food and Commercial Workers	228.05	275.09	268.83	256.20	304.07	268.41	283.03	24.1
Government Employees AFGE	64.61	82.65	113.03	115.73	134.89	138.73	137.28	112.5
Insulators	11.35	10.69	11.19	12.59	19.78	12.86	13.52	19.1

(Continued)

Table 7.1 (Continued)

Union	*Cycle*							*% Change from 2006–2007 to 2018–2019 (%)*
	2006–2007 ($)	*2008–2009 ($)*	*2010–2011 ($)*	*2012–2013 ($)*	*2014–2015 ($)*	*2016–2017 ($)*	*2018–2019 ($)*	
Iron workers	91.27	90.61	91.77	81.23	70.35	92.63	224.34	145.8
Journeymen and allied trades	3.78	4.19	4.74	4.42	4.43	5.45	6.89	82.4
Laborers	121.43	87.38	90.24	88.37	101.00	110.56	104.50	−13.9
Letter Carriers, National Association	217.56	196.33	236.73	241.05	265.52	261.46	205.04	−5.8
Letter carriers, rural	29.05	32.22	35.40	38.59	41.87	46.04	48.55	67.1
Longshore and Warehouse Union	6.75	7.01	6.92	6.78	6.25	7.11	8.23	21.9
Longshoremen's Association	30.63	29.48	25.97	29.38	38.25	35.41	42.98	40.3
Machinists	122.36	143.48	140.86	164.66	176.58	187.99	193.50	58.1
Mine workers, united	41.57	55.37	134.88	78.36	99.20	64.01	54.56	31.3
Musicians	13.76	15.73	14.78	13.26	14.43	18.26	24.10	75.1
National Education Association	349.59	366.00	391.24	352.46	357.04	386.48	388.33	11.1
Novelty and production workers	2.72	2.81	3.67	2.87	4.29	4.16	3.66	34.4
Office and professional employees	13.89	14.77	18.25	17.60	18.11	16.04	14.32	3.1
Painters	77.07	46.76	47.92	40.55	49.68	46.34	49.42	−35.9
Plasterers and cement masons	28.50	32.58	15.94	12.56	14.09	18.21	20.15	−29.3
Plumbers	143.87	181.22	174.49	180.52	221.22	247.23	161.15	12.0
Postal workers, American	158.26	149.77	132.94	120.08	113.18	120.99	128.53	−18.8
Roofers	9.21	8.80	9.49	8.62	9.08	9.92	11.58	25.7
Seafarers	1.43	1.47	1.57	1.48	1.47	1.47	1.44	0.3
Security police, fire professionals	6.69	6.44	6.83	5.51	6.63	8.07	7.83	17.0

Service employees	268.51	313.83	326.78	374.06	307.87	293.75	343.85	28.1
Sheet metal, air, rail, and transportation workers	99.50	67.19	75.73	87.41	178.39	151.57	172.80	73.7
Stage and picture operators	79.34	81.48	58.55	63.64	66.92	86.84	96.67	21.8
State, county, and municipal employees	159.89	203.74	198.73	201.26	200.41	200.91	194.78	21.8
Steelworkers	857.79	448.31	422.41	469.45	537.78	525.15	588.40	−31.4
Teachers	205.45	200.82	221.13	325.54	332.06	324.57	302.57	47.3
Teamsters	192.55	170.69	190.60	170.91	185.01	199.58	209.12	8.6
Transit Union	40.92	30.05	30.12	30.07	128.20	70.25	88.76	116.9
Transport workers	65.34	65.37	49.73	47.27	43.66	116.15	160.53	145.7
Treasury Employees Union	32.73	35.28	52.35	49.32	37.93	41.64	44.16	34.9
Unite Here	146.11	118.53	139.20	87.77	94.83	101.62	112.16	−23.2
University Professors	6.92	6.92	6.47	6.47	6.55	7.94	9.04	30.6
Utility workers	9.47	9.85	17.62	14.92	14.24	13.61	13.89	46.7
Writers Guild West	41.59	50.62	54.19	56.78	52.80	61.56	76.20	83.2
Average	**127.40**	**106.14**	**112.10**	**110.45**	**120.51**	**129.56**	**137.01**	**7.5**

106.14 million in 2008–2009. Despite the rise in the average level of spending over these 14 years overall, 13 unions ended the period with less in the two-year averaged total receipts than at the beginning two-year span.

Net disbursements appear in Table 7.2. Excluding transmittals, only four unions spent more than $300 million in 2018–2019. Just another six unions had net disbursements between $200 and $300 million. Twenty-four unions, on the other hand, had net spending below $50 million averaged over these two years, with eight of these reporting less than $10 million in net disbursements. Paralleling the pattern in receipts, the unions' net disbursements, on average, declined considerably between 2006–2007 and 2018–2019, dropping 23.5 percent from around $115 million to less than $88 million. Over the entire 14-year span, the unions' averaged net receipts rose 7.7 percent, comparing 2018–2019 to 2006–2007. Fifteen unions ended the period with lower averaged net disbursements than they had at the beginning.

Disbursements on Administration, Compensation, and Operating Budgets

Table 7.3 displays the unions' administrative expenditures. It shows that only six unions spent more than $100 million on administration in 2008–2009 (two-year average). Thirty-three unions spent less than $20 million. Over the 14 years, spending rose 18 percent for the two-year averaged periods, rising from $18.52 in 2006–2007 to $21.86 in 2018–2019. The rise is continual, suggesting that administrative spending defied the downturn in overall expenditures associated with the recession years. Sixteen unions spent less on administration in 2018–2019 than in 2006–2007.

We cover compensation expenditures in Table 7.4. It reveals that unions, overall, spent considerably more on compensation than administration *per se*. These expenditures grew continually, climbing 15 percent to almost $31 million averaged for 2018–2019. While only three unions spent more than $100 million on compensation for officers and employees combined for 2018–2019, 17 had compensation budgets less than $10 million. Eleven unions spent less on compensation in 2018–2019 than in 2006–2007.

The unions spent, on average, between about $47 million to $55 million on their operating budgets over the seven two-year averages (see Table 7.5). These expenditures, on average, rose almost 18 percent, comparing 2018–2019 to 2006–2007. Only two unions spent more than $200 million on their operations in 2018–2019, but 17 devoted less than $20 million. Ten unions spent less on their operating budgets in 2018–2019 than in 2006–2007.

Administration, Compensation, and Operating Budgets as Percentage of Net Disbursements

Table 7.6 shows the percentage of net disbursements going to administration across the 53 unions. Such expenditures fell within a relatively narrow band of 25.5 percent through 27.2 percent over these seven two-year averaged intervals.

Table 7.2 Net Disbursements

Union	*Cycles*							*% Change from 2006–2007 to 2018–2019 (%)*
	2006–2007 ($)	*2008–2009 ($)*	*2010–2011 ($)*	*2012–2013 ($)*	*2014–2015 ($)*	*2016–2017 ($)*	*2018–2019 (%)*	
Air Line Pilots Association	222.12	195.50	147.81	173.55	196.39	249.24	301.00	35.5
Air traffic controllers	21.20	23.56	24.77	24.85	27.11	29.32	30.10	42.0
Aircraft Mechanics Association	7.97	4.08	1.95	2.25	2.01	2.79	2.96	−62.9
Allied Pilots Association	42.49	32.95	30.39	31.01	40.07	37.35	44.58	4.9
Auto workers	304.60	283.75	254.12	225.16	240.08	253.73	262.09	−14.0
Bakery, tobacco, and grain	27.81	32.99	19.13	18.01	23.35	19.27	12.11	−56.4
Boilermakers	35.76	45.46	58.53	58.24	44.64	81.75	82.03	129.4
Bricklayers	47.98	50.77	39.52	36.55	40.28	37.16	41.69	−13.1
Carpenters	190.29	89.10	197.39	112.80	141.93	103.79	152.82	−19.7
Communications workers	641.01	501.67	355.67	156.38	152.53	222.87	151.21	−76.4
Directors Guild of America Inc	45.32	47.54	52.58	56.05	56.36	60.53	65.05	43.6
Electrical Workers IBEW	843.87	241.10	247.80	281.62	298.21	336.84	247.00	−70.7
Elevator constructors	11.56	11.47	10.12	14.48	12.45	13.25	23.21	100.8
Engineers, operating	54.01	96.75	68.91	68.37	77.24	124.89	203.85	277.4
Engineers, professional, and technical	4.22	4.33	4.72	4.95	5.21	5.47	5.10	21.0
Firefighters	49.49	50.42	52.77	55.76	61.00	66.41	77.24	56.1
Food and Commercial Workers	223.61	270.06	264.16	251.17	298.57	262.11	276.81	23.8
Government Employees AFGE	48.72	60.02	82.88	78.52	91.40	91.85	84.78	74.0
Insulators	11.35	10.69	11.19	12.59	19.78	12.86	13.52	19.1

(*Continued*)

Table 7.2 (Continued)

Union	*Cycles*							*% Change from 2006–2007 to 2018–2019 (%)*
	2006–2007 ($)	*2008–2009 ($)*	*2010–2011 ($)*	*2012–2013 ($)*	*2014–2015 ($)*	*2016–2017 ($)*	*2018–2019 (%)*	
Iron workers	91.27	90.61	91.77	81.23	70.35	92.63	224.13	145.6
Journeymen and allied trades	3.77	4.16	4.72	4.42	4.43	5.44	6.89	82.7
Laborers	121.41	87.37	90.24	88.37	101.00	110.56	104.50	−13.9
Letter Carriers, National Association	153.22	118.83	176.11	169.83	198.20	188.70	120.86	−21.1
Letter carriers, rural	13.19	13.56	14.32	19.40	30.81	34.87	36.55	177.0
Longshore and Warehouse Union	6.75	7.01	6.89	6.78	6.25	7.11	8.23	21.9
Longshoremen's Association	25.46	23.33	21.28	21.21	28.29	25.35	32.11	26.1
Machinists	121.77	140.01	128.08	145.18	150.10	161.11	161.95	33.0
Mine workers, united	34.44	35.09	114.51	58.45	80.01	48.12	36.99	7.4
Musicians	11.53	12.00	12.06	11.30	11.52	12.16	12.84	11.4
National Education Association	349.50	365.89	391.18	352.36	356.87	386.37	388.31	11.1
Novelty and production workers	2.72	2.81	3.67	2.01	4.29	4.16	3.66	34.4
Office and professional employees	13.83	14.32	17.35	16.72	17.27	15.20	13.55	−2.0
Painters	77.07	45.76	47.92	40.55	49.68	46.34	49.42	−35.9
Plasterers and cement masons	28.50	32.58	15.86	12.54	14.08	18.21	20.15	−29.3
Plumbers	143.87	181.22	174.49	180.52	221.22	247.23	161.15	12.0
Postal workers, American	84.23	80.51	71.09	61.87	57.76	61.23	67.07	−20.4
Roofers	9.21	8.79	9.49	8.61	9.08	9.91	11.55	25.3
Seafarers	1.43	1.47	1.57	1.48	1.47	1.47	1.44	0.5
Security police, fire professionals	5.56	5.13	4.80	4.86	5.01	5.49	5.19	−6.7

Service employees	268.29	313.39	326.51	373.77	306.99	292.72	343.24	27.9
Sheet metal, air, rail, and transportation workers	99.50	67.19	75.73	56.34	110.25	83.98	103.84	4.4
Stage and picture operators	79.34	81.48	58.55	63.64	66.68	86.68	96.54	21.7
State, county, and municipal employees	158.69	203.21	198.50	201.13	200.08	200.71	194.45	22.5
Steelworkers	708.71	294.98	264.64	295.22	362.85	354.32	409.44	−42.2
Teachers	176.77	169.52	188.70	290.33	295.10	284.83	260.79	47.5
Teamsters	184.95	161.39	180.95	160.43	174.95	190.74	199.36	7.8
Transit Union	40.90	30.03	30.05	30.03	128.20	70.25	88.76	117.0
Transport workers	49.19	50.48	34.10	33.78	30.37	101.23	143.97	192.7
Treasury Employees Union	29.26	31.17	47.46	44.46	32.92	36.27	38.72	32.3
Unite Here	111.52	108.69	131.23	84.55	90.70	94.09	105.07	−5.8
University Professors	6.77	6.73	6.36	6.45	6.55	7.94	9.04	33.4
Utility workers	8.95	9.34	17.01	14.55	13.87	13.33	13.60	52.0
Writers Guild West	41.59	50.62	54.19	42.77	52.80	61.56	76.20	83.2
Average	**115.03**	**92.47**	**93.13**	**87.69**	**96.58**	**101.35**	**106.16**	**−7.7**

Table 7.3 Administrative Budget

Union	*Cycle*							*% Change from 2006–2007 to 2018–2019 (%)*
	2006–2007 ($)	*2008–2009 ($)*	*2010–2011 ($)*	*2012–2013 ($)*	*2014–2015 ($)*	*2016–2017 ($)*	*2018–2019 ($)*	
Air Line Pilots Association	55.26	52.62	48.73	55.82	62.34	66.88	80.45	45.6
Air traffic controllers	6.39	8.19	8.00	8.24	8.78	9.65	9.16	43.3
Aircraft Mechanics Association	3.11	1.78	0.58	0.61	0.63	0.70	0.74	−76.2
Allied Pilots Association	9.45	10.93	9.05	9.75	10.31	12.51	16.50	74.7
Auto workers	52.70	45.47	38.71	26.09	25.00	28.78	38.53	−26.9
Bakery, tobacco, and grain	3.44	2.71	3.40	2.40	3.13	2.31	3.19	−7.3
Boilermakers	12.99	13.70	18.13	17.26	13.74	18.06	16.81	29.4
Bricklayers	14.92	15.29	12.72	11.07	14.12	12.58	13.10	−12.2
Carpenters	30.71	28.22	31.39	31.40	45.63	41.05	42.30	37.7
Communications workers	54.57	47.91	43.48	65.31	53.81	60.91	58.64	7.4
Directors Guild of America Inc	8.87	8.84	10.55	10.08	10.87	11.20	11.11	25.3
Electrical Workers IBEW	24.58	18.89	19.41	28.73	20.14	32.60	27.23	10.8
Elevator constructors	2.15	2.03	1.93	2.81	2.96	3.21	3.13	45.6
Engineers, operating	12.91	13.87	10.13	12.39	12.83	15.01	28.41	120.0
Engineers, professional, and technical	1.91	1.72	2.23	2.05	1.76	2.21	2.05	7.8
Firefighters	23.91	24.06	27.37	29.11	32.87	37.58	44.94	87.9
Food and Commercial Workers	28.43	35.79	31.37	34.95	34.09	32.64	35.24	24.0
Government Employees AFGE	11.66	14.92	23.18	19.87	28.16	24.03	22.49	92.8
Insulators	7.82	6.46	7.11	7.66	6.88	7.20	7.17	−8.3
Iron workers	20.46	16.84	18.61	24.37	20.47	28.39	25.76	25.9
Journeymen and allied trades	0.21	0.22	0.25	0.25	0.25	0.28	0.31	50.8

Laborers	34.72	31.62	36.86	31.26	30.16	34.93	29.49	−15.1
Letter Carriers, National Association	11.43	11.23	13.56	15.02	16.43	16.22	17.57	53.8
Letter carriers, rural	7.47	6.22	6.72	6.38	7.45	7.93	6.78	−9.2
Longshore and Warehouse Union	2.69	3.04	2.42	2.63	2.43	2.86	4.01	49.3
Longshoremen's Association	12.45	11.29	11.65	9.45	9.23	9.55	12.85	3.2
Machinists	35.21	41.35	41.55	43.52	41.21	42.20	39.73	12.8
Mine workers, united	5.18	4.79	7.11	4.78	6.85	6.34	10.55	103.6
Musicians	6.00	6.71	5.61	5.22	5.73	5.91	6.27	4.5
National Education Association	122.89	120.30	113.93	97.88	104.79	121.66	105.59	−14.1
Novelty and production workers	0.51	0.50	0.51	0.35	0.38	0.48	0.32	−37.8
Office and professional employees	4.41	5.51	7.00	6.44	6.24	5.10	4.64	5.2
Painters	10.34	15.52	11.60	11.46	14.11	11.89	16.92	63.7
Plasterers and cement masons	3.85	4.65	3.97	3.50	4.43	4.12	6.40	66.3
Plumbers	24.46	14.95	20.75	28.40	24.31	36.60	23.92	−2.2
Postal workers, American	16.29	15.69	12.51	12.37	12.14	12.98	14.39	−11.7
Roofers	3.75	3.90	3.18	3.35	4.18	3.43	4.25	13.3
Seafarers	0.33	0.25	0.33	0.35	0.31	0.28	0.25	−23.9
Security police, fire professionals	1.49	1.33	1.42	1.16	1.27	1.73	1.45	−2.6
Service employees	51.82	69.73	84.17	98.62	57.00	55.63	50.83	−1.9
Sheet metal, air, rail, and transportation workers	10.41	12.72	13.32	17.44	29.09	23.21	27.48	164.1
Stage and picture operators	8.09	8.56	13.05	13.27	10.02	9.01	12.34	52.4
State, county, and municipal employees	39.00	37.73	42.35	42.11	41.04	39.58	39.19	0.5

(Continued)

Table 7.3 (Continued)

Union	*Cycle*							*% Change from 2006–2007 to 2018–2019 (%)*
	2006–2007 ($)	*2008–2009 ($)*	*2010–2011 ($)*	*2012–2013 ($)*	*2014–2015 ($)*	*2016–2017 ($)*	*2018–2019 ($)*	
Steelworkers	34.73	33.50	31.02	31.50	35.64	33.99	35.47	2.2
Teachers	39.70	38.06	41.72	42.81	44.61	48.84	35.73	−10.0
Teamsters	52.53	42.71	47.99	38.13	39.72	51.05	41.00	−21.9
Transit Union	5.98	8.08	8.31	6.82	9.58	10.51	9.27	55.0
Transport workers	10.85	9.85	11.18	8.60	8.24	6.17	53.57	393.7
Treasury Employees Union	7.96	8.55	8.94	9.23	9.42	9.61	12.26	54.0
Unite Here	14.43	18.34	36.80	21.90	22.96	21.97	24.50	69.8
University Professors	3.70	4.34	4.09	4.02	3.63	4.99	6.09	64.5
Utility workers	2.99	3.38	5.99	4.99	5.20	4.81	5.72	91.4
Writers Guild West	9.29	9.25	9.26	9.49	10.07	11.35	12.68	36.4
Average	**18.52**	**18.38**	**19.34**	**19.48**	**19.37**	**20.80**	**21.86**	**18.1**

Table 7.4 Compensation Budget

Union	*Cycle*							*% Change from 2006–2007 to 2018–2019 (%)*
	2006–2007 ($)	*2008–2009 ($)*	*2010–2011 ($)*	*2012–2013 ($)*	*2014–2015 ($)*	*2016–2017 ($)*	*2018–2019 ($)*	
Air Line Pilots Association	56.72	58.60	54.88	59.74	66.10	69.29	77.79	37.1
Air traffic controllers	6.15	8.86	9.68	8.80	9.88	8.08	7.50	21.9
Aircraft Mechanics Association	3.06	0.87	0.54	0.61	0.68	0.76	0.86	−71.8
Allied Pilots Association	8.90	13.27	10.23	11.24	13.33	17.22	23.44	163.5
Auto workers	125.21	111.08	119.04	95.21	128.36	78.68	79.02	−36.9
Bakery, tobacco, and grain	6.19	10.01	6.66	5.89	5.44	5.27	5.41	−12.7
Boilermakers	18.78	22.56	27.86	24.66	21.51	23.75	25.38	35.1
Bricklayers	19.77	21.24	19.09	17.57	17.74	18.60	21.44	8.5
Carpenters	17.16	18.27	20.98	20.79	24.47	21.52	24.62	43.5
Communications workers	76.86	60.43	69.20	53.69	63.15	60.55	62.00	−19.3
Directors Guild of America Inc	6.68	9.38	13.54	14.51	16.47	17.86	18.63	179.0
Electrical Workers IBEW	59.36	63.44	68.84	75.06	76.80	82.31	87.60	47.6
Elevator constructors	3.98	5.09	5.31	5.67	5.94	6.40	8.99	126.1
Engineers, operating	27.04	26.65	34.15	31.77	33.61	33.80	36.34	34.4
Engineers, professional, and technical	1.90	1.76	1.96	2.18	2.56	2.30	2.25	18.4
Firefighters	16.49	17.63	19.52	22.01	22.82	24.84	28.22	71.1
Food and Commercial Workers	130.52	145.42	153.90	140.00	166.81	123.34	121.79	−6.7
Government Employees AFGE	21.37	27.97	31.48	31.79	34.39	38.54	40.14	87.8
Insulators	4.05	4.88	5.36	5.50	5.31	4.91	5.00	23.6

(*Continued*)

Table 7.4 (Continued)

Union	*Cycle*							*% Change from 2006–2007 to 2018–2019 (%)*
	2006–2007 ($)	*2008–2009 ($)*	*2010–2011 ($)*	*2012–2013 ($)*	*2014–2015 ($)*	*2016–2017 ($)*	*2018–2019 ($)*	
Iron workers	27.66	27.36	24.18	24.76	25.53	28.61	28.67	3.7
Journeymen and allied trades	0.74	0.90	1.16	1.18	1.38	1.99	2.90	292.4
Laborers	33.87	36.72	41.15	43.03	43.53	44.03	46.48	37.3
Letter Carriers, National Association	13.06	13.53	14.78	16.55	16.54	18.13	20.97	60.6
Letter carriers, rural	3.44	4.54	4.85	9.09	20.48	23.32	26.43	668.8
Longshore and Warehouse Union	2.96	4.29	3.97	4.01	3.61	4.06	5.01	69.1
Longshoremen's Association	14.18	13.52	13.18	12.57	10.79	11.15	12.73	−10.2
Machinists	53.45	50.35	49.91	57.17	46.86	63.70	55.08	3.0
Mine workers, united	20.04	16.15	16.91	15.88	16.39	15.78	13.86	−30.8
Musicians	4.58	4.09	4.43	4.12	4.36	4.55	4.93	7.5
National Education Association	93.43	99.59	109.71	111.09	105.98	105.97	107.26	14.8
Novelty and production workers	0.38	0.33	0.35	0.38	0.36	0.41	0.34	−10.1
Office and professional employees	3.31	4.02	4.78	5.24	6.17	6.27	6.06	82.7
Painters	13.92	15.60	14.82	15.58	14.53	16.12	19.66	41.2
Plasterers and cement masons	8.71	9.14	9.13	7.20	6.70	7.31	8.79	0.9
Plumbers	30.49	29.32	32.94	33.90	36.17	37.18	40.01	31.2
Postal workers, American	21.74	24.75	21.88	24.18	24.10	21.36	20.50	−5.7
Roofers	3.97	3.98	4.19	4.41	4.33	4.46	4.58	15.3
Seafarers	0.14	0.17	0.21	0.23	0.20	0.22	0.22	54.1
Security police, fire professionals	2.65	2.24	2.21	2.61	2.63	2.73	2.85	7.6

Service employees	61.12	79.74	71.91	63.44	60.07	62.99	52.81	−13.6
Sheet metal, air, rail, and transportation workers	17.84	20.57	23.48	30.16	34.28	32.55	33.65	88.7
Stage and picture operators	9.77	9.16	8.08	8.93	12.01	13.34	14.50	48.4
State, county, and municipal employees	50.83	55.60	61.22	62.15	59.87	58.54	56.88	11.9
Steelworkers	131.38	143.28	123.05	144.28	143.40	150.09	144.79	10.2
Teachers	36.12	38.57	43.73	45.40	48.18	43.81	50.11	38.7
Teamsters	66.64	64.03	66.07	69.26	72.05	76.53	86.51	29.8
Transit Union	10.85	15.40	17.66	16.33	10.53	12.27	15.55	43.4
Transport workers	9.33	13.17	11.69	12.33	10.98	10.14	12.46	33.6
Treasury Employees Union	10.28	12.27	15.74	13.43	13.16	14.49	15.31	48.9
Unite Here	38.78	40.56	27.92	28.25	27.60	28.01	28.30	−27.0
University Professors	2.14	2.78	3.26	2.35	2.44	2.65	2.61	21.9
Utility workers	3.71	4.05	4.98	5.41	4.99	5.03	5.65	52.3
Writers Guild West	12.10	14.92	14.44	14.25	15.22	16.35	15.95	31.8
Average	**26.86**	**28.34**	**29.06**	**28.98**	**30.58**	**29.85**	**30.92**	**15.1**

Table 7.5 Operating Budget

Union	*Cycle*							*% Change from 2006–2007 to 2018–2019 (%)*
	2006–2007 ($)	*2008–2009 ($)*	*2010–2011 ($)*	*2012–2013 ($)*	*2014–2015 ($)*	*2016–2017 ($)*	*2018–2019 ($)*	
Air Line Pilots Association	122.66	113.08	105.34	124.63	150.40	130.24	153.48	25.1
Air traffic controllers	18.21	20.52	20.94	21.43	22.56	25.13	25.51	40.1
Aircraft Mechanics Association	5.73	3.24	1.38	1.81	1.36	1.80	2.05	−64.3
Allied Pilots Association	24.74	17.88	13.30	18.07	26.45	22.37	27.53	11.3
Auto workers	181.33	178.22	154.46	151.79	133.25	139.08	150.88	−16.8
Bakery, tobacco, and grain	8.33	7.36	7.81	6.81	7.28	7.12	7.59	−8.9
Boilermakers	21.64	25.05	30.20	28.53	24.59	30.37	29.62	36.9
Bricklayers	32.14	33.34	23.99	20.59	24.92	23.70	25.91	−19.4
Carpenters	50.35	50.14	55.95	50.69	64.59	60.88	62.03	23.2
Communications workers	111.21	112.46	109.25	116.88	106.86	116.09	109.53	−1.5
Directors Guild of America Inc	38.40	39.58	45.87	47.58	47.13	52.71	52.36	36.4
Electrical Workers IBEW	81.50	81.88	82.48	98.92	94.93	108.10	103.96	27.6
Elevator constructors	6.21	6.43	6.82	9.20	9.37	9.92	12.32	98.5
Engineers, operating	28.49	30.46	24.90	30.10	36.69	41.54	55.20	93.8
Engineers, professional, and technical	3.03	3.15	3.38	3.53	3.24	3.81	3.63	19.7
Firefighters	35.40	38.19	38.63	43.36	47.87	54.33	61.83	74.7
Food and Commercial Workers	85.61	109.84	101.17	104.46	98.49	94.66	96.56	12.8
Government Employees AFGE	31.40	39.40	53.26	49.05	61.57	65.53	58.34	85.8
Insulators	9.20	8.15	8.81	10.21	10.42	10.89	11.84	28.6
Iron workers	27.14	25.27	27.36	34.06	32.31	42.32	42.37	56.1
Journeymen and allied trades	2.39	3.82	4.28	3.98	3.90	4.65	5.71	139.1

Laborers	51.48	56.68	57.99	51.01	48.87	54.48	48.20	−6.4
Letter Carriers, National Association	25.12	26.77	29.50	36.99	35.19	36.12	39.93	59.0
Letter carriers, rural	11.64	11.41	12.32	16.16	26.47	29.34	30.65	163.2
Longshore and Warehouse Union	4.85	4.99	4.81	4.61	4.69	5.36	5.93	22.3
Longshoremen's Association	17.17	15.67	15.80	15.43	16.52	15.84	19.33	12.6
Machinists	84.57	89.92	88.31	97.66	98.93	96.25	95.46	12.9
Mine workers, united	16.45	15.92	18.38	19.53	20.43	18.49	22.16	34.7
Musicians	9.36	9.72	9.27	8.55	9.28	9.67	9.50	1.4
National Education Association	279.38	295.55	291.14	273.61	283.11	311.46	291.33	4.3
Novelty and production workers	0.59	0.59	0.60	0.44	0.47	0.60	0.45	−24.3
Office and professional employees	9.08	11.30	13.16	12.61	12.36	11.21	9.20	1.3
Painters	21.07	29.71	27.29	26.95	28.89	28.80	36.36	72.6
Plasterers and cement masons	9.62	10.86	9.59	7.72	8.36	7.81	11.13	15.7
Plumbers	44.11	34.17	42.00	57.55	58.33	71.54	59.77	35.5
Postal workers, American	40.04	37.74	37.76	38.75	34.15	34.37	35.32	−11.8
Roofers	5.52	5.81	5.25	5.42	6.13	5.38	6.27	13.7
Seafarers	0.43	0.37	0.44	0.43	0.40	0.42	0.35	−19.4
Security police, fire professionals	4.03	4.00	3.56	3.33	3.33	3.96	3.63	−9.9
Service employees	219.18	254.10	253.56	275.03	252.46	251.33	220.98	0.8
Sheet metal, air, rail, and transportation workers	25.34	29.97	31.27	36.08	49.46	43.78	48.27	90.5
Stage and picture operators	13.65	14.46	19.22	21.00	19.02	18.62	22.86	67.5
State, county, and municipal employees	112.80	145.48	148.56	141.21	132.63	120.46	114.37	1.4

(*Continued*)

Table 7.5 (Continued)

Union	*Cycle*							*% Change from 2006–2007 to 2018–2019 (%)*
	2006–2007 ($)	*2008–2009 ($)*	*2010–2011 ($)*	*2012–2013 ($)*	*2014–2015 ($)*	*2016–2017 ($)*	*2018–2019 ($)*	
Steelworkers	150.93	142.85	130.48	139.93	147.57	142.60	147.82	−2.1
Teachers	113.98	130.67	143.07	146.96	153.34	164.15	154.79	35.8
Teamsters	113.07	113.28	106.32	98.18	100.25	112.41	112.60	−0.4
Transit Union	12.56	15.29	15.90	15.59	25.13	21.74	20.69	64.7
Transport workers	16.64	19.06	20.80	20.59	15.63	14.35	63.92	284.2
Treasury Employees Union	20.60	23.14	27.20	24.67	24.73	26.39	29.32	42.4
Unite Here	64.96	71.37	78.97	52.56	54.04	57.92	69.33	6.7
University Professors	5.00	5.30	5.41	5.44	5.56	6.96	8.09	61.6
Utility workers	6.07	6.53	10.22	9.14	7.98	7.73	9.37	54.5
Writers Guild West	36.79	43.64	48.81	51.26	47.62	55.76	60.52	64.5
Average	**46.63**	**49.51**	**49.56**	**50.76**	**51.69**	**53.41**	**54.83**	**17.6**

Table 7.6 Administrative Budget as a Percentage of Net Disbursements

Union	*Cycle*							*% Change from 2006–2007 to 2018–2019 (%)*
	2006–2007 (%)	*2008–2009 (%)*	*2010–2011 (%)*	*2012–2013 (%)*	*2014–2015 (%)*	*2016–2017 (%)*	*2018–2019 (%)*	
Air Line Pilots Association	24.9	26.9	33.0	32.2	31.7	26.8	26.7	7.4
Air traffic controllers	30.1	34.8	32.3	33.1	32.4	32.9	30.4	0.9
Aircraft Mechanics Association	39.0	43.6	29.5	27.3	31.5	25.2	25.0	−35.9
Allied Pilots Association	22.2	33.2	29.8	31.5	25.7	33.5	37.0	66.5
Auto workers	17.3	16.0	15.2	11.6	10.4	11.3	14.7	−15.0
Bakery, tobacco, and grain	12.4	8.2	17.8	13.3	13.4	12.0	26.3	112.7
Boilermakers	36.3	30.1	31.0	29.6	30.8	22.1	20.5	−43.6
Bricklayers	31.1	30.1	32.2	30.3	35.0	33.8	31.4	1.0
Carpenters	16.1	31.7	15.9	27.8	32.2	39.5	27.7	71.5
Communications workers	8.5	9.6	12.2	41.8	35.3	27.3	38.8	355.5
Directors Guild of America Inc	19.6	18.6	20.1	18.0	19.3	18.5	17.1	−12.7
Electrical Workers IBEW	2.9	7.8	7.8	10.2	6.8	9.7	11.0	278.5
Elevator constructors	18.6	17.7	19.0	19.4	23.8	24.3	13.5	−27.5
Engineers, operating	23.9	14.3	14.7	18.1	16.6	12.0	13.9	−41.7
Engineers, professional, and technical	45.2	39.8	47.2	41.4	33.7	40.4	40.3	−10.9
Firefighters	48.3	47.7	51.9	52.2	53.9	56.6	58.2	20.4
Food and Commercial Workers	12.7	13.3	11.9	13.9	11.4	12.5	12.7	0.1
Government Employees AFGE	23.9	24.9	28.0	25.3	30.8	26.2	26.5	10.8
Insulators	68.9	60.4	63.5	60.9	34.8	56.0	53.0	−23.0

(*Continued*)

Table 7.6 (Continued)

Union	*Cycle*							*% Change from 2006–2007 to 2018–2019 (%)*
	2006–2007 (%)	*2008–2009 (%)*	*2010–2011 (%)*	*2012–2013 (%)*	*2014–2015 (%)*	*2016–2017 (%)*	*2018–2019 (%)*	
Iron workers	22.4	18.6	20.3	30.0	29.1	30.6	11.5	−48.7
Journeymen and allied trades	5.5	5.3	5.3	5.6	5.7	5.2	4.5	−17.5
Laborers	28.6	36.2	40.9	35.4	29.9	31.6	28.2	−1.3
Letter Carriers, National Association	7.5	9.5	7.7	8.8	8.3	8.6	14.5	94.9
Letter carriers, rural	56.6	45.9	46.9	32.9	24.2	22.7	18.6	−67.2
Longshore and Warehouse Union	39.8	43.4	35.2	38.8	38.9	40.2	48.7	22.4
Longshoremen's Association	48.9	48.4	54.7	44.5	32.6	37.7	40.0	−18.2
Machinists	28.9	29.5	32.4	30.0	27.5	26.2	24.5	−15.2
Mine workers, united	15.0	13.7	6.2	8.2	8.6	13.2	28.5	89.6
Musicians	52.1	55.9	46.5	46.2	49.8	48.7	48.9	−6.2
National Education Association	35.2	32.9	29.1	27.8	29.4	31.5	27.2	−22.7
Novelty and production workers	18.9	17.9	14.0	17.6	8.9	11.6	8.8	−53.7
Office and professional employees	31.9	38.5	40.3	38.5	36.1	33.5	34.2	7.3
Painters	13.4	33.9	24.2	28.3	28.4	25.6	34.2	155.2
Plasterers and cement masons	13.5	14.3	25.0	28.0	31.4	22.6	31.8	135.2
Plumbers	17.0	8.3	11.9	15.7	11.0	14.8	14.8	−12.7
Postal workers, American	19.3	19.5	17.6	20.0	21.0	21.2	21.4	10.9
Roofers	40.7	44.3	33.5	38.9	46.0	34.6	36.8	−9.6
Seafarers	23.1	17.1	20.8	23.7	21.2	19.3	17.5	−24.3
Security police, fire professionals	26.8	25.9	29.6	23.9	25.4	31.4	28.0	4.4

Service employees	19.3	22.2	25.8	26.4	18.6	19.0	14.8	−23.3
Sheet metal, air, rail, and transportation workers	10.5	18.9	17.6	31.0	26.4	27.6	26.5	153.0
Stage and picture operators	10.2	10.5	22.3	20.8	15.0	10.4	12.8	25.3
State, county, and municipal employees	24.6	18.6	21.3	20.9	20.5	19.7	20.2	−18.0
Steelworkers	4.9	11.4	11.7	10.7	9.8	9.6	8.7	76.8
Teachers	22.5	22.5	22.1	14.7	15.1	17.1	13.7	−39.0
Teamsters	28.4	26.5	26.5	23.8	22.7	26.8	20.6	−27.6
Transit Union	14.6	26.9	27.6	22.7	7.5	15.0	10.4	−28.6
Transport workers	22.1	19.5	32.8	25.4	27.1	6.1	37.2	68.7
Treasury Employees Union	27.2	27.4	18.8	20.8	28.6	26.5	31.7	16.4
Unite Here	12.9	16.9	28.0	25.9	25.3	23.3	23.3	80.3
University Professors	54.7	64.5	64.3	62.3	55.3	62.8	67.4	23.3
Utility workers	33.4	36.2	35.2	34.3	37.5	36.1	42.1	25.9
Writers Guild West	22.3	18.3	17.1	22.2	19.1	18.4	16.6	−25.5
Average	**25.6**	**26.6**	**26.9**	**27.2**	**25.5**	**25.5**	**26.3**	**2.9**

Table 7.7 Compensation Budget as a Percentage of Net Disbursements

Union	*Cycle*							*% Change from 2006–2007 to 2018–2019 (%)*
	2006–2007 (%)	*2008–2009 (%)*	*2010–2011 (%)*	*2012–2013 (%)*	*2014–2015 (%)*	*2016–2017 (%)*	*2018–2019 (%)*	
Air Line Pilots Association	25.5	30.0	37.1	34.4	33.7	27.8	25.8	1.2
Air traffic controllers	29.0	37.6	39.1	35.4	36.4	27.5	24.9	−14.2
Aircraft Mechanics Association	38.4	21.3	27.8	27.0	33.6	27.4	29.2	−24.0
Allied Pilots Association	20.9	40.3	33.7	36.3	33.3	46.1	52.6	151.2
Auto workers	41.1	39.1	46.8	42.3	53.5	31.0	30.2	−26.7
Bakery, tobacco, and grain	22.3	30.3	34.8	32.7	23.3	27.3	44.7	100.5
Boilermakers	52.5	49.6	47.6	42.3	48.2	29.0	30.9	−41.1
Bricklayers	41.2	41.8	48.3	48.1	44.0	50.1	51.4	24.8
Carpenters	9.0	20.5	10.6	18.4	17.2	20.7	16.1	78.7
Communications workers	12.0	12.0	19.5	34.3	41.4	27.2	41.0	241.9
Directors Guild of America Inc	14.7	19.7	25.8	25.9	29.2	29.5	28.6	94.3
Electrical Workers IBEW	7.0	26.3	27.8	26.7	25.8	24.4	35.5	404.2
Elevator constructors	34.4	44.4	52.5	39.2	47.7	48.3	38.7	12.6
Engineers, operating	50.1	27.5	49.6	46.5	43.5	27.1	17.8	−64.4
Engineers, professional, and technical	45.1	40.6	41.7	44.1	49.1	42.0	44.1	−2.2
Firefighters	33.3	35.0	37.0	39.5	37.4	37.4	36.5	9.6
Food and Commercial Workers	58.4	53.8	58.3	55.7	55.9	47.1	44.0	−24.6
Government Employees AFGE	43.9	46.6	38.0	40.5	37.6	42.0	47.3	7.9
Insulators	35.7	45.6	47.8	43.7	26.9	38.2	37.0	3.7
Iron workers	30.3	30.2	26.4	30.5	36.3	30.9	12.8	−57.8
Journeymen and allied trades	19.6	21.6	24.7	26.7	31.1	36.5	42.1	114.7

Laborers	27.9	42.0	45.6	48.7	43.1	39.8	44.5	59.5
Letter Carriers, National Association	8.5	11.4	8.4	9.7	8.3	9.6	17.4	103.6
Letter carriers, rural	26.1	33.5	33.8	46.8	66.5	66.9	72.3	177.6
Longshore and Warehouse Union	43.9	61.2	57.6	59.2	57.8	57.1	60.9	38.7
Longshoremen's Association	55.7	58.0	62.0	59.2	38.2	44.0	39.7	−28.8
Machinists	43.9	36.0	39.0	39.4	31.2	39.5	34.0	−22.5
Mine workers, united	58.2	46.0	14.8	27.2	20.5	32.8	37.5	−35.6
Musicians	39.7	34.0	36.7	36.4	37.9	37.4	38.4	−3.5
National Education Association	26.7	27.2	28.0	31.5	29.7	27.4	27.6	3.3
Novelty and production workers	13.8	11.8	9.5	18.9	8.3	9.8	9.3	−33.1
Office and professional employees	24.0	28.1	27.5	31.3	35.7	41.2	44.7	86.4
Painters	18.1	34.1	30.9	38.4	29.2	34.8	39.8	120.2
Plasterers and cement masons	30.6	28.1	57.5	57.4	47.6	40.2	43.6	42.8
Plumbers	21.2	16.2	18.9	18.8	16.4	15.0	24.8	17.2
Postal workers, American	25.8	30.7	30.8	39.1	41.7	34.9	30.6	18.4
Roofers	43.1	45.3	44.1	51.2	47.7	44.9	39.6	−8.0
Seafarers	10.0	11.4	13.4	15.8	13.7	14.9	15.3	53.4
Security police, fire professionals	47.6	43.6	45.9	53.6	52.4	49.7	54.9	15.3
Service employees	22.8	25.4	22.0	17.0	19.6	21.5	15.4	−32.5
Sheet metal, air, rail, and transportation workers	17.9	30.6	31.0	53.5	31.1	38.8	32.4	80.8
Stage and picture operators	12.3	11.2	13.8	14.0	18.0	15.4	15.0	21.9
State, county, and municipal employees	32.0	27.4	30.8	30.9	29.9	29.2	29.2	−8.7

(Continued)

Table 7.7 (Continued)

Union	*Cycle*							*% Change from 2006–2007 to 2018–2019 (%)*
	2006–2007 (%)	*2008–2009 (%)*	*2010–2011 (%)*	*2012–2013 (%)*	*2014–2015 (%)*	*2016–2017 (%)*	*2018–2019 (%)*	
Steelworkers	18.5	48.6	46.5	48.9	39.5	42.4	35.4	90.8
Teachers	20.4	22.8	23.2	15.6	16.3	15.4	19.2	−6.0
Teamsters	36.0	39.7	36.5	43.2	41.2	40.1	43.4	20.4
Transit Union	26.5	51.3	58.8	54.4	8.2	17.5	17.5	−33.9
Transport workers	19.0	26.1	34.3	36.5	36.2	10.0	8.7	−54.4
Treasury Employees Union	35.1	39.4	33.2	30.2	40.0	40.0	39.5	12.5
Unite Here	34.8	37.3	21.3	33.4	30.4	29.8	26.9	−22.5
University Professors	31.6	41.3	51.3	36.4	37.2	33.3	28.8	−8.6
Utility workers	41.5	43.4	29.3	37.2	35.9	37.7	41.6	0.2
Writers Guild West	29.1	29.5	26.7	33.3	28.8	26.6	20.9	−28.1
Average	**30.3**	**33.7**	**34.7**	**36.6**	**34.4**	**33.1**	**33.6**	**10.8**

Table 7.8 Operating Budget as a Percentage of Net Disbursements

Union	*Cycle*							*% Change from 200620–2007 to 2018–2019 (%)*
	2006–2007 (%)	*2008–2009 (%)*	*2010–2011 (%)*	*2012–2013 (%)*	*2014–2015 (%)*	*2016–2017 (%)*	*2018–2019 (%)*	
Air Line Pilots Association	55.2	57.8	71.3	71.8	76.6	52.3	51.0	−7.7
Air traffic controllers	85.9	87.1	84.5	86.2	83.2	85.7	84.8	−1.3
Aircraft Mechanics Association	72.0	79.3	70.7	80.6	67.8	64.5	69.3	−3.6
Allied Pilots Association	58.2	54.3	43.8	58.3	66.0	59.9	61.8	6.1
Auto workers	59.5	62.8	60.8	67.4	55.5	54.8	57.6	−3.3
Bakery, tobacco, and grain	29.9	22.3	40.8	37.8	31.2	36.9	62.7	109.3
Boilermakers	60.5	55.1	51.6	49.0	55.1	37.2	36.1	−40.3
Bricklayers	67.0	65.7	60.7	56.3	61.9	63.8	62.2	−7.2
Carpenters	26.5	56.3	28.3	44.9	45.5	58.7	40.6	53.4
Communications workers	17.3	22.4	30.7	74.7	70.1	52.1	72.4	317.5
Directors Guild of America Inc	84.7	83.3	87.2	84.9	83.6	87.1	80.5	−5.0
Electrical Workers IBEW	9.7	34.0	33.3	35.1	31.8	32.1	42.1	335.8
Elevator constructors	53.7	56.1	67.4	63.5	75.3	74.9	53.1	−1.2
Engineers, operating	52.7	31.5	36.1	44.0	47.5	33.3	27.1	−48.7
Engineers, professional, and technical	71.9	72.9	71.7	71.3	62.1	69.7	71.1	−1.1
Firefighters	71.5	75.7	73.2	77.8	78.5	81.8	80.0	11.9
Food and Commercial Workers	38.3	40.7	38.3	41.6	33.0	36.1	34.9	−8.9
Government Employees AFGE	64.5	65.6	64.3	62.5	67.4	71.3	68.8	6.8
Insulators	81.1	76.3	78.8	81.1	52.7	84.7	87.6	8.0

(*Continued*)

Table 7.8 (Continued)

Union	*Cycle*							*% Change from 200620–2007 to 2018–2019 (%)*
	2006–2007 (%)	*2008–2009 (%)*	*2010–2011 (%)*	*2012–2013 (%)*	*2014–2015 (%)*	*2016–2017 (%)*	*2018–2019 (%)*	
Iron workers	29.7	27.9	29.8	41.9	45.9	45.7	18.9	−36.4
Journeymen and allied trades	63.4	91.8	90.7	89.9	87.9	85.5	82.9	30.9
Laborers	42.4	64.9	64.3	57.7	48.4	49.3	46.1	8.8
Letter Carriers, National Association	16.4	22.5	16.8	21.8	17.8	19.1	33.0	101.6
Letter carriers, rural	88.3	84.2	86.0	83.3	85.9	84.1	83.9	−5.0
Longshore and Warehouse Union	71.9	71.1	69.7	68.0	75.0	75.4	72.1	0.3
Longshoremen's Association	67.4	67.1	74.3	72.7	58.4	62.5	60.2	−10.7
Machinists	69.5	64.2	68.9	67.3	65.9	59.7	58.9	−15.1
Mine workers, united	47.8	45.4	16.0	33.4	25.5	38.4	59.9	25.4
Musicians	81.2	81.0	76.9	75.7	80.6	79.6	74.0	−8.9
National Education Association	79.9	80.8	74.4	77.7	79.3	80.6	75.0	−6.1
Novelty and production workers	21.8	20.9	16.2	22.1	10.9	14.4	12.3	−43.6
Office and professional employees	65.7	78.9	75.8	75.4	71.5	73.7	67.8	3.3
Painters	27.3	64.9	56.9	66.5	58.2	62.2	73.6	169.2
Plasterers and cement masons	33.8	33.3	60.5	61.6	59.4	42.9	55.2	63.7
Plumbers	30.7	18.9	24.1	31.9	26.4	28.9	37.1	21.0
Postal workers, American	47.5	46.9	53.1	62.6	59.1	56.1	52.7	10.8
Roofers	59.9	66.1	55.3	62.9	67.5	54.3	54.3	−9.3
Seafarers	30.0	25.4	28.3	29.3	27.3	28.9	24.1	−19.8

Security police, fire professionals	72.4	78.1	74.2	68.5	66.5	72.1	69.9	−3.4
Service employees	81.7	81.1	77.7	73.6	82.2	85.9	64.4	−21.2
Sheet metal, air, rail, and transportation workers	25.5	44.6	41.3	64.0	44.9	52.1	46.5	82.6
Stage and picture operators	17.2	17.7	32.8	33.0	28.5	21.5	23.7	37.7
State, county, and municipal employees	71.1	71.6	74.8	70.2	66.3	60.0	58.8	−17.3
Steelworkers	21.3	48.4	49.3	47.4	40.7	40.2	36.1	69.5
Teachers	64.5	77.1	75.8	50.6	52.0	57.6	59.4	−7.9
Teamsters	61.1	70.2	58.8	61.2	57.3	58.9	56.5	−7.6
Transit Union	30.7	50.9	52.9	51.9	19.6	31.0	23.3	−24.1
Transport workers	33.8	37.8	61.0	60.9	51.5	14.2	44.4	31.3
Treasury Employees Union	70.4	74.3	57.3	55.5	75.1	72.8	75.7	7.6
Unite Here	58.3	65.7	60.2	62.2	59.6	61.6	66.0	13.3
University Professors	73.9	78.7	85.0	84.3	84.8	87.6	89.5	21.1
Utility workers	67.8	69.9	60.1	62.8	57.5	58.0	69.0	1.7
Writers Guild West	88.5	86.2	90.1	119.8	90.2	90.6	79.4	−10.2
Average	**54.2**	**58.6**	**58.2**	**61.4**	**58.0**	**57.4**	**57.5**	**6.1**

Comparing 2018–2019 to 2006–2007, the unions' average share of spending on administration rose by a modest three percent. Though only three unions devoted more than 50 percent of their net spending to administration in 2018–2019, 19 unions allocated less than 20 percent. Twenty-six unions spent relatively less money on administration in 2018–2019 than in 2006–2007.

The unions' relative spending on compensation is reported in Table 7.7. The data indicate that these personnel costs comprised, on average, between 30.3 percent and 33.6 percent of net spending. Overall, the unions spent 10 percent more at the end of the 14-year period than at the start. Only five unions devoted more than 50 percent of net disbursements to compensation in 2018–2019, but 11 spent less than 20 percent. Eighteen unions ended the period spending relatively less on compensation than at the beginning.

Over this period, operating budgets, on average, consumed anywhere from 53.5 percent to 61.4 percent (the peak being in 2012–2013 at the tail end of the recession). Thirty-eight unions allocated more than 50 percent of their net disbursements to operations in 2018–2019 compared to just two which devoted less than 20 percent. Twenty-six unions ended the 14-year span spending relatively less on their operating budgets than they did in 2006–2007.

8 Financial Performance

This chapter reports the financial ratios for the 53 unions over the seven two-year intervals. In each of the five reported ratios, the unions' average performance improved comparing the end to beginning periods. The unions' average OPCAP, which shows the capacity of the unions to fund their operating budgets with MBI, rose 12 percent over the seven intervals. Liquid ratios, on average, climbed 91 percent to over 222, meaning that the unions' current assets tended to vastly exceed their current liabilities. The unions' average net assets over operating budgets (SURVIVE) rose 22 percent comparing end to beginning periods to 2.85. Only seven unions had SURVIVE ratios less than 1.0 in 2018–2019. Stress is the ratio between operating budgets to current assets, meaning a higher ratio connotes more stress with less capacity to finance operations with current assets. Over the seven intervals, the average ratio fell 17 percent suggesting a generally improved financial position on this dimension. The EFFICIENCY ratio captures the ratio of MBI to administrative budget. Over the seven intervals, EFFICIENCY on average rose from 3.01 in 2006–2007 to 3.54 in 2018–2019. In 2018–2019, only one union had an EFFICIENCY ratio less than 1.0.

We examine the unions' disaggregated financial performance ratios. The five ratios include: operating capacity (OPCAP), liquidity (LIQUID), survivability (SURVIVE), stress, and efficiency (EFFICIENCY), each as previously measured. These ratios provide a measure of the relative financial health of the organization, reflecting their ability to (1) fund operations from recurring and relatively stable sources of revenue (i.e. member-based income [MBI]), (2) maintain operations if income were disrupted (due to a strike or an unexpected emergency such as a pandemic), and (3) operate relatively efficiently in terms of managing administrative costs.

Operating Capacity

This ratio measures the extent to which unions can fund their operating budgets with MBI. Compared to the recent trends in business income (BI), MBI appears more resilient to economic downturn, having risen more or less steadily since 2006–2007. Table 8.1 reports the unions' OPCAP ratios, which shows that 40

DOI: 10.4324/9781003335474-9

Table 8.1 Operating Capacity

Union	*Cycle*							*% Change from 2006–2007 to 2018–2019 (%)*
	2006–2007	*2008–2009*	*2010–2011*	*2012–2013*	*2014–2015*	*2016–2017*	*2018–2019*	
Air Line Pilots Association	0.86	0.89	1.02	0.98	0.92	1.42	1.38	60.0
Air traffic controllers	1.05	0.98	1.03	1.08	1.04	0.99	1.05	−0.9
Aircraft Mechanics Association	0.36	0.33	0.76	0.63	0.91	0.73	0.74	105.9
Allied Pilots Association	0.66	0.99	1.30	0.95	0.63	1.27	1.49	126.9
Auto workers	0.99	0.81	0.78	0.76	1.07	1.29	1.20	20.6
Bakery, tobacco, and grain	1.20	1.38	1.29	1.46	1.28	1.26	1.19	−1.3
Boilermakers	1.31	1.52	1.18	1.28	1.58	1.27	1.45	10.9
Bricklayers	1.22	1.13	1.23	1.44	1.31	1.59	1.57	28.7
Carpenters	1.02	1.07	0.94	1.25	0.99	1.09	1.17	15.4
Communications workers	1.25	1.27	1.24	1.09	1.18	1.02	1.14	−9.0
Directors Guild of America Inc	0.46	0.50	0.45	0.45	0.53	0.51	0.56	22.8
Electrical Workers IBEW	1.06	1.14	1.23	1.14	1.34	1.26	1.40	31.5
Elevator constructors	1.41	1.75	1.59	1.11	1.17	1.34	1.74	23.9
Engineers, operating	1.52	1.50	1.99	1.75	1.56	1.45	1.21	−20.9
Engineers, professional, and technical	1.31	1.37	1.40	1.32	1.44	1.31	1.38	5.1
Fire Fighters	0.86	0.93	0.99	0.95	0.92	0.85	0.82	−4.5
Food and commercial workers	2.18	1.87	2.09	2.01	2.28	2.32	2.34	7.1
Government Employees AFGE	1.33	1.26	1.16	1.36	1.14	1.18	1.38	3.1
Insulators	1.02	1.33	1.25	1.20	1.24	1.17	1.17	14.8
Iron workers	1.24	1.50	1.25	1.15	1.31	1.04	1.17	−4.9
Journeymen and allied trades	1.55	1.10	1.03	1.02	1.06	1.01	1.11	−28.4

Laborers	1.38	1.35	1.28	1.50	1.62	1.54	1.91	38.0
Letter Carriers, National Association	1.42	1.46	1.37	0.97	1.06	1.12	1.10	−22.5
Letter carriers, rural	0.88	0.93	0.88	1.02	1.06	1.05	1.15	29.7
Longshore and Warehouse Union	1.42	1.39	1.40	1.55	1.53	1.46	1.37	−3.8
Longshoremen's Association	0.77	1.38	1.18	1.54	1.47	1.56	1.18	53.7
Machinists	1.08	1.10	1.29	1.32	1.37	1.40	1.49	38.3
Mine workers, united	1.14	1.22	1.12	1.13	0.96	0.78	0.67	−41.6
Musicians	0.99	1.01	0.98	1.05	0.99	0.98	1.00	1.6
National Education Association	1.10	1.17	1.26	1.34	1.28	1.18	1.27	16.2
Novelty and production workers	1.20	1.02	0.98	1.68	1.91	1.50	2.07	72.5
Office and professional employees	1.27	1.07	1.00	1.11	1.22	1.44	1.80	42.1
Painters	1.15	0.89	0.95	0.94	0.94	1.07	0.90	−22.1
Plasterers and cement masons	1.62	1.39	1.18	1.57	1.68	2.17	1.68	3.7
Plumbers	1.53	2.19	1.77	1.40	1.48	1.22	1.71	11.8
Postal workers, American	1.33	1.39	1.30	1.31	1.49	1.63	1.63	22.4
Roofers	1.30	1.29	1.41	1.33	1.21	1.52	1.39	6.7
Seafarers	2.91	2.99	2.64	2.80	3.08	3.15	4.51	55.1
Security police, fire professionals	1.04	1.06	1.47	1.57	1.56	1.34	1.63	56.6
Service employees	1.09	1.02	1.15	1.09	1.15	1.11	1.27	16.6
Sheet metal, air, rail, and transportation workers	1.50	1.35	1.37	1.51	1.31	1.59	1.58	5.8
Stage and picture operators	1.22	1.28	1.03	1.01	1.32	1.52	1.42	16.8
State, county, and municipal employees	1.33	1.27	1.27	1.27	1.34	1.53	1.59	19.8

(*Continued*)

Table 8.1 (Continued)

Union	*Cycle*							*% Change from 2006–2007 to 2018–2019 (%)*
	2006–2007	*2008–2009*	*2010–2011*	*2012–2013*	*2014–2015*	*2016–2017*	*2018–2019*	
Steelworkers	1.49	1.59	1.90	2.02	1.93	1.93	2.02	35.4
Teachers	1.10	1.12	1.10	1.09	1.07	1.13	1.21	10.5
Teamsters	1.41	1.42	1.52	1.65	1.69	1.59	1.69	20.1
Transit Union	1.42	1.30	1.32	1.40	0.94	1.25	1.43	0.9
Transport workers	1.00	0.94	0.90	0.93	1.32	1.61	0.40	−60.2
Treasury Employees Union	1.00	1.20	1.20	1.32	1.34	1.13	1.02	2.0
Unite Here	0.95	0.82	0.60	0.98	0.99	0.98	0.90	−4.7
University Professors	0.98	1.11	1.05	1.06	1.25	1.06	0.91	−7.1
Utility workers	1.30	1.40	0.96	1.06	1.40	1.53	1.38	6.4
Writers Guild West	0.54	0.47	0.43	0.45	0.53	0.50	0.58	8.0
Average	**1.20**	**1.23**	**1.22**	**1.25**	**1.29**	**1.32**	**1.37**	**13.8**

unions had an OPCAP greater than 1.0 for the 2018–2019 years averaged. Only nine unions had ratios indicating that their operating budgets exceeded available MBI during this period. The unions' average OPCAP rose nearly 12 percent from 1.23 to 1.37 between 2006–2007 and 2018–2019. Fifteen unions ended the reported period with lower operating capacity (OPCAP) ratios than they had at the start.

Liquidity

Liquid is the ratio between a union's current assets and current liabilities. It measures the capacity to pay down relatively immediate liabilities with liquid (and unencumbered) assets. The data reveal that unions, overall, are extremely liquid, with the average being 222.58 in 2018–2019, which was 91 percent higher than in 2006–2007 (Table 8.2). Considerable fluctuation existed in the unions' average ratios during the period, with the lowest point being in 2012–2013 as the nation was emerging from the depths of the Great Recession. No union had a ratio below 1.0 in 2018–2019, and only 13 showed LIQUID at less than 10.0 in this interval.

Survivability

Survive measures the extent to which unions can fund operating budgets from net assets. This ratio indicates how unions might cope with a sudden disruption in income in the event, for example, of a major strike or pandemic resulting in the closure of businesses resulting in mass layoffs and union membership losses. One union had a ratio greater than 10 in 2018–2019, while seven showed a ratio above 5.0. Seven unions reported a SURVIVE of less than 1.0 (Table 8.3). On average, the ratios dipped to their lowest at 2.08 in the peak recession years (2008–2009 and 2010–2011), ending the period at 2.85 or 22 percent higher than the 2.33 at the start. Unions possessed 2.85 times the amount of net assets in 2018–2019 than they had in operating expenditures.

Stress

A union's stress ratio shows the extent to which its current assets exceed operating budgets. This measure provides a more immediate indicator of financial wherewithal. Current assets are by definition comparatively liquid and can be used readily to pay bills if income were interrupted (Table 8.4). Stress represents a union's operating budget divided by its current assets. As noted, a higher score indicates more financial stress, in that the operating expenditures are relatively more than current assets. In 2018–2019, three unions showed a stress ratio above 3.0, while another 22 had a ratio between 1.0 and 3.0. Twenty-three unions' ratios fell below 1.0, which suggests less financial stress. Eighteen unions ended the period with higher ratios than at the start. Comparing 2018–2019 to 2006–2007, the average ratio across unions fell 17 percent from 2.0 to 1.66.

Table 8.2 Liquidity Ratio

Union	*Cycle*							*% Change from 2006–2007 to 2018–2019*
	2006–2007	*2008–2009*	*2010–2011*	*2012–2013*	*2014–2015*	*2016–2017*	*2018–2019*	
Air Line Pilots Association	0.97	1.53	1.06	0.71	1.28	1.70	1.58	0.63
Air traffic controllers	10.32	10.79	8.97	16.51	6.95	5.13	2.79	−0.73
Aircraft Mechanics Association	2.34	2.68	2.86	3.70	5.85	4.56	5.42	1.31
Allied Pilots Association	38.99	13.20	23.03	6.07	11.42	7.50	10.89	−0.72
Auto workers	438.66	266.87	267.04	29.09	40.63	75.16	103.18	−0.76
Bakery, tobacco, and grain	65.80	45.73	96.00	89.14	122.17	68.72	138.97	1.11
Boilermakers	228.03	146.57			56.95	16.03	30.39	−0.87
Bricklayers	12.83	17.83	12.67	34.33	30.17	50.63	73.23	4.71
Carpenters	15.31	26.04	74.11	36.71	28.10	28.95	43.79	1.86
Communications workers	78.64	56.39	25.51	40.92	24.23	6.48	7.26	−0.91
Directors Guild of America Inc	19.56	35.62	23.02	22.82	27.46	31.66	16.97	−0.13
Electrical Workers IBEW	23.50	13.13	17.80	21.28	25.20	16.40	34.30	0.46
Elevator constructors	20.24	75.90	72.32	67.18	40.96	62.65	55.34	1.73
Engineers, operating	97.96	35.65	10.04	4.52	4.75	10.57	5.49	−0.94
Engineers, professional, and technical	32.73	15.28	41.14	80.08	29.33	152.76	5562.89	168.96
Firefighters	7.71	7.41	7.29	10.59	12.60	12.74	9.26	0.20
Food and commercial workers	20.61	21.83	23.50	18.43	16.05	20.85	25.93	0.26
Government Employees AFGE	6.14	4.38	7.88	8.41	6.91	4.57	8.70	0.42
Insulators	49.91	197.49	689.58	588.70	193.52	166.66		
Iron workers	80.90	74.78	157.07	35.18	31.45	22.72	22.10	−0.73
Journeymen and allied trades	7.13	5.05	3.52	4.41	7.94	9.59	14.48	1.03
Laborers	15.66	20.36	14.59	15.27	9.57	74.85	68.35	3.37

Letter Carriers, National Association	22.87	25.87	29.37	13.67	21.62	79.97	34.80	0.52
Letter carriers, rural	23.71	82.88	15.65	9.14	6.34	8.01	14.60	−0.38
Longshore and Warehouse Union	13.32	11.19	12.17	9.57	23.40	20.92	29.43	1.21
Longshoremen's Association					9.98	6.19	5.58	
Machinists	2424.35	1593.14	759.19	100.98	159.98	140.10	43.29	−0.98
Mine workers, united	385.43	356.87	325.57	174.01	366.64	1052.02	89.91	−0.77
Musicians	19.26	25.48	37.83	62.12	126.77	188.68	200.78	9.43
National Education Association	3.93	4.48	3.48	5.18	8.45	7.97	8.97	1.28
Novelty and production workers	10.99	4.85	5.31	12.14	15.49	12.42	28.18	1.56
Office and professional employees	16.63	16.54	30.46	21.66	34.01	43.72	57.08	2.43
Painters	25.60	8.75	10.23	24.87	19.04	13.35	11.32	−0.56
Plasterers and cement masons	437.14					86.00	46.35	−0.89
Plumbers	47.78	42.07	59.87	32.84	33.27	35.30	42.49	−0.11
Postal workers, American	54.16	19.48	57.15	39.75	41.87	26.88	84.10	0.55
Roofers	26.98	51.81	143.73	207.75	114.32	84.24	63.11	1.34
Seafarers	49.67	66.95	47.03	43.32	37.71	30.74	64.94	0.31
Security police, fire professional	949.40	7906.74	1920.70	7585.90	92488.10	4757.20	3841.26	3.05
Service employees	4.41	3.68	22.32	23.25	48.05	35.97	122.51	26.81
Sheet metal, air, rail, and transportation workers	6.72	3.90	2.07	6.54	25.66	19.61	31.65	3.71
Stage and picture operators	55.31	69.70	84.77	38.57	40.07	61.90	47.88	−0.13
State, county, and municipal employees	7.27	11.44	16.39	20.07	22.07	31.70	62.10	7.54

(Continued)

Table 8.2 (Continued)

Union	*Cycle*							*% Change from 2006–2007 to 2018–2019*
	2006–2007	*2008–2009*	*2010–2011*	*2012–2013*	*2014–2015*	*2016–2017*	*2018–2019*	
Steelworkers	7.86	7.14	16.70	22.73	29.67	23.59	23.75	2.02
Teachers	3.40	3.58	1.71	3.13	3.12	3.58	4.17	0.22
Teamsters	2.47	1.84	1.87	2.76	2.45	4.01	2.21	−0.10
Transit Union	18.78	26.70	6.66	6.77	9.31	30.21	9.14	−0.51
Transport workers								
Treasury Employees Union	5.65	3.49	18.84	17.21	11.13	12.62	6.91	0.22
Unite Here	2.05	1.79	2.71	8.57		37.15	18.39	7.97
University Professors	6.24	8.53	14.81	17.80	23.54	32.48	45.77	6.33
Utility workers	5.08	11.92	2.73	4.75	7.13	23.08	34.83	5.86
Writers Guild West	17.45	28.24	30.32	27.28	45.63	51.47	34.65	0.99
Average	**116.23**	**229.87**	**107.32**	**197.48**	**1890.17**	**150.23**	**222.58**	**0.91**

Table 8.3 Survivability Ratio

Union	*Cycle*							*% Change from 2006–2007 to 2018–2019*
	2006–2007	*2008–2009*	*2010–2011*	*2012–2013*	*2014–2015*	*2016–2017*	*2018–2019*	
Air Line Pilots Association	1.13	0.78	0.58	0.29	0.23	0.77	1.35	0.19
Air traffic controllers	0.92	0.74	0.62	0.59	0.57	0.41	0.34	−0.63
Aircraft Mechanics Association	0.10	0.04	0.73	0.59	1.07	0.98	1.02	8.79
Allied Pilots Association	1.24	1.59	2.36	2.02	1.58	1.86	1.77	0.42
Auto workers	6.83	6.50	6.83	6.52	7.16	6.50	6.62	−0.03
Bakery, tobacco, and grain	4.13	2.46	2.21	3.04	2.76	3.65	3.62	−0.13
Boilermakers	2.75	2.92	2.15	1.95	2.34	1.85	1.83	−0.34
Bricklayers	1.82	1.74	2.05	2.72	2.55	3.26	3.69	1.03
Carpenters	7.47	10.28	9.85	12.07	10.07	11.12	11.87	0.59
Communications workers	3.29	2.98	2.56	1.65	2.59	2.19	2.86	−0.13
Directors Guild of America Inc	1.15	1.25	1.12	1.11	1.18	1.10	1.24	0.07
Electrical Workers IBEW	4.73	2.95	2.71	1.88	3.12	3.59	4.05	−0.14
Elevator constructors	2.58	2.87	3.20	1.92	1.87	1.31	1.91	−0.26
Engineers, operating	9.59	7.63	10.39	9.93	9.00	8.08	6.12	−0.36
Engineers, professional, and technical	0.39	0.45	0.48	0.28	0.62	0.67	0.88	1.26
Firefighters	0.61	0.26	0.04	−0.06	−0.04	−0.57	0.39	−0.35
Food and commercial workers	1.77	1.42	1.72	1.84	2.00	2.84	3.77	1.13
Government Employees AFGE	−0.04	−0.69	−0.49	−0.53	−0.44	−0.58	−0.75	17.80
Insulators	1.51	1.69	1.60	1.34	1.62	1.80	1.91	0.27
Iron workers	3.59	3.73	3.53	2.77	3.36	2.53	2.76	−0.23
Journeymen and allied trades	0.44	0.33	0.20	0.20	0.31	0.34	0.51	0.18
Laborers	2.22	2.17	2.41	3.20	3.78	3.94	5.49	1.47

(*Continued*)

Table 8.3 (Continued)

Union	*Cycle*							*% Change from 2006–2007 to 2018–2019*
	2006–2007	*2008–2009*	*2010–2011*	*2012–2013*	*2014–2015*	*2016–2017*	*2018–2019*	
Letter Carriers, National Association	7.09	7.30	7.97	6.70	8.11	8.33	7.93	0.12
Letter carriers, rural	0.86	0.88	0.68	0.46	0.28	0.23	0.26	−0.70
Longshore and Warehouse Union	0.37	0.46	0.58	0.75	1.23	1.37	1.02	1.73
Longshoremen's Association	1.69	1.08	0.81	1.47	2.20	2.98	2.94	0.74
Machinists	2.57	1.58	1.65	1.52	1.72	1.97	2.42	−0.06
Mine workers, united	9.82	10.45	9.47	9.08	8.42	8.70	6.38	−0.35
Musicians	0.95	0.96	0.93	1.26	1.38	1.60	2.14	1.27
National education Association	0.43	0.48	0.56	0.79	1.04	1.02	1.22	1.86
Novelty and production workers	1.13	1.06	0.03	0.06	2.20	1.99	4.43	2.94
Office and professional employees	1.11	1.08	1.10	1.06	1.04	1.49	2.54	1.28
Painters	2.52	2.65	2.73	2.75	2.52	2.86	2.29	−0.09
Plasterers and cement masons	2.14	1.79	1.53	1.94	2.19	3.88	3.53	0.65
Plumbers	2.10	4.20	4.12	3.26	4.00	3.17	4.54	1.16
Postal workers, American	0.85	1.06	1.29	1.40	1.86	2.44	3.27	2.86
Roofers	4.88	4.93	5.71	5.78	5.09	6.34	5.97	0.22
Seafarers	0.87	0.46	0.05	−0.39	−0.19	−0.25	1.99	1.29
Security police, fire professional	0.72	0.39	0.94	1.54	2.01	1.90	2.83	2.94
Service employees	0.29	0.20	0.43	0.44	0.63	0.89	1.57	4.38
Sheet metal, air, rail, and transportation workers	1.95	0.86	0.88	0.58	1.78	2.27	2.85	0.46
Stage and picture operators	2.61	2.86	2.10	1.79	2.26	2.63	2.19	−0.16

State, county, and municipal employees	0.14	0.17	0.17	0.14	0.23	0.65	1.47	9.16
Steelworkers	−1.02	−2.23	−3.44	−1.27	0.25	2.17	3.91	−4.83
Teachers	0.52	0.45	0.30	0.33	0.20	0.08	0.26	−0.50
Teamsters	0.96	0.67	1.16	1.67	2.14	2.53	3.06	2.19
Transit Union	9.93	7.65	6.49	6.28	5.80	7.28	8.25	−0.17
Transport workers	3.02	2.16	1.39	1.19	1.55	7.84	1.02	−0.66
Treasury Employees Union	1.06	0.72	0.58	0.95	1.06	1.17	1.22	0.15
Unite Here	3.09	2.78	1.55	1.74	2.19	2.44	2.51	−0.19
University Professors	0.18	0.16	0.20	0.11	−0.04	0.15	0.59	2.36
Utility workers	0.58	0.82	0.61	0.64	1.07	1.58	1.76	2.01
Writers Guild West	0.86	0.66	0.64	0.70	0.99	1.01	1.20	0.40
Average	**2.31**	**2.13**	**2.08**	**2.08**	**2.31**	**2.65**	**2.85**	**0.23**

Table 8.4 Stress Ratio

Union	*Cycle*							*% Change from 2006–2007 to 2018–2019*
	2006–2007	*2008–2009*	*2010–2011*	*2012–2013*	*2014–2015*	*2016–2017*	*2018–2019*	
Air Line Pilots Association	6.84	3.80	5.14	7.56	5.38	3.12	3.55	−0.48
Air traffic controllers	2.27	2.68	3.22	3.17	3.93	8.00	7.94	2.50
Aircraft Mechanics Association	3.40	5.70	2.26	2.63	1.54	2.01	1.57	−0.54
Allied Pilots Association	1.56	1.68	1.16	1.96	2.08	2.24	1.60	0.03
Auto workers	0.23	0.27	0.46	1.85	1.57	0.85	0.70	2.07
Bakery, tobacco, and grain	0.80	0.49	0.60	0.46	0.45	0.37	0.38	−0.53
Boilermakers	1.37	1.79	8.22	6.03	3.88	3.44	3.36	1.46
Bricklayers	0.93	1.18	1.52	1.02	1.11	0.72	0.53	−0.43
Carpenters	1.73	1.15	0.57	0.98	1.39	0.79	0.67	−0.61
Communications workers	1.03	1.03	0.79	0.76	0.88	3.68	2.65	1.57
Directors Guild of America Inc	1.35	1.15	1.46	1.52	1.64	1.64	1.40	0.04
Electrical Workers IBEW	1.66	2.44	1.82	2.10	1.79	1.79	1.24	−0.25
Elevator constructors	1.54	0.69	0.39	0.64	0.79	0.64	0.56	−0.63
Engineers, operating	0.22	0.37	0.91	2.10	2.68	1.18	2.94	12.31
Engineers, professional, and technical	3.32	2.59	2.44	1.92	1.79	2.23	2.17	−0.35
Firefighters	2.91	2.46	2.44	2.82	3.43	3.38	3.89	0.33
Food and commercial workers	1.26	0.97	1.04	1.23	1.28	0.86	0.67	−0.47
Government Employees AFGE	3.41	5.19	4.71	3.51	6.51	4.72	3.29	−0.04
Insulators	0.73	0.59	0.56	0.70	0.90	1.40	1.08	0.48
Iron workers	1.02	0.77	0.92	1.34	1.13	1.46	1.18	0.15
Journeymen and allied trades	2.42	2.57	3.78	4.35	3.07	2.85	1.92	−0.21
Laborers	2.49	3.13	2.29	1.56	1.34	1.50	0.97	−0.61
Letter Carriers, National Association	0.28	0.24	0.34	0.78	0.52	0.53	0.88	2.10

Letter carriers, rural	1.18	1.28	1.40	2.24	3.16	3.27	2.41	1.05
Longshore and Warehouse Union	2.44	2.01	1.57	1.13	0.76	0.69	0.75	−0.69
Longshoremen's Association	0.64	1.07	1.63	0.67	0.55	0.39	0.51	−0.20
Machinists	2.80	2.78	2.73	2.52	2.48	3.03	3.59	0.28
Mine workers, united	0.22	0.74	2.08	1.65	3.23	1.90	4.40	18.67
Musicians	0.83	0.76	0.81	0.63	0.58	0.47	0.37	−0.56
National education Association	3.10	2.88	3.04	1.92	1.35	1.43	1.24	−0.60
Novelty and production workers	0.81	1.07	1.63	0.60	0.59	0.80	0.27	−0.67
Office and professional employees	1.17	1.05	1.01	1.04	1.03	0.69	0.40	−0.65
Painters	0.98	1.75	1.53	1.05	1.15	1.69	1.93	0.98
Plasterers and cement masons	2.16	1.59	3.16	1.85	1.65	0.60	0.84	−0.61
Plumbers	0.81	0.45	0.61	0.89	0.73	0.84	0.53	−0.35
Postal workers, American	3.26	2.87	3.49	3.69	2.84	2.73	1.88	−0.42
Roofers	2.73	1.59	0.67	0.59	0.76	0.72	0.98	−0.64
Seafarers	0.37	0.43	0.63	0.68	0.38	0.48	0.24	−0.36
Security police, fire professional	5.03	3.38	0.92	0.44	0.34	0.34	0.22	−0.96
Service employees	4.19	3.44	2.27	2.97	2.15	1.71	0.94	−0.78
Sheet metal, air, rail, and transportation workers	1.99	2.97	3.77	1.53	1.29	1.48	1.34	−0.33
Stage and picture operators	0.68	0.63	0.64	0.69	0.91	0.84	0.89	0.31
State, county, and municipal employees	2.04	1.89	1.61	1.38	1.11	0.69	0.44	−0.78
Steelworkers	2.34	2.69	1.38	0.85	0.67	0.71	0.60	−0.74
Teachers	2.91	2.90	3.35	3.99	4.06	2.80	2.42	−0.17
Teamsters	2.54	2.28	2.61	1.59	1.53	1.95	1.92	−0.25
Transit Union	1.20	0.65	3.45	3.33	2.73	0.93	2.57	1.15

(Continued)

Table 8.4 (Continued)

Union	*Cycle*							*% Change from 2006–2007 to 2018–2019*
	2006–2007	*2008–2009*	*2010–2011*	*2012–2013*	*2014–2015*	*2016–2017*	*2018–2019*	
Transport workers	1.29	3.04	5.37	6.52	2.38	1.25	1.54	0.19
Treasury Employees Union	6.72	8.44	3.84	3.60	4.50	4.65	4.72	−0.30
Unite Here	4.32	2.64	2.65	1.61	2.14	1.88	1.35	−0.69
University Professors	2.39	2.69	2.26	2.18	1.93	1.48	0.95	−0.60
Utility workers	2.98	1.81	4.81	4.53	3.01	1.29	1.26	−0.58
Writers Guild West	1.86	1.41	1.37	1.49	1.17	1.11	1.04	−0.44
Average	**2.05**	**2.00**	**2.14**	**2.05**	**1.89**	**1.74**	**1.66**	**−0.19**

Table 8.5 Efficiency Ratio

Union	*Cycle*							*% Change from 2006–2007 to 2018–2019*
	2006–2007	*2008–2009*	*2010–2011*	*2012–2013*	*2014–2015*	*2016–2017*	*2018–2019*	
Air Line Pilots Association	1.91	1.91	2.21	2.20	2.22	2.77	2.63	0.38
Air traffic controllers	3.00	2.45	2.69	2.80	2.67	2.58	2.91	−0.03
Aircraft Mechanics Association	0.66	0.60	1.83	1.85	1.96	1.87	2.04	2.09
Allied Pilots Association	1.72	1.61	1.91	1.77	1.61	2.27	2.49	0.45
Auto workers	3.42	3.18	3.12	4.41	5.70	6.22	4.69	0.37
Bakery, tobacco, and grain	2.91	3.75	2.96	4.15	2.97	3.89	2.83	−0.03
Boilermakers	2.19	2.79	1.96	2.11	2.83	2.13	2.56	0.17
Bricklayers	2.63	2.46	2.32	2.67	2.32	3.00	3.11	0.18
Carpenters	1.67	1.90	1.67	2.01	1.40	1.62	1.72	0.03
Communications workers	2.55	2.99	3.11	1.96	2.35	1.94	2.12	−0.17
Directors Guild of America Inc	1.98	2.23	1.95	2.14	2.28	2.41	2.65	0.34
Electrical Workers IBEW	3.52	4.93	5.21	3.94	6.31	4.19	5.33	0.51
Elevator constructors	4.07	5.54	5.63	3.64	3.70	4.15	6.87	0.69
Engineers, operating	3.36	3.30	4.89	4.24	4.45	4.01	2.34	−0.30
Engineers, professional, and technical	2.08	2.51	2.12	2.27	2.65	2.26	2.43	0.17
Firefighters	1.28	1.47	1.39	1.42	1.34	1.23	1.13	−0.11
Food and commercial workers	6.58	5.74	6.74	6.02	6.58	6.72	6.41	−0.03
Government Employees AFGE	3.59	3.31	2.67	3.37	2.50	3.21	3.57	−0.01
Insulators	1.20	1.68	1.55	1.60	1.88	1.77	1.93	0.61
Iron workers	1.64	2.25	1.84	1.61	2.06	1.55	1.93	0.18
Journeymen and allied trades	17.98	19.15	17.60	16.32	16.29	16.77	20.42	0.14
Laborers	2.05	2.42	2.01	2.45	2.63	2.40	3.12	0.52
Letter Carriers, National Association	3.12	3.48	2.99	2.38	2.26	2.49	2.50	−0.20

(*Continued*)

Table 8.5 (Continued)

Union	*Cycle*							*% Change from 2006–2007 to 2018–2019*
	2006–2007	*2008–2009*	*2010–2011*	*2012–2013*	*2014–2015*	*2016–2017*	*2018–2019*	
Letter carriers, rural	1.38	1.71	1.61	2.58	3.77	3.88	5.18	2.76
Longshore and Warehouse Union	2.57	2.28	2.78	2.71	2.95	2.75	2.03	−0.21
Longshoremen's Association	1.06	1.92	1.60	2.51	2.63	2.59	1.77	0.68
Machinists	2.59	2.39	2.73	2.97	3.28	3.19	3.59	0.38
Mine workers, united	3.62	4.07	2.90	4.64	2.86	2.27	1.40	−0.61
Musicians	1.54	1.46	1.62	1.72	1.61	1.59	1.52	−0.01
National Education Association	2.49	2.88	3.22	3.75	3.46	3.03	3.52	0.41
Novelty and production workers	1.38	1.19	1.14	2.11	2.33	1.85	2.90	1.10
Office and professional employees	2.60	2.20	1.89	2.17	2.41	3.17	3.56	0.37
Painters	2.35	1.70	2.23	2.21	1.92	2.59	1.93	−0.18
Plasterers and cement masons	4.05	3.25	2.86	3.46	3.17	4.12	2.92	−0.28
Plumbers	2.75	5.00	3.59	2.84	3.54	2.38	4.26	0.55
Postal workers, American	3.27	3.35	3.94	4.11	4.19	4.33	4.00	0.22
Roofers	1.92	1.92	2.33	2.15	1.77	2.39	2.05	0.07
Seafarers	3.78	4.43	3.59	3.45	3.95	4.72	6.21	0.64
Security police, fire professional	2.80	3.21	3.70	4.50	4.08	3.08	4.06	0.45
Service employees	4.61	3.72	3.46	3.03	5.10	5.02	5.52	0.20
Sheet metal, air, rail, and transportation workers	3.64	3.18	3.21	3.12	2.23	2.99	2.78	−0.24
Stage and picture operators	2.05	2.16	1.51	1.60	2.50	3.15	2.63	0.28
State, county, and municipal employees	3.85	4.89	4.46	4.26	4.32	4.67	4.65	0.21

Steelworkers	6.48	6.79	8.01	8.98	8.00	8.10	8.41	0.30
Teachers	3.15	3.85	3.76	3.73	3.68	3.78	5.26	0.67
Teamsters	3.03	3.76	3.36	4.24	4.25	3.49	4.64	0.53
Transit Union	2.98	2.45	2.52	3.20	2.46	2.58	3.19	0.07
Transport workers	1.53	1.82	1.67	2.22	2.50	3.75	0.47	−0.69
Treasury Employees Union	2.58	3.26	3.64	3.52	3.52	3.11	2.43	−0.06
Unite Here	4.26	3.21	1.29	2.34	2.32	2.57	2.55	−0.40
University Professors	1.32	1.35	1.38	1.43	1.91	1.48	1.21	−0.09
Utility workers	2.64	2.71	1.63	1.94	2.14	2.45	2.26	−0.14
Writers Guild West	2.12	2.20	2.27	2.42	2.51	2.48	2.77	0.30
Average	**3.01**	**3.21**	**3.10**	**3.23**	**3.33**	**3.38**	**3.54**	**0.18**

Efficiency

This ratio shows the extent to which the unions' MBI exceed their administrative costs. In 2018–2019, only one union had a ratio less than 1.0. Eight unions' ratios exceeded 5.0. On average, the range across the seven intervals extended from 3.01 to 3.54, which occurred during the beginning and end periods, respectively. Nineteen unions ended the period with a lower ratio than at the start.

9 Union Membership and Financial Wherewithal

To capture the unions' financial resources on a per-member basis, we report the per-member net assets, net receipts, member-based income (MBI), and business income (BI) over the seven two-year intervals. On this basis, the unions' net assets rose 48 percent from beginning to end periods to $833 per member. In 2018–2019, only four unions, however, possessed more than $3k in net assets per member. Six unions had between zero and $100, with one reporting a negative number or liabilities in excess of assets. In terms of average net receipts, the amount rose slightly over 15 percent for the 14 years to $718. Thirteen unions endred the period with a lower amount of net receipts than at the beginning. The amount the unions raised per-member from MBI varied widely, from $53 to $3427 in 2018–2019. The unions, on average, experienced a 53 percent rise in MBI to $454 in 2018–2019.

The unions' total financial wherewithal provides a baseline by which to compare their overall capacity to generate services. Because unions derive a considerable amount of their revenue and hence financial capacity from their members, their overall wealth should be positively correlated with membership. But absolute numbers do not reflect unions in terms of their relative capacity given differences in membership size. To provide such a comparison, we compute the unions' net assets, net receipts, and member-based income (MBI) on a per-member basis for the seven intervals between 2006 and 2019. We show the average amounts for each time period across the 53 nationals and percentage change comparing end to beginning intervals.

Table 9.1 shows the unions' net assets per member. It reveals that the average per members assets rose 48.4 percent from 2006–2007 to 2018–2019, climbing to $833 at the end. Four unions had per-member net assets above $3,000, while seven had between $1k and $2k, with 14 in the range of $500 to $1k in 2018–2019. Only one union (AFGE) reported a negative number for this interval, with six showing per-member net assets between zero and $100. Five unions had less per-member net assets in 2018–2019 than at the start.

The national unions' per-member net receipts appear in Table 9.2. The data show a 5.3 percent decrease from 2006–2007 to 2012–2013 to an average low of $592.2 before rising to almost $718 in 2018–2019 (or about 15 percent comparing

DOI: 10.4324/9781003335474-10

Table 9.1 Net Assets per Member

Union	*Cycle*							*% Change from 2006–2007 to 2018–2019 (%)*
	2006–2007 ($)	*2008–2009 ($)*	*2010–2011 ($)*	*2012–2013 ($)*	*2014–2015 ($)*	*2016–2017 ($)*	*2018–2019 ($)*	
Air Line Pilots Association	2,267.96	1,578.68	1,020.45	744.21	688.91	1,781.69	3,343.44	47.4
Air traffic controllers	1,144.94	995.79	803.52	776.64	777.77	600.43	472.80	−58.7
Aircraft Mechanics Association	58.19	32.55	358.77	339.00	452.05	519.50	587.93	910.4
Allied Pilots Association	2,787.66	2,990.09	3,354.03	3,766.68	3,400.67	2,862.41	3,402.84	22.1
Auto workers	2,469.95	2,948.73	2,785.15	2,556.85	2,348.39	2,136.08	2,515.97	1.9
Bakery, tobacco, and grain	368.73	205.30	206.29	269.02	280.94	386.68	423.70	14.9
Boilermakers	929.50	1,143.50	1,081.42	984.72	1,052.26	1,080.25	1,100.16	18.4
Bricklayers	614.86	619.21	588.90	727.33	870.17	1,051.09	1,300.22	111.5
Carpenters	718.10	1,046.36	1,260.21	1,480.06	1,512.98	1,554.47	1,685.23	134.7
Communications workers	571.35	643.66	574.60	410.02	442.21	393.98	485.80	−15.0
Directors Guild of America Inc	3,271.44	3,441.53	3,476.48	3,474.67	3,464.23	3,418.02	3,597.41	10.0
Electrical Workers IBEW	551.56	342.07	332.76	281.70	447.79	580.17	623.08	13.0
Elevator constructors	607.04	632.80	783.70	696.11	693.75	478.92	821.17	35.3
Engineers, operating	681.83	574.09	669.38	786.47	878.56	885.78	848.60	24.5
Engineers, professional, and technical	19.51	22.43	23.74	15.91	33.00	43.04	54.56	179.7
Firefighters	76.75	33.56	5.20	(9.15)	(6.17)	(101.60)	76.77	0.0
Food and commercial workers	115.89	118.60	135.18	150.61	155.27	214.22	294.11	153.8
Government Employees AFGE	(5.39)	(106.06)	(91.67)	(86.20)	(86.36)	(116.18)	(133.24)	2374.1
Insulators	667.45	621.21	671.22	622.93	759.10	877.25	1,011.46	51.5
Iron workers	745.78	682.44	773.26	774.55	859.92	836.47	906.05	21.5

Journeymen and allied trades	20.88	22.08	15.30	14.18	20.72	24.26	37.83	81.2
Laborers	178.20	188.95	234.38	288.98	337.63	370.70	461.79	159.1
Letter Carriers, National Association	617.82	676.63	835.10	926.27	1,041.21	1,035.88	1,094.84	77.2
Letter carriers, rural	91.75	89.07	77.59	72.63	71.30	61.13	68.22	−25.6
Longshore and Warehouse Union	47.14	55.23	61.65	92.95	166.21	207.13	167.52	255.4
Longshoremen's Association	667.38	389.30	588.86	523.10	928.75	1,302.40	1,767.85	164.9
Machinists	335.27	226.34	247.57	258.89	298.52	336.26	400.48	19.5
Mine workers, united	1,944.73	2,138.30	2,226.19	2,400.12	2,369.54	2,462.14	2,364.86	21.6
Musicians	98.74	104.91	97.02	135.72	166.18	208.07	279.60	183.2
National Education Association	40.23	44.42	50.93	70.91	99.69	106.71	119.03	195.9
Novelty and production workers	38.57	42.92	1.14	1.70	53.53	65.94	117.61	204.9
Office and professional employees	97.34	115.16	143.57	133.48	124.57	153.83	246.45	153.2
Painters	406.34	609.54	662.89	710.18	691.83	748.63	743.47	83.0
Plasterers and cement masons	484.10	451.68	369.50	392.11	478.68	725.14	887.00	83.2
Plumbers	281.42	415.84	512.29	567.88	705.64	669.64	770.39	173.7
Postal workers, American	121.28	155.50	196.28	223.19	261.30	340.09	502.68	314.5
Roofers	1,150.35	1,232.22	1,353.11	1,476.24	1,501.32	1,584.21	1,666.29	44.9
Seafarers	10.16	5.06	0.65	(5.48)	(2.62)	(3.66)	23.46	130.9
Security police, fire professionals	145.85	60.18	132.34	289.81	392.98	441.43	569.12	290.2
Service employees	39.16	27.42	56.59	65.37	83.50	116.55	178.68	356.3
Sheet metal, air, rail, and transportation workers	330.36	172.62	200.46	124.61	428.58	489.04	671.21	103.2
Stage and picture operators	333.30	370.92	358.76	326.52	356.03	376.11	352.20	5.7

(Continued)

Table 9.1 (Continued)

Union	*Cycle*							*% Change from 2006–2007 to 2018–2019 (%)*
	2006–2007 ($)	*2008–2009 ($)*	*2010–2011 ($)*	*2012–2013 ($)*	*2014–2015 ($)*	*2016–2017 ($)*	*2018–2019 ($)*	
State, county, and municipal employees	11.21	16.38	17.60	14.34	22.73	59.17	125.75	1021.9
Steelworkers	(212.19)	(479.34)	(740.15)	(292.35)	62.31	547.21	999.72	−571.1
Teachers	71.28	67.72	49.01	39.56	18.74	8.30	23.61	−66.9
Teamsters	76.74	54.97	93.43	130.33	166.05	222.54	253.65	230.5
Transit Union	683.55	618.40	540.80	511.96	754.59	797.08	849.99	24.3
Transport workers	431.64	339.20	244.89	211.54	207.63	886.42	476.70	10.4
Treasury Employees Union	280.04	204.37	185.00	285.21	333.90	388.24	447.70	59.9
Unite Here	436.85	653.42	528.56	355.60	448.06	511.61	570.78	30.7
University Professors	21.38	19.95	26.94	15.85	(6.48)	25.54	107.70	403.7
Utility workers	70.76	107.66	124.42	117.60	170.26	269.60	368.15	420.3
Writers Guild West	1,722.37	1,515.81	1,567.41	1,720.04	2,178.17	2,444.67	3,003.74	74.4
Average	**561.08**	**552.44**	**563.64**	**584.17**	**640.69**	**706.88**	**832.76**	**48.4**

Table 9.2 Net Receipts per Member

Union	*Cycle*							*% Change from 2006–2007 to 2018–2019 (%)*
	2006–2007 ($)	*2008–2009 ($)*	*2010–2011 ($)*	*2012–2013 ($)*	*2014–2015 ($)*	*2016–2017 ($)*	*2018–2019 ($)*	
Air Line Pilots Association	3,786.77	3,727.50	2,559.30	3,665.29	3,976.19	4,298.83	4,897.39	29.3
Air traffic controllers	1,451.49	1,556.02	1,531.28	1,592.77	1,568.87	1,746.02	1,656.61	14.1
Aircraft Mechanics Association	781.70	1,027.22	701.20	781.86	626.69	813.50	888.36	13.6
Allied Pilots Association	4,081.51	3,195.36	3,496.28	2,905.45	3,382.79	2,778.55	3,453.90	−15.4
Auto workers	604.21	725.24	671.51	581.08	593.27	597.79	704.16	16.5
Bakery, tobacco, and grain	297.50	370.34	227.08	244.84	319.98	290.18	184.96	−37.8
Boilermakers	556.34	733.49	884.80	1,057.06	825.11	1,550.98	1,714.20	208.1
Bricklayers	547.74	493.40	436.79	498.61	550.66	611.64	666.71	21.7
Carpenters	367.66	198.47	459.05	284.93	308.14	257.14	349.30	−5.0
Communications workers	991.57	987.85	697.94	361.85	238.85	331.62	235.68	−76.2
Directors Guild of America Inc	3,524.73	3,490.49	3,368.67	3,672.37	3,464.93	3,749.11	3,634.75	3.1
Electrical Workers IBEW	1,188.56	341.95	373.46	426.24	442.93	516.59	395.50	−66.7
Elevator constructors	453.54	553.03	439.35	440.12	519.76	544.48	798.85	76.1
Engineers, operating	205.44	166.52	172.28	183.35	204.27	329.77	511.79	149.1
Engineers, professional, and technical	70.62	70.69	71.00	78.64	83.96	87.46	89.84	27.2
Firefighters	171.35	173.07	176.80	192.54	202.89	219.74	242.97	41.8
Food and commercial workers	173.53	193.34	207.20	216.06	216.12	218.04	236.35	36.2
Government Employees AFGE	213.91	231.90	294.12	270.45	285.88	278.97	273.93	28.1
Insulators	506.84	527.73	566.07	597.10	652.13	635.97	684.91	35.1

(Continued)

Table 9.2 (Continued)

Union	*Cycle*							*% Change from 2006–2007 to 2018–2019 (%)*
	2006–2007 ($)	*2008–2009 ($)*	*2010–2011 ($)*	*2012–2013 ($)*	*2014–2015 ($)*	*2016–2017 ($)*	*2018–2019 ($)*	
Iron workers	677.99	678.18	735.52	664.58	573.05	712.77	1,731.55	155.4
Journeymen and allied trades	77.22	74.46	80.33	79.67	80.33	84.77	98.57	27.6
Laborers	188.18	134.68	151.84	159.07	191.95	184.33	189.05	0.5
Letter Carriers, National Association	526.51	423.76	613.72	630.03	717.71	658.29	404.31	−23.2
Letter carriers, rural	111.51	115.11	134.94	183.90	307.29	312.47	339.98	204.9
Longshore and Warehouse Union	186.91	170.96	159.94	194.71	208.60	222.84	230.31	23.2
Longshoremen's Association	511.09	635.58	912.40	601.00	754.86	797.64	804.96	57.5
Machinists	188.59	222.37	219.69	261.01	265.14	270.72	282.83	50.0
Mine workers, united	460.57	439.04	1,410.25	827.78	1,042.83	813.92	548.48	19.1
Musicians	147.20	136.01	131.72	147.69	162.81	182.21	191.06	29.8
National Education Association	117.26	114.08	125.07	127.53	130.76	129.70	130.70	11.5
Novelty and production workers	160.34	192.05	256.34	200.10	213.53	228.92	249.10	55.4
Office and professional employees	149.06	156.84	167.07	170.81	165.44	160.32	187.13	25.5
Painters	608.55	357.94	432.26	392.58	406.01	412.36	452.68	−25.6
Plasterers and cement masons	704.53	755.66	373.87	351.88	393.00	437.10	456.73	−35.2
Plumbers	446.94	538.49	525.01	543.20	683.24	745.73	488.82	9.4
Postal workers, American	307.49	314.04	279.96	259.65	244.25	249.92	294.10	−4.4
Roofers	382.78	423.77	415.38	422.31	445.37	476.05	459.97	20.2
Seafarers	42.07	41.53	45.27	50.51	53.35	52.57	57.58	36.9

Security police, fire professional	279.44	198.65	236.98	337.31	334.92	339.75	357.62	28.0
Service employees	168.34	177.63	173.71	193.49	169.68	161.25	192.21	14.2
Sheet metal, air, rail, and transportation workers	679.02	450.87	545.36	390.85	530.90	404.00	522.99	−23.0
Stage and picture operators	739.88	741.17	524.41	535.28	553.61	666.99	679.18	−8.2
State, county, and municipal employees	113.11	133.12	141.82	143.35	149.22	153.03	147.73	30.6
Steelworkers	957.21	439.47	479.70	540.95	594.39	628.43	677.14	−29.3
Teachers	213.99	194.70	210.08	238.72	185.27	185.99	156.70	−26.8
Teamsters	128.74	132.92	137.25	140.43	143.56	151.70	152.93	18.8
Transit Union	240.35	171.46	155.25	162.57	676.20	410.98	382.39	59.1
Transport workers	426.75	413.04	285.16	286.92	275.60	816.16	1,035.35	142.6
Treasury Employees Union	371.44	431.89	655.34	584.22	473.25	451.68	483.97	30.3
Unite Here	228.90	349.84	567.36	342.26	327.63	359.21	382.24	67.0
University Professors	166.83	168.80	161.84	175.21	197.11	222.57	261.10	56.5
Utility workers	186.03	215.00	307.44	291.28	290.36	329.75	312.73	68.1
Writers Guild West	2,288.11	3,107.33	2,605.56	2,705.16	2,599.76	2,852.37	3,082.30	34.7
Average	**625.62**	**604.04**	**597.96**	**592.20**	**622.72**	**662.70**	**717.82**	**14.7**

Table 9.3 Member Based Income (MBI) per Member

Union	*Cycle*							*% Change from 2006–2007 to 2018–2019 (%)*
	2006–2007 ($)	*2008–2009 ($)*	*2010–2011 ($)*	*2012–2013 ($)*	*2014–2015 ($)*	*2016–2017 ($)*	*2018–2019 ($)*	
Air Line Pilots Association	1,726.23	1,798.54	1,810.09	2,502.13	2,723.03	3,295.03	3,426.97	98.5
Air traffic controllers	1,314.47	1,325.31	1,332.91	1,425.22	1,423.00	1,443.73	1,441.69	9.7
Aircraft Mechanics Association	200.44	290.45	374.52	361.48	385.98	388.45	425.98	112.5
Allied Pilots Association	1,473.92	1,851.76	1,850.33	1,777.74	1,347.95	1,955.83	2,866.45	94.5
Auto workers	358.81	367.37	318.74	297.32	351.09	423.04	454.80	26.8
Bakery, tobacco, and grain	107.39	115.31	120.53	129.48	130.07	133.47	139.21	29.6
Boilermakers	442.78	596.87	591.57	646.79	711.60	739.25	874.79	97.6
Bricklayers	413.26	401.92	353.24	383.85	448.45	512.30	555.17	34.3
Carpenters	97.80	109.17	119.78	152.68	148.14	152.95	166.65	70.4
Communications workers	217.32	274.75	278.36	271.64	201.95	183.40	193.27	−11.1
Directors Guild of America Inc	1,297.24	1,367.48	1,396.38	1,412.80	1,546.65	1,581.88	1,635.90	26.1
Electrical Workers IBEW	123.93	131.90	150.94	171.47	192.38	204.44	214.99	73.5
Elevator constructors	330.87	386.26	389.22	402.61	434.95	493.28	748.62	126.3
Engineers, operating	108.29	112.92	128.09	138.19	152.00	158.95	167.09	54.3
Engineers, professional, and technical	65.66	67.61	69.73	75.09	77.02	83.76	85.40	30.1
Firefighters	108.87	120.33	129.21	140.37	147.53	151.56	160.94	47.8
Food and commercial workers	143.06	156.17	164.10	165.22	176.39	174.58	182.39	27.5
Government Employees AFGE	180.26	192.38	217.15	222.67	224.72	234.15	244.68	35.7
Insulators	450.12	488.34	523.94	558.81	583.85	570.52	616.99	37.1
Iron workers	256.45	274.49	273.94	321.74	334.43	344.08	385.01	50.1

Journeymen and allied trades	74.37	73.73	78.54	73.45	71.33	72.13	81.97	10.2
Laborers	110.93	117.55	124.55	135.93	144.97	145.09	160.67	44.8
Letter Carriers, National Association	123.72	135.34	143.82	133.74	135.42	138.75	151.99	22.9
Letter carriers, rural	93.82	94.25	99.88	159.39	271.09	277.20	303.49	223.5
Longshore and Warehouse Union	179.64	166.87	149.65	191.92	206.30	220.93	224.77	25.1
Longshoremen's Association	302.51	497.65	856.41	545.57	620.93	680.29	708.40	134.2
Machinists	140.91	157.17	192.91	225.34	237.29	238.64	247.15	75.4
Mine workers, united	225.77	250.49	264.18	299.98	269.98	220.15	246.97	9.4
Musicians	102.98	110.15	102.28	112.42	119.62	126.46	130.76	27.0
National Education Association	103.25	107.43	115.08	121.00	122.67	123.75	124.24	20.3
Novelty and production workers	41.08	41.66	40.48	45.36	46.49	49.77	54.89	33.6
Office and professional employees	110.45	114.84	131.65	139.24	145.25	148.80	174.47	58.0
Painters	185.71	203.75	229.78	242.28	256.80	280.19	291.28	56.9
Plasterers and cement masons	366.30	352.34	285.02	317.43	366.92	406.13	422.46	15.3
Plumbers	204.22	216.89	220.29	244.47	260.91	256.92	289.58	41.8
Postal workers, American	190.67	203.68	198.06	210.12	209.06	227.83	250.81	31.5
Roofers	306.99	321.97	335.35	340.17	355.70	380.10	388.02	26.4
Seafarers	33.92	32.81	36.34	39.51	42.03	45.71	53.12	56.6
Security police, fire professional	210.53	162.71	207.37	295.40	304.16	312.47	326.69	55.2
Service employees	146.13	141.58	151.93	159.57	153.68	146.15	144.63	−1.0
Sheet metal, air, rail, and transportation workers	252.94	272.24	311.02	322.62	316.23	341.70	372.89	47.4
Stage and picture operators	155.43	165.85	175.23	183.83	207.77	218.01	228.26	46.9

(Continued)

Table 9.3 (Continued)

Union	*Cycle*							*% Change from 2006–2007 to 2018–2019 (%)*
	2006–2007 ($)	*2008–2009 ($)*	*2010–2011 ($)*	*2012–2013 ($)*	*2014–2015 ($)*	*2016–2017 ($)*	*2018–2019 ($)*	
State, county, and municipal employees	103.29	124.35	130.87	129.73	134.18	139.72	136.57	32.2
Steelworkers	309.43	341.60	410.02	465.99	483.02	486.68	515.52	66.6
Teachers	151.25	167.96	178.27	132.36	102.19	117.89	111.71	−26.1
Teamsters	112.76	116.13	122.27	128.42	130.75	139.65	140.22	24.3
Transit Union	97.53	104.74	109.75	114.19	122.14	136.62	147.27	51.0
Transport workers	142.74	147.60	157.77	164.83	177.16	182.13	185.26	29.8
Treasury employees union	263.90	342.93	380.46	396.03	422.15	373.92	372.59	41.2
Unite Here	133.76	193.94	204.32	199.76	201.59	204.14	205.21	53.4
University Professors	119.32	142.38	142.89	153.13	179.81	180.21	166.25	39.3
Utility workers	157.53	183.41	195.74	193.65	223.23	259.71	289.41	83.7
Writers Guild West	1,080.23	1,066.60	1,051.13	1,096.81	1,164.12	1,223.51	1,454.11	34.6
Average	**297.19**	**326.45**	**342.00**	**363.60**	**376.34**	**409.92**	**454.50**	**52.9**

the end to beginning periods). The per-member net receipts varied widely across unions, from a high of nearly $4,900 in 2018–2019 to a low of $57.5. Four unions reported per-member net receipts over $3,000 at the two-year end point, with another four between $1,000 and $3,000. Eleven unions had per-member net receipts between $500 and $1k. Three unions had less than $100 in 2018–2019. Thirteen unions had less per-member net receipts in 2018–2019 than at the beginning.

The range in the unions' per-member MBI extends from $53 to $3,427 in 2018–2019 (see Table 9.3). On average, MBI rose more or less continually across the seven time periods from roughly $297 to $454, or about 53 percent. Only three unions ended the period with lower MBI per member than at the beginning. Only one union had more than $3,000 in per-member MBI in 2018–2019, with another four between $1,000 and $3,000. Four unions reported less than $100 per-member MBI.

10 Union Political Spending

This chapter examines the unions' political spending based on data from their LM-2 disclosures and from reports filed with the Federal Election Commission (FEC) under federal election laws. The non-profit Center for Responsive Politics collects and analyzes the FEC data which are made available in its Opensecrets website. Union political spending deserves special treatment because of constitutional issues and concerns about the potential for corrupting elections and lawmaking. The data reveal that the unions' average spending from their treasury funds across two-year intervals varied from $3.55 million to $6.27 million. In 2018–2019, five unions spent more than $30 million while 21 expended less than $1 million. As a percentage of net disbursements from treasury funds, the unions' average allocations to politics ranged from 2.99 percent in 2006–2007 to a high of 4.22 percent in 2008–2009. In 2018–2019, six unions allocated more than 10 percent of their net disbursements to politics while 26 spent less than two percent. As a percentage of member-based income (MBI) in the last two-year interval, ten unions spent more than 10 percent on politics while 34 devoted less than 5 percent. In electoral contributions to federal candidates, the 53 unions' total donations more than tripled from $60 million in the 2005–2006 election cycle to over $192 million in 2019–2020. The average electoral contributions rose from $1.1 million from the 2005–2006 cycle to $3.6 million or 2.5 times increase.

Unions engage in a variety of political activities which fall into the main categories of electioneering and lobbying. Federal law regulates the extent to which unions (and corporations) may use their treasury funds to participate in politics. In general, such law forbids unions from using their treasuries to give contributions to federal candidates (congressional and presidential); state laws, to varying degrees, may apply similar restrictions. However, the law allows unions to use their treasuries to finance lobbying and certain types of electoral activities that are non-partisan or uncoordinated with political candidates. Notwithstanding prior restrictions on the use of treasury funds for partisan political activities such as campaign advertising, the US Supreme Court ruled in a landmark 2010 *Citizens United* that labor unions and corporations could make unlimited use of their treasuries to finance campaign advertising as long as it was conducted independently of political candidates.

DOI: 10.4324/9781003335474-11

In this chapter, we review data on union political spending: (1) from their treasuries, (2) on contributions to electoral activities from both their treasuries and separately formed accounts from donations made by union members and their families, which are often referred to as political action committees, PACs, (3) on lobbying, which is generally funded from treasuries. Data on political spending from treasuries are obtained from the unions' LM-2 financial disclosures. Electioneering contributions and lobbying expenditures come from the website of the Center for Responsive Politics: opensecrets.com.

Treasury Expenditures

Table 10.1 reports the amount of money the nationals spent on politics. It shows the range in two-year averages extends from $3.55 million (2006–2007) to $6.27 million in 2016–2017. Comparing the end to beginning periods, the average spending rose 64 percent. The highest levels of such spending, on average, occurred in 2014–2015 and 2018–2019, both of which coincided with a mid-term election. Five unions spent more than $30 million in the 2018–2019 period (averaged), with another four spending between $10 and $11 million. Twenty-one unions spent less than $1 million, with another 15 spending between $1 and $5 million. Eleven 11 unions spent less money on politics in 2018–2019 than in 2006–2007.

The unions' political spending as a percentage of net disbursements appears in Table 10.2. It ranges from a low of 2.99 percent (2006–2007) to a high of 4.22 (2008–2009). The averaged percentage for 2018–2019 represented a 27 percent increase over 2006–2007. Only six unions spent more than 10 percent of net disbursements on politics in 2018–2019, with just one exceeding 20 percent. Twenty-six unions spent less than two percent on politics in the last two-year interval, while 14 unions spent less at the end of the 14-year span than at the beginning.

Table 10.3 shows how much the unions devoted to politics as share of member-based income (MBI). The average percentage ranged from 4.4 percent to 5.84 percent and rose 18 percent comparing 2018–2019 to 2006–2007. Ten unions allocated more than 10 percent to politics in 2018–2019, but only two of these exceeded 20 percent. Thirty-four of the unions devoted less than 5 percent of their MBI to politics. Twenty-three spent a relatively smaller share in 2018–2019 than in 2006–2007.

Union per-member political spending varied considerably across the two-year intervals (see Table 10.4). It ranged from a low of just under $12 in 2006–2007 to a high of just above $18 in 2018–2019. Such spending jumped sharply in 2008–2009, which included a presidential election. Overall, comparing the end-to-start periods, the average per-member spending rose 52 percent. Interestingly, both of these periods included mid-term election years. One union (NATCA) spent over $100 per member, with two others spending over $50 per member in 2018–2019 (ALPA and APA). Each of the top three ranked unions on this dimension represents workers in the airline-transportation sector. Parenthetically, among the top ten unions in per-member political spending in 2018–2019, five represented the public sector (NATCA, NTEU, IAFF, AFSCME, and AFGE), three of which are mainly of federal employees.

Table 10.1 Political Spending

Union	*Cycle*							*% Change from 2006–2007 to 2018–2019*
	2006–2007 ($)	*2008–2009 ($)*	*2010–2011 ($)*	*2012–2013 ($)*	*2014–2015 ($)*	*2016–2017 ($)*	*2018–2019 ($)*	
Air Line Pilots Association	4.18	3.33	4.12	4.02	4.43	6.25	5.32	27.2
Air traffic controllers	1.37	2.61	1.81	1.54	2.13	2.09	2.50	82.6
Aircraft Mechanics Association	0.08	0.05	0.06	0.05	0.04	0.03	0.04	−49.0
Allied Pilots Association	0.94	1.14	0.97	0.92	0.95	1.25	1.39	47.7
Auto workers	8.25	10.12	8.66	8.66	19.80	8.26	10.15	23.2
Bakery, tobacco, and grain	0.13	0.18	0.10	0.14	0.05	0.05	0.03	−75.4
Boilermakers	0.81	1.83	1.39	1.36	1.48	1.36	1.60	99.1
Bricklayers	0.81	1.16	0.74	0.45	0.37	0.93	0.66	−19.0
Carpenters	2.72	1.89	2.85	1.52	4.93	5.96	10.00	268.1
Communications workers	1.65	2.88	3.92	1.76	4.03	3.83	6.33	282.7
Directors Guild of America Inc	0.47	0.45	0.56	0.60	0.60	0.47	0.50	5.6
Electrical Workers IBEW	6.22	4.72	6.50	3.90	5.68	4.61	4.76	−23.4
Elevator constructors	0.01	0.01	0.02	0.01	0.03	0.26	0.24	2172.6
Engineers, operating	2.98	4.17	4.40	2.56	4.54	6.34	9.31	212.3
Engineers, professional, and technical	0.13	0.25	0.17	0.17	0.21	0.20	0.31	142.3
Firefighters	5.78	8.36	6.96	5.86	9.51	9.47	10.34	78.7
Food and commercial workers	3.85	7.43	5.53	6.50	9.03	6.34	5.26	36.6
Government Employees AFGE	4.64	5.51	4.31	4.42	5.18	6.55	8.87	91.2
Insulators	0.00	0.00	0.00	0.00	0.01	0.04	0.08	0.0
Iron workers	0.83	1.40	0.98	0.88	1.40	1.18	1.56	86.6
Journeymen and allied trades	0.00	0.00	0.00	0.00	0.00	0.00	0.02	1721.8
Laborers	4.62	8.68	5.84	4.74	5.40	5.11	5.91	27.8

Letter Carriers, National Association	1.37	2.66	1.45	1.82	5.04	2.21	2.10	53.3
Letter carriers, rural	1.16	1.12	1.31	1.06	1.21	1.21	1.02	−11.6
Longshore and Warehouse Union	0.09	0.04	0.14	0.18	0.19	0.20	0.13	44.7
Longshoremen's Association	0.53	0.68	0.65	0.67	0.92	0.96	0.84	58.8
Machinists	2.42	2.52	2.34	2.44	2.67	3.30	3.43	41.6
Mine workers, united	0.91	1.86	1.29	1.03	1.07	1.85	1.85	104.3
Musicians	0.15	0.18	0.13	0.16	0.14	0.16	0.23	53.7
National Education Association	29.59	39.92	30.98	36.08	42.33	36.20	48.17	62.8
Novelty and production workers	0.00	0.00	0.00	0.00	0.00	0.00	0.00	0.0
Office and professional employees	0.32	0.32	0.25	0.31	0.25	0.26	0.19	−40.9
Painters	0.59	0.83	1.47	1.52	2.75	1.93	2.35	298.6
Plasterers and cement masons	0.08	0.12	0.07	0.09	0.37	0.06	0.07	−17.2
Plumbers	0.83	1.27	1.26	1.24	5.08	5.75	6.44	672.6
Postal workers, American	1.31	1.79	1.37	1.54	2.54	1.21	1.36	3.5
Roofers	0.15	0.16	0.15	0.15	0.17	0.15	0.16	6.6
Seafarers	0.03	0.03	0.03	0.03	0.03	0.04	0.03	8.2
Security police, fire professional	0.01	0.01	0.00	0.01	0.00	0.00	0.00	−100.0
Service employees	29.75	62.54	44.02	40.53	82.73	37.82	47.43	59.4
Sheet metal, air, rail, and transportation workers	1.05	1.65	1.41	1.23	1.30	1.67	1.55	46.8
Stage and picture operators	0.24	0.26	0.28	0.38	0.55	0.74	0.95	295.6
State, county, and municipal employees	31.69	55.42	47.84	41.61	51.13	45.87	40.90	29.1
Steelworkers	5.83	9.43	5.74	7.01	9.44	12.37	10.69	83.4

(Continued)

Table 10.1 (Continued)

Union	*Cycle*							*% Change from 2006–2007 to 2018–2019*
	2006–2007 ($)	*2008–2009 ($)*	*2010–2011 ($)*	*2012–2013 ($)*	*2014–2015 ($)*	*2016–2017 ($)*	*2018–2019 ($)*	
Teachers	14.62	21.55	17.04	22.56	24.88	31.22	34.31	134.6
Teamsters	6.71	10.16	5.98	7.42	8.74	8.23	8.14	21.4
Transit Union	1.22	1.76	1.38	1.48	2.13	1.89	1.79	46.0
Transport workers	1.34	1.72	1.49	1.64	1.29	0.99	1.23	−7.9
Treasury Employees Union	1.73	2.05	1.78	1.75	1.98	2.07	3.36	93.9
Unite Here	3.54	2.77	3.89	1.45	2.90	2.79	4.17	18.0
University Professors	0.10	0.11	0.10	0.21	0.03	0.00	0.00	−97.3
Utility workers	0.17	0.19	0.25	0.39	0.40	0.15	0.15	−10.0
Writers Guild West	0.04	0.23	0.18	0.26	0.36	0.48	0.41	827.2
Average	**3.55**	**5.46**	**4.42**	**4.27**	**6.27**	**5.14**	**5.82**	**64.1**

Table 10.2 Political Spending as a Percentage of Net Disbursements

Union	*Cycle*							*% Change from 2006–2007 to 2018–2019 (%)*
	2006–2007 (%)	*2008–2009 (%)*	*2010–2011 (%)*	*2012–2013 (%)*	*2014–2015 (%)*	*2016–2017 (%)*	*2018–2019 (%)*	
Air Line Pilots Association	1.88	1.70	2.79	2.31	2.26	2.51	1.77	−6.1
Air traffic controllers	6.47	11.10	7.32	6.18	7.87	7.11	8.32	28.6
Aircraft Mechanics Association	0.97	1.25	3.12	2.28	1.87	1.25	1.34	37.6
Allied Pilots Association	2.22	3.45	3.19	2.97	2.37	3.35	3.12	40.8
Auto workers	2.71	3.57	3.41	3.85	8.25	3.25	3.87	43.1
Bakery, tobacco, and grain	0.46	0.55	0.51	0.75	0.21	0.26	0.26	−43.4
Boilermakers	2.25	4.03	2.37	2.33	3.31	1.67	1.95	−13.2
Bricklayers	1.69	2.29	1.88	1.23	0.91	2.49	1.58	−6.7
Carpenters	1.43	2.12	1.44	1.35	3.47	5.74	6.54	358.3
Communications workers	0.26	0.57	1.10	1.12	2.64	1.72	4.18	1522.3
Directors Guild of America Inc	1.04	0.94	1.06	1.06	1.07	0.77	0.76	−26.4
Electrical Workers IBEW	0.74	1.96	2.62	1.39	1.91	1.37	1.93	161.8
Elevator constructors	0.09	0.05	0.17	0.07	0.26	1.94	1.03	1031.6
Engineers, operating	5.52	4.31	6.39	3.75	5.87	5.08	4.57	−17.2
Engineers, professional, and technical	3.03	5.69	3.62	3.38	4.06	3.75	6.06	100.2
Firefighters	11.69	16.58	13.19	10.52	15.59	14.26	13.39	14.5
Food and commercial workers	1.72	2.75	2.09	2.59	3.02	2.42	1.90	10.4
Government Employees AFGE	9.52	9.18	5.20	5.63	5.67	7.13	10.46	9.9
Insulators	0.00	0.02	0.04	0.03	0.04	0.29	0.60	

(*Continued*)

Table 10.2 (Continued)

Union	*Cycle*							*% Change from 2006–2007 to 2018–2019 (%)*
	2006–2007 (%)	*2008–2009 (%)*	*2010–2011 (%)*	*2012–2013 (%)*	*2014–2015 (%)*	*2016–2017 (%)*	*2018–2019 (%)*	
Iron workers	0.91	1.54	1.06	1.09	1.99	1.28	0.69	−24.0
Journeymen and allied trades	0.03	0.03	0.03	0.03	0.02	0.00	0.33	897.0
Laborers	3.81	9.94	6.47	5.36	5.35	4.62	5.65	48.5
Letter Carriers, National Association	0.89	2.24	0.83	1.07	2.54	1.17	1.74	94.3
Letter carriers, rural	8.77	8.26	9.15	5.45	3.92	3.47	2.80	−68.1
Longshore and Warehouse Union	1.31	0.60	1.98	2.72	2.99	2.83	1.56	18.7
Longshoremen's Association	2.09	2.92	3.03	3.17	3.25	3.78	2.63	25.9
Machinists	1.99	1.80	1.82	1.68	1.78	2.05	2.12	6.4
Mine workers, united	2.63	5.31	1.13	1.75	1.34	3.85	5.01	90.2
Musicians	1.31	1.50	1.08	1.42	1.26	1.33	1.80	37.9
National Education Association	8.47	10.91	7.92	10.24	11.86	9.37	12.40	46.5
Novelty and production workers	0.00	0.00	0.00	0.00	0.00	0.00	0.00	
Office and professional employees	2.34	2.27	1.46	1.88	1.43	1.69	1.41	−39.7
Painters	0.76	1.81	3.08	3.75	5.53	4.17	4.75	521.7
Plasterers and cement masons	0.29	0.38	0.45	0.69	2.61	0.36	0.35	17.2
Plumbers	0.58	0.70	0.72	0.69	2.30	2.33	4.00	589.7
Postal workers, American	1.56	2.22	1.93	2.49	4.39	1.97	2.03	30.0
Roofers	1.67	1.81	1.56	1.74	1.88	1.46	1.42	−15.0
Seafarers	2.05	2.33	1.98	2.34	2.07	2.43	2.21	7.7

Security police, fire professional	0.19	0.20	0.10	0.12	0.00	0.01	0.00	−100.0
Service employees	11.09	19.95	13.48	10.84	26.95	12.92	13.82	24.6
Sheet metal, air, rail, and transportation workers	1.06	2.45	1.86	2.19	1.18	1.99	1.49	40.7
Stage and picture operators	0.30	0.32	0.48	0.60	0.83	0.85	0.98	225.2
State, county, and municipal employees	19.97	27.27	24.10	20.69	25.55	22.86	21.03	5.3
Steelworkers	0.82	3.20	2.17	2.37	2.60	3.49	2.61	217.5
Teachers	8.27	12.72	9.03	7.77	8.43	10.96	13.16	59.0
Teamsters	3.63	6.30	3.31	4.62	5.00	4.31	4.08	12.6
Transit Union	2.99	5.88	4.60	4.91	1.66	2.69	2.01	−32.7
Transport workers	2.72	3.40	4.36	4.87	4.25	0.98	0.86	−68.5
Treasury Employees Union	5.92	6.56	3.76	3.94	6.03	5.71	8.68	46.5
Unite Here	3.17	2.55	2.97	1.71	3.20	2.97	3.97	25.2
University Professors	1.52	1.64	1.64	3.30	0.44	0.00	0.03	−97.9
Utility workers	1.86	2.01	1.48	2.68	2.86	1.09	1.10	−40.8
Writers Guild West	0.11	0.46	0.34	0.62	0.69	0.78	0.53	406.1
Average	**3.00**	**4.22**	**3.41**	**3.24**	**4.09**	**3.51**	**3.79**	**26.5**

Table 10.3 Political Spending as a Percentage of Member-based Income (MBI)

Union	*Cycle*							*% Change from 2006–2007 to 2018–2019 (%)*
	2006–2007 (%)	*2008–2009 (%)*	*2010–2011 (%)*	*2012–2013 (%)*	*2014–2015 (%)*	*2016–2017 (%)*	*2018–2019 (%)*	
Air Line Pilots Association	3.96	3.32	3.82	3.28	3.20	3.38	2.51	−36.5
Air traffic controllers	7.14	13.01	8.43	6.66	9.10	8.37	9.39	31.5
Aircraft Mechanics Association	3.77	4.76	5.78	4.50	3.03	2.65	2.62	−30.7
Allied Pilots Association	5.79	6.46	5.60	5.34	5.72	4.41	3.39	−41.5
Auto workers	4.58	7.01	7.18	7.53	13.89	4.61	5.62	22.7
Bakery, tobacco, and grain	1.28	1.79	0.96	1.36	0.54	0.55	0.35	−72.6
Boilermakers	2.84	4.80	3.91	3.72	3.79	3.54	3.72	31.2
Bricklayers	2.07	3.09	2.51	1.52	1.13	2.45	1.61	−21.9
Carpenters	5.31	3.52	5.44	2.41	7.74	8.95	13.74	158.9
Communications workers	1.19	2.01	2.89	1.37	3.19	3.24	5.08	327.2
Directors Guild of America Inc	2.67	2.26	2.70	2.77	2.43	1.74	1.68	−36.9
Electrical Workers IBEW	7.18	5.07	6.42	3.45	4.47	3.37	3.28	−54.3
Elevator constructors	0.12	0.05	0.16	0.11	0.30	1.93	1.12	824.1
Engineers, operating	6.87	9.11	8.89	4.88	7.94	10.53	14.00	103.6
Engineers, professional, and technical	3.22	5.71	3.61	3.60	4.54	4.11	6.19	92.6
Firefighters	18.93	23.56	18.24	14.19	21.64	20.40	20.28	7.1
Food and commercial workers	2.06	3.62	2.61	3.09	4.02	2.89	2.33	13.1
Government Employees AFGE	11.07	11.15	6.98	6.60	7.37	8.50	11.05	−0.2
Insulators	0.00	0.02	0.04	0.03	0.06	0.29	0.59	
Iron workers	2.49	3.69	2.85	2.26	3.31	2.68	3.13	25.7

Journeymen and allied trades	0.03	0.03	0.03	0.03	0.02	0.00	0.36	964.1
Laborers	6.49	11.35	7.87	6.18	6.80	6.09	6.42	−1.1
Letter Carriers, National Association	3.84	6.80	3.59	5.10	13.57	5.49	4.78	24.3
Letter carriers, rural	11.23	10.52	12.13	6.41	4.30	3.94	2.91	−74.1
Longshore and warehouse union	1.28	0.60	2.03	2.58	2.61	2.56	1.58	23.1
Longshoremen's Association	4.04	3.14	3.47	2.83	3.78	3.88	3.71	−8.2
Machinists	2.66	2.55	2.06	1.89	1.98	2.45	2.41	−9.3
Mine workers, united	4.83	9.56	6.27	4.63	5.46	12.88	12.54	159.5
Musicians	1.63	1.84	1.44	1.79	1.57	1.71	2.43	49.1
National Education Association	9.66	11.52	8.45	9.82	11.66	9.82	12.97	34.3
Novelty and production workers	0.00	0.00	0.00	0.00	0.00	0.00	0.00	
Office and professional employees	2.81	2.67	1.92	2.25	1.64	1.59	1.16	−58.9
Painters	2.43	3.14	5.71	6.01	10.17	6.27	7.20	196.4
Plasterers and cement masons	0.54	0.81	0.63	0.72	2.62	0.38	0.37	−31.0
Plumbers	1.24	1.70	1.70	1.54	5.89	6.60	6.32	410.1
Postal workers, American	2.46	3.40	2.79	3.03	5.00	2.15	2.36	−4.2
Roofers	2.14	2.13	2.00	2.07	2.31	1.77	1.89	−12.1
Seafarers	2.35	3.07	2.66	2.86	2.47	2.66	2.03	−13.4
Security police, fire professional	0.25	0.24	0.09	0.11	0.00	0.01	0.00	−100.0
Service employees	12.46	24.10	15.10	13.57	28.47	13.55	16.90	35.6
Sheet metal, air, rail, and transportation workers	2.78	4.07	3.29	2.27	2.00	2.40	2.03	−27.1
Stage and picture operators	1.44	1.41	1.42	1.79	2.21	2.61	2.92	102.2

(Continued)

Table 10.3 (Continued)

Union	*Cycle*							*% Change from 2006–2007 to 2018–2019 (%)*
	2006–2007 (%)	*2008–2009 (%)*	*2010–2011 (%)*	*2012–2013 (%)*	*2014–2015 (%)*	*2016–2017 (%)*	*2018–2019 (%)*	
State, county, and municipal employees	21.13	30.03	25.31	23.20	28.84	24.81	22.46	6.3
Steelworkers	2.59	4.15	2.31	2.48	3.31	4.49	3.58	38.3
Teachers	11.69	14.70	10.86	14.11	15.17	16.89	18.27	56.3
Teamsters	4.22	6.32	3.71	4.59	5.17	4.61	4.28	1.5
Transit Union	6.88	8.90	6.59	6.75	9.01	6.96	6.05	−12.2
Transport workers	8.06	9.56	7.97	8.63	6.25	4.28	4.85	−39.8
Treasury Employees Union	8.45	7.36	5.48	5.38	5.98	6.94	11.29	33.6
Unite Here	5.75	4.71	8.22	2.82	5.46	4.94	6.67	16.0
University Professors	2.10	1.88	1.85	3.69	0.41	0.00	0.04	−98.2
Utility workers	2.11	2.05	2.57	4.02	3.56	1.24	1.16	−45.3
Writers Guild West	0.22	1.15	0.87	1.15	1.43	1.70	1.16	421.8
Average	**4.57**	**5.84**	**4.89**	**4.39**	**5.78**	**4.99**	**5.37**	**17.5**

Table 10.4 Political Spending per Member

Union	*Cycle*							*% Change from 2006–2007 to 2018–2019 (%)*
	2006–2007 ($)	*2008–2009 ($)*	*2010–2011 ($)*	*2012–2013 ($)*	*2014–2015 ($)*	*2016–2017 ($)*	*2018–2019 ($)*	
Air Line Pilots Association	68.29	59.74	69.19	81.98	87.19	111.22	86.15	26.1
Air traffic controllers	93.84	172.41	112.35	94.86	129.55	120.90	135.32	44.2
Aircraft Mechanics Association	7.56	13.84	21.66	16.28	11.70	10.31	11.15	47.4
Allied Pilots Association	85.41	119.60	103.71	94.92	77.16	86.26	97.17	13.8
Auto workers	16.44	25.74	22.88	22.39	48.77	19.50	25.56	55.5
Bakery, tobacco, and grain	1.37	2.06	1.16	1.76	0.70	0.73	0.49	−64.5
Boilermakers	12.56	28.64	23.10	24.06	26.98	26.17	32.54	159.1
Bricklayers	8.54	12.42	8.86	5.82	5.05	12.57	8.97	4.9
Carpenters	5.19	3.84	6.52	3.68	11.47	13.69	22.89	341.1
Communications workers	2.58	5.52	8.05	3.73	6.44	5.93	9.82	279.9
Directors Guild of America Inc	34.64	30.95	37.68	39.11	37.64	27.47	27.56	−20.4
Electrical Workers IBEW	8.90	6.68	9.70	5.91	8.61	6.89	7.05	−20.7
Elevator constructors	0.40	0.20	0.61	0.42	1.29	9.50	8.36	1990.9
Engineers, operating	7.44	10.28	11.38	6.74	12.07	16.74	23.39	214.2
Engineers, professional, and technical	2.11	3.86	2.52	2.70	3.50	3.45	5.29	150.5
Firefighters	20.61	28.35	23.57	19.92	31.93	30.92	32.63	58.3
Food and commercial workers	2.95	5.65	4.29	5.10	7.10	5.05	4.25	44.2
Government Employees AFGE	19.95	21.45	15.15	14.70	16.57	19.90	27.03	35.4
Insulators	0.00	0.11	0.20	0.15	0.34	1.66	3.62	

(*Continued*)

Table 10.4 (Continued)

Union	*Cycle*							*% Change from 2006–2007 to 2018–2019 (%)*
	2006–2007 ($)	*2008–2009 ($)*	*2010–2011 ($)*	*2012–2013 ($)*	*2014–2015 ($)*	*2016–2017 ($)*	*2018–2019 ($)*	
Iron workers	6.38	10.12	7.82	7.26	11.07	9.23	12.05	88.8
Journeymen and allied trades	0.02	0.02	0.02	0.02	0.02	0.00	0.29	1072.7
Laborers	7.19	13.34	9.80	8.40	9.86	8.83	10.31	43.3
Letter Carriers, National Association	4.76	9.20	5.16	6.82	18.38	7.62	7.26	52.7
Letter carriers, rural	10.54	9.92	12.12	10.21	11.66	10.92	8.84	−16.2
Longshore and Warehouse Union	2.30	1.01	3.03	4.96	5.39	5.66	3.55	54.0
Longshoremen's Association	12.22	15.65	29.69	15.44	23.50	26.39	26.27	114.9
Machinists	3.74	4.01	3.97	4.26	4.69	5.85	5.95	59.0
Mine workers, united	10.91	23.94	16.57	13.88	14.75	28.36	30.98	183.9
Musicians	1.68	2.02	1.47	2.01	1.88	2.16	3.18	89.3
National Education Association	9.97	12.38	9.72	11.88	14.31	12.16	16.11	61.6
Novelty and production workers	0.00	0.00	0.00	0.00	0.00	0.00	0.00	
Office and professional employees	3.11	3.07	2.53	3.13	2.38	2.36	2.02	−35.1
Painters	4.51	6.41	13.13	14.55	26.11	17.58	20.98	364.9
Plasterers and cement masons	1.98	2.85	1.78	2.27	9.62	1.55	1.57	−20.4
Plumbers	2.53	3.68	3.73	3.76	15.38	16.97	18.29	623.3
Postal workers, American	4.69	6.94	5.53	6.36	10.44	4.90	5.92	26.1
Roofers	6.58	6.86	6.71	7.06	8.22	6.73	7.32	11.1
Seafarers	0.80	1.01	0.97	1.13	1.04	1.22	1.08	35.6

Security police, fire professional	0.53	0.39	0.19	0.32	0.00	0.02	0.00	−100.0
Service employees	18.21	34.13	22.94	21.65	43.75	19.80	24.44	34.2
Sheet metal, air, rail, and transportation workers	7.04	11.08	10.24	7.32	6.34	8.21	7.56	7.4
Stage and picture operators	2.24	2.34	2.49	3.29	4.59	5.68	6.66	197.0
State, county, and municipal employees	21.83	37.34	33.12	30.09	38.70	34.67	30.67	40.5
Steelworkers	8.02	14.16	9.46	11.55	15.99	21.87	18.48	130.4
Teachers	17.68	24.70	19.35	18.68	15.50	19.91	20.41	15.5
Teamsters	4.75	7.35	4.54	5.89	6.76	6.44	6.00	26.2
Transit Union	6.71	9.32	7.23	7.71	11.01	9.51	8.90	32.6
Transport workers	11.50	14.11	12.57	14.23	11.08	7.80	8.99	−21.8
Treasury Employees Union	22.31	25.22	20.83	21.32	25.25	25.94	42.07	88.6
Unite Here	7.69	9.14	16.80	5.63	11.00	10.09	13.69	78.0
University Professors	2.51	2.68	2.64	5.66	0.74	0.00	0.06	−97.5
Utility workers	3.32	3.75	5.02	7.79	7.94	3.21	3.34	0.6
Writers Guild West	2.40	12.26	9.10	12.57	16.70	20.84	16.83	602.4
Average	**11.88**	**16.83**	**14.96**	**13.99**	**17.51**	**16.82**	**18.10**	**52.4**

Twenty-eight unions spent less than $10 per member in the last two-year interval. Only seven unions ended the period spending less than at the beginning. What is perhaps most striking about these data is the seemingly small amount most unions spend on a per-member basis on politics. We can demonstrate this reality in another way by examining the percent of time union officers and employees devote their time to politics. In 2018–2019, the national unions' officers spent an average of 2.7 percent of their time on politics. For union employees, the average fell less than 6.2 percent.

National Unions Electoral Contributions

Table 10.5 reports the national unions' contributions to federal elections. These contributions are made from money raised by the union's political action committees (PACs) and from outside spending sources (which can include money from

Table 10.5 National Unions' Electoral Contributions in Federal Elections 2006–2020

Union	*2005–2006 ($)*	*2019–2020 ($)*	*% Change*
CARP	26,06,963	3,36,69,232	11.91512
NEA	24,62,759	2,57,94,758	9.473927
AFT	26,51,727	1,67,83,909	5.329426
LIU	30,31,426	1,49,84,411	3.943024
AFSCME	24,52,888	1,39,21,906	4.67572
UNITE	9,72,309	96,98,550	8.974761
CWA	16,17,730	77,37,115	3.782699
IBEW	33,74,455	75,99,445	1.252051
SEIU	17,35,811	59,21,237	2.411222
IUOE	28,54,439	56,47,668	0.978556
Plumber	20,70,765	48,52,402	1.34329
USW	12,37,550	47,64,865	2.85024
UFCW	16,68,240	45,04,774	1.700315
NATCA	21,70,570	26,36,581	0.214695
ALPA	18,48,800	25,26,284	0.366445
IBT	22,45,106	24,73,624	0.101785
AFGE	6,92,369	23,68,036	2.420194
IAM	21,06,360	21,37,010	0.014551
IAFF	21,96,305	20,76,993	−0.05432
NALC	17,41,550	19,75,998	0.13462
Painter	14,66,265	18,34,317	0.251013
UAW	23,55,589	17,27,316	−0.26672
TU	7,67,330	17,04,678	1.221571
SHEET	17,57,012	16,51,851	−0.05985
TWU	8,82,400	15,89,171	0.800964
SIU	17,19,115	13,77,013	−0.199
APWU	17,15,150	13,47,405	−0.21441
Brick	10,46,775	11,08,406	0.058877
APA	1,90,000	10,90,407	4.738984
Stage	1,18,710	10,54,265	7.881013
Iron	16,35,125	9,15,405	−0.44016

(*Continued*)

Table 10.5 (Continued)

Union	*2005–2006 ($)*	*2019–2020 ($)*	*% Change*
NRLCA	9,05,600	7,11,680	−0.21413
NTEU	5,64,610	7,02,951	0.24502
UMW	4,94,050	5,52,535	0.118379
BIOLER	6,39,940	5,51,916	−0.13755
Music	50,350	4,10,049	7.143972
ILA	5,46,500	2,62,687	−0.51933
OPEIU	1,09,250	1,85,658	0.699387
ILWU	2,52,150	1,78,595	−0.29171
Writer	-	1,71,809	0
Utility	62,813	1,70,763	1.718593
Insulate	1,07,390	1,68,456	0.568638
Plaster	13,720	1,47,400	9.74344
Director	87,000	1,39,182	0.599793
EPT	33,650	96,300	1.861813
Elevator	21,500	94,800	3.409302
Roofer	1,550	46,022	28.69161
Bakery	2,71,000	30,750	−0.88653
SPFP	-	2,800	0
AMA	-	-	0
Journey	-	-	0
Novelty	-	-	0
AAUP	-	-	0
Total	5,95,52,666	19,20,00,000	2.225706
Average	11,23,635	36,24,517	2.421723

the unions' treasuries). Only PAC money, which must be raised by unions from members and their families on a purely voluntary basis, can be given to federal candidates for Congress or the presidency, within specified statutory limits. Treasury funds can be used to fund candidacies if they are not coordinated with the campaigns, i.e., they are made "independently."

The data reveal that the 53 nationals' total electoral contributions more than tripled between the election cycle of 2006 and 2020, rising from just under $60 million to over $192 million. The average contributions made rose from roughly $1.1 million to $3.6 million, or nearly 2.5 times. Five unions contributed more than $10 million in the 2019–2020 cycle, with three of them being public sector (NEA, AFT, and AFSCME) and other two building trades (CARP and LIU). Thirty-two unions made more than $1 million in contributions in this last cycle, but four made no contributions. Eight unions contributed less money in 2019–2020 than they did in 2005–2006.

11 Compensation and Benefits

This chapter examines the amount the unions spent on compensation for their officers and employees. It reported the aggregated amount to total income spent in 2007 and 2019 (this includes gross salary and expenses). We also report the total amount spent by the unions on benefits for officers and employees over the seven two-year intervals. The data indicate that the average officer across the 53 unions earned slightly over $79,000 in gross salary and expenses in 2007, compared to just under $102,000 in 2019, for a 28.5 percent hike. The average salary and expenses paid to employees rose from about $65,000 to nearly $95,000 over this time period, or 46 percent. The average total of gross salaries and expenses for officers and employees over the seven intervals climbed from $14.5 million in 2006–2007 to $16.4 million in 2018–2019, or 13 percent. In 2018–2019, two unions spent more than $50 million on gross salaries and expenses to officers and employees, while ten spent more than $30 million.

This chapter reviews issues relating to the compensation of officers and employees of the 53 national unions. First, we report the total income, excluding benefits, received by the officers and employees of these national organizations in 2007 and 2019, on an aggregated basis. Total income includes gross salary plus expenses. The totals enable us to compute the average salaries paid to officers and employees at this point in time, along with the total number of officers and employees in each union. [The LM-2 disclosure forms require that unions itemize the salaries and expenses of all their officers and employees earning more than $10,000 in gross pay, including wages and expenses.] Second, we report the amount that each union spent on benefits for the seven two-year averaged periods. The financial disclosure forms require the unions to disclose the total amount spent on benefits for their employees and officers combined. [These benefit expenditures include not only benefits provided to current employees and officers but also those provided to retirees each year.]

Aggregated Employees' and Officers' Compensation

Table 11.1 reports the total amount of money the 53 unions spent on gross salaries plus expenses at aggregated levels for 2007 and 2019. It reveals that the unions spent almost $133.45 million in salary and expenses for 2,062 reported officers in

DOI: 10.4324/9781003335474-12

Table 11.1 National Unions' Expenditures on Compensation in 2007 and 2019

	Total		*Average*		*Range**		*Count*	
	2007 ($)	*2019 ($)*	*2007 ($)*	*2019 ($)*	*2007 ($)*	*2019 ($)*	*2007 ($)*	*2019 ($)*
Officers	133,447,392	155,790,540	79,281	101,835	667,681	840,652	2,062	1,873
Employees	109,231,198	1,051,038,762	64,749	94,648	772,286	730,336	11,597	10,327

* Low end of range was $0 for all four cells.

2007, yielding an average of just about $79,281. Officers in total received almost $156 million in compensation in 2019, for an average of just above $101,834 (based on 1,873 reported officers). In 2007, the highest paid officer received $667,681, compared to $840,652 in 2019. The average compensation of officers thus increased by almost 28.5 percent.

In 2019, the nationals spent roughly $1.051 billion on 10,327 reported employees. This is just slightly below the $1.059 billion spent in 2007 on 11,587 listed employees. The average compensation rose about 46 percent from 2007 to 2019, climbing from about $64,749 to $94,648. Comparing 2019 to 2007, the total number of officers reported by the unions shrank 9.1 percent. The unions employed 10.95 percent fewer people in 2019 than in 2007.

Table 11.2 reports the amount of money the unions spent on total compensation (officers and employees) in terms of gross salary for the seven intervals. Two unions (the USW and ALPA) spent more than $50 million in 2018–2019, with ten expending more than $30 million. Twenty-three unions spent less than $10 million in this two-year interval. The range in average amounts spent across the 53 nationals ranged from $14.5 million (2006–2007) to $16.4 million in 2018–2019, reflecting a 13 percent rise. Thirteen unions spent a smaller amount on total salary compensation for officers and employees in 2018–2019 than at the beginning of the 14-year span.

Table 11.3 shows the amount the 53 unions spent on compensation for officers. In 2018–2019, three unions spent more than $5 million, while 19 spent less than $ 1 million. The average amount spent on compensation rose 13.1 percent from $1.9 million to $2.15 million between 2006–2007 and 2018–2019. Seventeen unions spent less on officers' compensation in 2018–2019 than in 2006–2007.

The total amount the unions spent on compensation for employees appears in Table 11.4. In 2018–2019, two unions spent more than $50 million (USW and ALPA), while 28 spent less than $10 million. The average amount spent on compensation rose 13.1 percent from $12.6 million to $14.25 million between 2006–2007 and 2018–2019. Fifteen unions spent less on employees' gross pay in the last reported interval than in 2006–2007.

In Table 11.5, we show the unions' expenditures on benefits for employees and officers combined, which includes direct and indirect spendings. In 2018–2019, three unions spent more than $50 million (NEA, UFCW, and USW) while 22 spent between less than$5 million. Ten unions spent between $20 and $50 million. The average amount spent on benefits rose from $12.36 million in 2006–2007 to $14.52 million in 2018−2019. Twelve unions spent more on benefits in 2018–2019 than at the start, but the absolute level of spending on benefits peaked at $15.38 million in 2014–2015.

Tables 11.6 and 11.7 report the percentage of net disbursements spent on (1) gross salary and expenses for officers and employees and (2) the total benefits spent on both groups. As shown in Table 11.6, one union spent more than 50 percent on gross compensation for officers and employees in 2018–2019, while 14 spent more than 25 percent. The average spent on compensation rose from 17.4 percent to 19.87 percent from 2006–2007 to 2018–2019. Twenty-five unions spent less on a percentage basis on total salary compensation in 2018–2019 than in 2006–2007.

Table 11.2 Total Compensation

Union	*Cycle*							*% Change from 2006–2007 to 2018–2019 (%)*
	2006–2007 ($)	*2008–2009 ($)*	*2010–2011 ($)*	*2012–2013 ($)*	*2014–2015 ($)*	*2016–2017 ($)*	*2018–2019 ($)*	
Air Line Pilots Association	43.65	43.98	39.46	42.84	48.48	48.84	56.01	28.3
Air traffic controllers	4.34	6.78	7.04	6.39	7.42	5.39	4.68	7.9
Aircraft Mechanics Association	0.95	0.80	0.49	0.55	0.61	0.69	0.78	−18.3
Allied Pilots Association	7.31	10.79	8.15	9.10	10.87	14.08	19.07	160.8
Auto workers	58.75	58.43	48.75	45.38	42.87	43.21	49.35	−16.0
Bakery, tobacco, and grain	4.01	3.66	3.86	3.37	3.44	3.27	3.50	−12.7
Boilermakers	10.27	11.61	13.80	10.74	8.49	9.46	10.08	−1.8
Bricklayers	10.34	11.10	9.19	8.03	7.86	8.30	9.09	−12.2
Carpenters	6.92	6.45	9.84	10.24	13.13	10.39	11.00	59.0
Communications workers	58.55	39.09	49.70	32.80	35.30	38.27	37.08	−36.7
Directors Guild of America Inc	4.94	7.41	11.36	12.23	13.90	15.04	15.58	215.4
Electrical Workers IBEW	28.70	33.53	34.69	38.03	38.44	40.98	43.28	50.8
Elevator constructors	2.35	2.55	2.83	3.34	3.70	3.98	5.40	130.2
Engineers, operating	10.18	13.43	10.37	11.37	12.54	12.65	14.48	42.3
Engineers, professional, and technical	1.46	1.39	1.54	1.63	1.63	1.72	1.62	11.1
Firefighters	10.87	10.10	11.35	13.95	14.64	16.70	18.45	69.7
Food and commercial workers	27.69	32.20	41.40	33.84	30.96	34.79	29.00	4.7
Government Employees AFGE	13.08	16.92	19.24	18.31	21.16	24.47	24.44	86.9
Insulators	2.51	3.07	3.52	3.66	3.69	3.57	3.91	56.1

(*Continued*)

Table 11.2 (Continued)

Union	*Cycle*							*% Change from 2006–2007 to 2018–2019 (%)*
	2006–2007 ($)	*2008–2009 ($)*	*2010–2011 ($)*	*2012–2013 ($)*	*2014–2015 ($)*	*2016–2017 ($)*	*2018–2019 ($)*	
Iron workers	8.09	8.92	10.08	11.04	12.25	13.53	14.47	78.9
Journeymen and allied trades	0.45	0.62	0.81	0.83	0.95	1.34	1.92	326.7
Laborers	18.09	21.29	21.48	21.72	20.94	20.88	21.11	16.7
Letter Carriers, National Association	8.69	9.27	9.98	11.19	11.30	11.99	14.18	63.2
Letter carriers, rural	2.73	3.85	4.08	7.59	16.85	18.73	20.99	669.6
Longshore and Warehouse Union	1.64	2.79	2.36	2.30	2.23	2.51	2.92	78.2
Longshoremen's Association	7.12	9.39	9.13	8.15	6.61	6.59	8.05	13.1
Machinists	41.23	36.57	34.41	38.94	25.49	36.80	25.47	−38.2
Mine workers, united	7.34	7.10	7.41	6.84	7.18	6.55	6.33	−13.7
Musicians	3.27	2.84	3.03	2.97	3.04	3.11	3.39	3.8
National Education Association	48.13	51.71	52.66	47.75	45.26	47.53	45.42	−5.6
Novelty and Production Workers	0.11	0.11	0.11	0.12	0.11	0.15	0.11	8.0
Office and professional employees	2.00	2.50	2.94	3.13	3.50	3.58	3.23	61.3
Painters	6.85	9.38	8.20	7.89	7.95	8.72	10.51	53.5
Plasterers and cement masons	4.85	5.27	4.68	3.72	3.65	3.63	4.18	−13.8
Plumbers	11.57	12.05	12.33	13.56	15.25	15.65	15.25	31.9
Postal workers, American	13.69	14.04	13.36	13.69	14.45	13.52	13.81	0.9
Roofers	2.17	2.11	2.23	2.44	2.43	2.42	2.50	15.2

Seafarers	0.10	0.11	0.12	0.12	0.12	0.12	0.13	25.9
Security police, fire professional	1.66	1.48	1.34	1.49	1.48	1.70	1.70	2.5
Service employees	44.40	61.03	52.68	43.39	40.01	41.97	35.48	−20.1
Sheet metal, air, rail, and transportation workers	8.84	9.72	10.85	14.33	19.08	16.35	16.54	87.2
Stage and picture operators	6.67	7.38	8.08	8.93	6.81	7.47	8.24	23.4
State, county, and municipal employees	34.27	38.72	42.17	42.41	37.76	35.16	33.27	−2.9
Steelworkers	61.50	61.87	55.81	61.19	60.55	58.22	75.00	22.0
Teachers	24.12	26.52	28.92	29.66	31.52	26.36	30.27	25.5
Teamsters	35.00	35.72	32.48	32.21	32.01	33.06	36.73	4.9
Transit Union	5.18	5.81	8.16	8.26	6.61	7.30	7.18	38.7
Transport workers	5.95	7.43	7.89	9.22	6.21	5.95	6.96	16.9
Treasury Employees Union	8.21	9.76	12.49	10.39	9.67	10.73	11.11	35.4
Unite Here	23.80	25.57	17.28	18.09	17.31	17.61	18.19	−23.6
University Professors	1.57	2.22	2.64	1.78	1.80	1.97	1.94	23.0
Utility workers	2.35	2.63	3.19	3.53	3.18	3.10	3.57	51.8
Writers Guild West	10.03	12.64	12.10	11.93	12.74	13.52	12.45	24.2
Average	**14.50**	**15.50**	**15.51**	**15.22**	**15.20**	**15.73**	**16.40**	**13**

Table 11.3 Compensation to Officers

Union	*Cycle*							*% Change from 2006–2007 to 2018–2019 (%)*
	2006–2007 ($)	*2008–2009 ($)*	*2010–2011 ($)*	*2012–2013 ($)*	*2014–2015 ($)*	*2016–2017 ($)*	*2018–2019 ($)*	
Air Line Pilots Association	3.53	3.54	3.18	3.61	3.57	3.83	4.54	28.8
Air traffic controllers	1.11	1.57	1.72	2.04	2.03	1.11	0.96	−13.1
Aircraft Mechanics Association	0.71	0.63	0.40	0.45	0.50	0.58	0.61	−13.9
Allied Pilots Association	1.58	1.87	1.38	2.20	2.16	2.45	3.51	122.1
Auto workers	1.66	1.62	1.62	1.34	1.25	1.20	2.25	36.1
Bakery, tobacco, and grain	1.39	1.30	1.46	1.25	1.32	1.16	1.34	−4.0
Boilermakers	2.55	2.69	3.33	3.10	2.87	2.78	2.94	15.4
Bricklayers	0.78	0.91	0.95	0.82	0.80	0.86	0.94	19.3
Carpenters	2.05	1.57	2.11	1.84	1.95	2.08	2.50	21.8
Communications workers	3.38	2.23	3.39	1.91	2.28	2.48	2.36	−30.4
Directors Guild of America Inc	0.04	0.04	0.03	0.07	0.04	0.05	0.03	−39.7
Electrical Workers IBEW	2.47	2.64	2.69	2.73	2.71	2.79	2.86	15.8
Elevator constructors	0.52	0.53	0.53	0.61	0.61	0.64	0.69	32.6
Engineers, operating	1.19	1.55	1.30	1.34	1.33	1.36	1.38	16.1
Engineers, professional, and technical	0.24	0.27	0.31	0.29	0.29	0.32	0.35	42.3
Firefighters	1.87	1.45	1.99	2.40	2.52	3.27	3.29	76.0
Food and commercial workers	3.71	3.57	4.24	3.87	3.79	3.39	3.35	−9.9
Government Employees AFGE	1.64	1.81	1.79	1.82	1.92	2.08	1.87	13.6
Insulators	2.12	2.61	2.98	3.12	3.03	2.73	2.97	40.6
Iron workers	1.76	1.92	1.91	2.09	2.22	2.13	2.22	26.6

Journeymen and allied trades	0.20	0.24	0.26	0.31	0.44	0.51	0.60	200.1
Laborers	2.87	3.25	3.27	3.29	3.35	3.54	3.73	29.8
Letter Carriers, National Association	2.25	2.34	2.10	2.46	3.89	5.45	5.69	152.4
Letter carriers, rural	1.29	1.78	1.53	1.53	1.57	1.68	1.83	41.6
Longshore and Warehouse Union	0.40	0.60	0.62	0.66	0.69	0.82	1.01	149.6
Longshoremen's Association	4.76	6.44	6.21	4.84	3.76	4.22	4.98	4.6
Machinists	2.36	2.02	2.08	2.67	2.30	2.89	2.26	−4.4
Mine workers, united	1.02	1.31	1.26	1.19	1.30	1.39	1.48	44.9
Musicians	0.40	0.42	0.42	0.45	0.41	0.40	0.40	0.9
National Education Association	4.11	4.65	4.16	3.48	3.25	3.42	3.03	−26.3
Novelty and Production Workers	0.11	0.11	0.11	0.12	0.11	0.15	0.11	8.0
Office and professional employees	0.49	0.56	0.70	0.55	0.59	0.65	0.54	10.7
Painters	1.54	1.54	1.65	1.70	1.62	1.49	1.54	−0.2
Plasterers and cement masons	1.63	1.74	1.60	1.63	1.82	1.99	2.17	32.8
Plumbers	6.83	7.23	7.51	8.67	9.40	9.30	8.68	27.1
Postal workers, American	6.67	7.31	7.20	7.88	7.73	7.82	8.14	22.1
Roofers	0.78	0.85	0.79	0.91	1.00	1.01	0.90	15.1
Seafarers	0.08	0.09	0.10	0.09	0.09	0.09	0.10	15.8
Security police, fire professional	0.88	0.72	0.55	0.52	0.57	0.72	0.68	−22.8
Service employees	1.58	2.17	3.18	2.02	−1.35	1.47	1.25	−21.2

(Continued)

Table 11.3 (Continued)

Union	*Cycle*							*% Change from 2006–2007 to 2018–2019 (%)*
	2006–2007 ($)	*2008–2009 ($)*	*2010–2011 ($)*	*2012–2013 ($)*	*2014–2015 ($)*	*2016–2017 ($)*	*2018–2019 ($)*	
Sheet metal, air, rail, and transportation workers	1.03	1.17	1.34	1.80	2.96	2.67	3.51	240.6
Stage and picture operators	5.49	6.00	6.48	7.16	1.85	1.83	1.68	−69.4
State, county, and municipal employees	1.15	0.93	1.09	1.02	0.71	0.76	0.79	−31.6
Steelworkers	3.12	2.99	2.51	2.42	2.65	2.44	3.40	9.0
Teachers	0.77	0.85	0.83	0.95	0.86	0.97	0.73	−4.9
Teamsters	3.08	3.19	2.62	2.60	2.41	2.57	2.52	−18.0
Transit Union	2.94	3.04	4.23	4.09	3.12	3.12	3.13	6.4
Transport workers	2.40	3.23	3.07	3.53	3.11	3.11	3.77	56.7
Treasury Employees Union	0.31	0.35	0.36	0.38	0.38	0.39	0.41	31.5
Unite Here	5.03	4.50	3.20	3.17	3.27	2.96	2.99	−40.7
University Professors	0.05	0.05	0.07	0.08	0.08	0.07	0.11	104.0
Utility workers	0.92	0.98	1.07	0.93	1.03	0.86	0.95	3.2
Writers Guild West	0.01	0.01	0.00	0.01	0.01	0.00	0.01	−15.2
Average	**1.90**	**2.02**	**2.07**	**2.08**	**1.93**	**2.04**	**2.15**	**13.1**

Table 11.4 Compensation to Employees

Union	*Cycle*							*% Change from 2006–2007 to 2018–2019 (%)*
	2006–2007 ($)	*2008–2009 ($)*	*2010–2011 ($)*	*2012–2013 ($)*	*2014–2015 ($)*	*2016–2017 ($)*	*2018–2019 ($)*	
Air Line Pilots Association	40.12	40.44	36.28	39.23	44.92	45.01	51.47	28.3
Air traffic controllers	3.23	5.20	5.33	4.35	5.39	4.27	3.72	15.1
Aircraft Mechanics Association	0.24	0.17	0.10	0.10	0.11	0.10	0.17	−31.2
Allied Pilots Association	5.73	8.92	6.77	6.89	8.70	11.63	15.56	171.4
Auto workers	57.09	56.81	47.14	44.04	41.63	42.01	47.10	−17.5
Bakery, tobacco, and grain	2.61	2.36	2.40	2.12	2.12	2.11	2.16	−17.4
Boilermakers	7.72	8.92	10.47	7.65	5.61	6.69	7.14	−7.5
Bricklayers	9.56	10.19	8.24	7.21	7.06	7.44	8.15	−14.7
Carpenters	4.87	4.88	7.73	8.40	11.18	8.31	8.51	74.7
Communications workers	55.17	36.86	46.31	30.89	33.03	35.78	34.73	−37.1
Directors Guild of America Inc	4.90	7.37	11.33	12.16	13.86	14.99	15.55	217.6
Electrical Workers IBEW	26.24	30.89	32.00	35.31	35.73	38.19	40.42	54.1
Elevator constructors	1.82	2.02	2.30	2.74	3.09	3.33	4.71	158.0
Engineers, operating	8.99	11.88	9.07	10.03	11.20	11.28	13.10	45.8
Engineers, professional, and technical	1.22	1.11	1.23	1.34	1.34	1.40	1.28	4.9
Firefighters	9.01	8.65	9.35	11.54	12.13	13.42	15.16	68.3
Food and commercial workers	23.97	28.62	37.16	29.96	27.17	31.39	25.65	7.0
Government Employees AFGE	11.43	15.11	17.45	16.50	19.24	22.38	22.57	97.4
Insulators	0.39	0.46	0.55	0.55	0.66	0.84	0.94	140.0

(Continued)

Table 11.4 (Continued)

Union	*Cycle*							*% Change from 2006–2007 to 2018–2019 (%)*
	2006–2007 ($)	*2008–2009 ($)*	*2010–2011 ($)*	*2012–2013 ($)*	*2014–2015 ($)*	*2016–2017 ($)*	*2018–2019 ($)*	
Iron workers	6.33	7.00	8.18	8.95	10.04	11.39	12.25	93.4
Journeymen and allied trades	0.25	0.38	0.55	0.52	0.50	0.84	1.32	427.4
Laborers	15.22	18.04	18.21	18.43	17.59	17.35	17.38	14.2
Letter Carriers, National Association	6.44	6.93	7.88	8.72	7.41	6.54	8.50	32.0
Letter carriers, rural	1.43	2.08	2.55	6.06	15.28	17.06	19.16	1236.9
Longshore and Warehouse Union	1.23	2.19	1.74	1.63	1.54	1.68	1.91	54.8
Longshoremen's Association	2.35	2.94	2.92	3.31	2.85	2.37	3.07	30.4
Machinists	38.87	34.55	32.33	36.27	23.19	33.91	23.21	−40.3
Mine workers, united	6.32	5.80	6.14	5.65	5.88	5.16	4.86	−23.1
Musicians	2.87	2.42	2.62	2.52	2.63	2.72	2.99	4.2
National Education Association	44.02	47.06	48.49	44.28	42.01	44.12	42.39	−3.7
Novelty and Production Workers	0.00	0.00	0.00	0.00	0.00	0.00	0.00	–
Office and professional employees	1.52	1.94	2.24	2.58	2.91	2.93	2.70	77.5
Painters	5.31	7.84	6.55	6.20	6.33	7.23	8.97	69.0
Plasterers and cement masons	3.22	3.53	3.08	2.08	1.83	1.64	2.01	−37.5
Plumbers	4.74	4.82	4.83	4.89	5.85	6.35	6.57	38.7
Postal workers, American	7.02	6.72	6.16	5.81	6.72	5.70	5.67	−19.3
Roofers	1.39	1.26	1.44	1.53	1.43	1.41	1.60	15.2
Seafarers	0.02	0.02	0.02	0.03	0.03	0.03	0.03	71.8

Security police, fire professional	0.78	0.75	0.79	0.97	0.91	0.98	1.03	30.9
Service employees	42.81	58.86	49.49	41.37	41.36	40.49	34.23	−20.0
Sheet metal, air, rail, and transportation workers	7.81	8.54	9.51	12.53	16.12	13.68	13.04	67.0
Stage and picture operators	1.19	1.38	1.60	1.77	4.96	5.64	6.56	452.4
State, county, and municipal employees	33.12	37.79	41.09	41.39	37.05	34.39	32.49	−1.9
Steelworkers	58.38	58.87	53.30	58.77	57.90	55.78	71.60	22.7
Teachers	23.35	25.67	28.09	28.71	30.66	25.39	29.54	26.5
Teamsters	31.92	32.53	29.86	29.60	29.59	30.48	34.21	7.2
Transit Union	2.23	2.77	3.93	4.16	3.48	4.18	4.05	81.1
Transport workers	3.55	4.20	4.82	5.69	3.09	2.84	3.19	−10.0
Treasury Employees Union	7.90	9.41	12.13	10.01	9.29	10.34	10.71	35.5
Unite Here	18.77	21.07	14.08	14.92	14.04	14.64	15.21	−19.0
University Professors	1.52	2.16	2.57	1.70	1.72	1.89	1.83	20.3
Utility workers	1.43	1.65	2.12	2.59	2.16	2.24	2.62	83.0
Writers Guild West	10.02	12.63	12.10	11.93	12.74	13.52	12.44	24.2
Average	**12.60**	**13.48**	**13.45**	**13.14**	**13.27**	**13.69**	**14.25**	**13.1**

Table 11.5 Benefits to Officers and Employees

Union	*Cycle*							*% Change from 2006–2007 to 2018–2019 (%)*
	2006–2007 ($)	*2008–2009 ($)*	*2010–2011 ($)*	*2012–2013 ($)*	*2014–2015 ($)*	*2016–2017 ($)*	*2018–2019 ($)*	
Air Line Pilots Association	13.08	14.61	15.42	16.91	17.61	20.45	21.78	66.5
Air traffic controllers	1.82	2.09	2.64	2.41	2.45	2.69	2.82	55.2
Aircraft Mechanics Association	2.10	0.07	0.05	0.06	0.07	0.08	0.08	−96.0
Allied Pilots Association	1.58	2.48	2.08	2.15	2.47	3.14	4.37	176.2
Auto workers	66.46	52.65	70.28	49.83	85.48	35.47	29.67	−55.4
Bakery, tobacco, and grain	2.19	6.35	2.80	2.52	2.01	1.99	1.91	−12.6
Boilermakers	8.52	10.95	14.05	13.91	13.02	14.28	15.29	79.6
Bricklayers	9.43	10.13	9.90	9.53	9.88	10.30	12.36	31.1
Carpenters	10.24	11.82	11.14	10.55	11.34	11.13	13.62	33.0
Communications workers	18.31	21.33	19.50	20.89	27.85	22.28	24.91	36.0
Directors Guild of America Inc	1.74	1.97	2.18	2.28	2.57	2.81	3.06	75.6
Electrical Workers IBEW	30.65	29.91	34.14	37.03	38.36	41.33	44.32	44.6
Elevator constructors	1.63	2.54	2.48	2.33	2.24	2.42	3.59	120.2
Engineers, operating	16.87	13.22	23.78	20.39	21.07	21.15	21.86	29.6
Engineers, professional, and technical	0.44	0.37	0.43	0.55	0.93	0.58	0.63	42.2
Firefighters	5.62	7.53	8.18	8.06	8.17	8.14	9.78	74.0
Food and commercial workers	102.83	113.22	112.50	106.17	135.85	88.56	92.79	−9.8
Government Employees AFGE	8.29	11.05	12.23	13.47	13.24	14.07	15.70	89.3
Insulators	1.54	1.81	1.83	1.83	1.63	1.34	1.09	−29.2
Iron workers	19.57	18.44	14.10	13.72	13.28	15.08	14.20	−27.4

Journeymen and allied trades	0.29	0.28	0.36	0.35	0.44	0.65	0.98	238.7
Laborers	15.78	15.44	19.67	21.30	22.59	23.14	25.37	60.8
Letter Carriers, National Association	4.37	4.25	4.80	5.36	5.25	6.14	6.79	55.3
Letter carriers, rural	0.71	0.68	0.76	1.49	3.64	4.59	5.43	665.7
Longshore and Warehouse Union	1.32	1.50	1.61	1.72	1.38	1.55	2.09	57.9
Longshoremen's Association	7.06	4.14	4.05	4.42	4.18	4.57	4.69	−33.6
Machinists	12.22	13.78	15.51	18.23	21.37	26.89	29.61	142.3
Mine workers, united	12.70	9.04	9.51	9.05	9.21	9.23	7.53	−40.7
Musicians	1.31	1.24	1.39	1.15	1.32	1.43	1.53	16.8
National Education Association	45.29	47.87	57.05	63.34	60.72	58.43	61.84	36.5
Novelty and Production Workers	0.27	0.22	0.24	0.26	0.25	0.26	0.22	−17.2
Office and professional employees	1.31	1.52	1.83	2.11	2.67	2.69	2.82	115.5
Painters	7.07	6.22	6.62	7.69	6.58	7.40	9.15	29.4
Plasterers and cement masons	3.86	3.87	4.45	3.48	3.05	3.68	4.61	19.5
Plumbers	18.92	17.27	20.61	20.34	20.92	21.53	24.76	30.9
Postal workers, American	8.05	10.71	8.52	10.49	9.65	7.84	6.69	−16.9
Roofers	1.81	1.87	1.96	1.97	1.90	2.03	2.08	15.3
Seafarers	0.04	0.06	0.09	0.12	0.08	0.10	0.09	121.6
Security police, fire professional	0.99	0.76	0.87	1.12	1.14	1.03	1.15	16.2
Service employees	16.72	18.72	19.23	20.04	20.06	21.02	17.33	3.6

(Continued)

Table 11.5 (Continued)

Union	*Cycle*							*% Change from 2006–2007 to 2018–2019 (%)*
	2006–2007 ($)	*2008–2009 ($)*	*2010–2011 ($)*	*2012–2013 ($)*	*2014–2015 ($)*	*2016–2017 ($)*	*2018–2019 ($)*	
Sheet metal, air, rail, and transportation workers	9.00	10.85	12.63	15.84	15.20	16.21	17.11	90.1
Stage and picture operators	3.10	1.78	0.00	0.00	5.21	5.86	6.26	102.0
State, county, and municipal employees	16.56	16.88	19.05	19.74	22.11	23.38	23.60	42.5
Steelworkers	69.88	81.42	67.24	83.10	82.84	91.87	69.79	−0.1
Teachers	12.00	12.05	14.81	15.74	16.66	17.44	19.84	65.4
Teamsters	31.64	28.31	33.60	37.05	40.05	43.47	49.78	57.3
Transit Union	5.67	9.59	9.49	8.07	3.93	4.96	8.38	47.7
Transport workers	3.38	5.74	3.80	3.11	4.77	4.19	5.50	62.9
Treasury Employees Union	2.07	2.51	3.24	3.05	3.50	3.76	4.19	102.5
Unite here	14.97	14.99	10.64	10.16	10.29	10.40	10.10	−32.5
University Professors	0.56	0.56	0.62	0.57	0.64	0.68	0.67	18.9
Utility workers	1.36	1.42	1.79	1.88	1.80	1.93	2.08	53.1
Writers Guild West	2.08	2.27	2.34	2.31	2.48	2.83	3.50	68.6
Average	**12.36**	**12.84**	**13.55**	**13.76**	**15.38**	**14.12**	**14.52**	**17.4**

Table 11.6 Total Compensation as a Percentage of Net Distributions

Union	*Cycle*							*% Change from 2006–2007 to 2018–2019 (%)*
	2006–2007 (%)	*2008–2009 (%)*	*2010–2011 (%)*	*2012–2013 (%)*	*2014–2015 (%)*	*2016–2017 (%)*	*2018–2019 (%)*	
Air Line Pilots Association	19.65	22.50	26.70	24.68	24.69	19.60	18.61	−5.3
Air traffic controllers	20.45	28.77	28.44	25.70	27.38	18.38	15.55	−24.0
Aircraft Mechanics Association	11.97	19.60	25.35	24.53	30.13	24.61	26.35	120.2
Allied Pilots Association	17.21	32.75	26.83	29.33	27.12	37.70	42.79	148.6
Auto workers	19.29	20.59	19.19	20.15	17.86	17.03	18.83	−2.4
Bakery, tobacco, and grain	14.40	11.10	20.16	18.72	14.72	16.97	28.87	100.4
Boilermakers	28.72	25.53	23.58	18.45	19.02	11.58	12.29	−57.2
Bricklayers	21.56	21.87	23.25	21.98	19.52	22.33	21.79	1.1
Carpenters	3.64	7.24	4.98	9.07	9.25	10.01	7.20	98.0
Communications workers	9.13	7.79	13.97	20.97	23.15	17.17	24.52	168.5
Directors Guild of America Inc	10.90	15.60	21.62	21.82	24.66	24.85	23.94	119.7
Electrical Workers IBEW	3.40	13.91	14.00	13.50	12.89	12.17	17.52	415.1
Elevator constructors	20.30	22.24	27.96	23.10	29.69	30.02	23.26	14.6
Engineers, operating	18.84	13.88	15.05	16.64	16.23	10.13	7.10	−62.3
Engineers, professional, and technical	34.60	32.08	32.56	32.96	31.26	31.46	31.78	−8.2
Firefighters	21.97	20.02	21.50	25.01	24.01	25.14	23.88	8.7
Food and commercial workers	12.38	11.92	15.67	13.47	10.37	13.27	10.48	−15.4
Government Employees AFGE	26.84	28.20	23.22	23.33	23.15	26.64	28.83	7.4

(*Continued*)

Table 11.6 (Continued)

Union	*Cycle*							*% Change from 2006–2007 to 2018–2019 (%)*
	2006–2007 (%)	*2008–2009 (%)*	*2010–2011 (%)*	*2012–2013 (%)*	*2014–2015 (%)*	*2016–2017 (%)*	*2018–2019 (%)*	
Insulators	22.08	28.73	31.48	29.10	18.64	27.75	28.93	31.0
Iron workers	8.86	9.85	10.99	13.59	17.42	14.60	6.46	−27.1
Journeymen and allied trades	11.96	14.86	17.11	18.79	21.33	24.68	27.92	133.6
Laborers	14.90	24.36	23.80	24.58	20.73	18.89	20.20	35.6
Letter Carriers, National Association	5.67	7.80	5.67	6.59	5.70	6.35	11.74	106.9
Letter carriers, rural	20.68	28.43	28.51	39.14	54.68	53.72	57.45	177.8
Longshore and Warehouse Union	24.26	39.79	34.20	33.84	35.69	35.25	35.46	46.1
Longshoremen's Association	27.95	40.22	42.91	38.42	23.37	25.98	25.07	−10.3
Machinists	33.86	26.12	26.86	26.82	16.98	22.84	15.73	−53.6
Mine workers, united	21.31	20.25	6.47	11.70	8.98	13.62	17.12	−19.6
Musicians	28.35	23.69	25.15	26.24	26.40	25.61	26.42	−6.8
National Education Association	13.77	14.13	13.46	13.55	12.68	12.30	11.70	−15.1
Novelty and Production Workers	3.89	3.82	2.96	5.81	2.52	3.57	3.13	−19.6
Office and professional employees	14.50	17.43	16.96	18.71	20.26	23.52	23.86	64.5
Painters	8.88	20.49	17.12	19.46	16.01	18.82	21.26	139.3
Plasterers and cement masons	17.03	16.18	29.49	29.64	25.92	19.93	20.76	21.9
Plumbers	8.04	6.65	7.07	7.51	6.89	6.33	9.47	17.7
Postal workers, American	16.25	17.43	18.79	22.13	25.01	22.09	20.59	26.7

Roofers	23.51	24.03	23.48	28.32	26.75	24.45	21.61	−8.1
Seafarers	7.03	7.33	7.71	7.98	8.13	7.93	8.81	25.3
Security police, fire professional	29.88	28.79	27.89	30.65	29.60	31.00	32.82	9.8
Service employees	16.55	19.47	16.13	11.61	13.03	14.34	10.34	−37.5
Sheet metal, air, rail, and transportation workers	8.88	14.46	14.32	25.43	17.31	19.46	15.93	79.4
Stage and picture operators	8.41	9.06	13.80	14.03	10.21	8.62	8.53	1.5
State, county, and municipal employees	21.59	19.06	21.25	21.09	18.87	17.52	17.11	−20.8
Steelworkers	8.68	20.97	21.09	20.73	16.69	16.43	18.32	111.1
Teachers	13.65	15.65	15.33	10.22	10.68	9.26	11.61	−14.9
Teamsters	18.92	22.13	17.95	20.08	18.29	17.33	18.43	−2.6
Transit Union	12.66	19.34	27.17	27.49	5.15	10.39	8.09	−36.1
Transport workers	12.10	14.72	23.13	27.29	20.44	5.88	4.84	−60.0
Treasury Employees Union	28.06	31.30	26.32	23.36	29.37	29.59	28.70	2.3
Unite Here	21.34	23.53	13.17	21.40	19.08	18.72	17.32	−18.9
University Professors	23.23	32.96	41.57	27.55	27.46	24.75	21.42	−7.8
Utility workers	26.28	28.15	18.73	24.24	22.96	23.29	26.24	−0.1
Writers Guild West	24.11	24.98	22.33	27.90	24.13	21.96	16.34	−32.2
Average	**17.40**	**20.22**	**20.65**	**21.48**	**20.05**	**19.73**	**19.87**	**14.2**

Table 11.7 Benefits as a Percentage of Net Disbursements

Union	*Cycle*							*% Change from 2006–2007 to 2018–2019 (%)*
	2006–2007 (%)	*2008–2009 (%)*	*2010–2011 (%)*	*2012–2013 (%)*	*2014–2015 (%)*	*2016–2017 (%)*	*2018–2019 (%)*	
Air Line Pilots Association	5.89	7.47	10.43	9.74	8.97	8.21	7.23	22.9
Air traffic controllers	8.56	8.86	10.64	9.70	9.05	9.17	9.36	9.3
Aircraft Mechanics Association	26.41	1.68	2.41	2.48	3.50	2.78	2.82	−89.3
Allied Pilots Association	3.72	7.51	6.84	6.92	6.16	8.41	9.80	163.3
Auto workers	21.82	18.55	27.66	22.13	35.60	13.98	11.32	−48.1
Bakery, tobacco, and grain	7.87	19.24	14.64	13.99	8.59	10.35	15.79	100.6
Boilermakers	23.82	24.09	24.01	23.89	29.17	17.47	18.64	−21.7
Bricklayers	19.65	19.96	25.06	26.09	24.53	27.72	29.64	50.8
Carpenters	5.38	13.27	5.64	9.35	7.99	10.73	8.91	65.6
Communications workers	2.86	4.25	5.48	13.36	18.26	10.00	16.48	476.8
Directors Guild of America Inc	3.84	4.14	4.14	4.06	4.56	4.65	4.70	22.4
Electrical Workers IBEW	3.63	12.40	13.78	13.15	12.86	12.27	17.94	394.0
Elevator constructors	14.12	22.13	24.52	16.07	18.00	18.26	15.48	9.6
Engineers, operating	31.22	13.66	34.51	29.83	27.28	16.94	10.72	−65.7
Engineers, professional, and technical	10.50	8.51	9.09	11.15	17.79	10.58	12.34	17.5
Firefighters	11.36	14.93	15.50	14.46	13.40	12.25	12.66	11.5
Food and commercial workers	45.99	41.92	42.59	42.27	45.50	33.79	33.52	−27.1
Government Employees AFGE	17.02	18.40	14.76	17.16	14.48	15.32	18.52	8.8
Insulators	13.61	16.91	16.37	14.55	8.23	10.40	8.08	−40.6
Iron workers	21.44	20.35	15.36	16.89	18.88	16.28	6.34	−70.4

Journeymen and allied trades	7.67	6.72	7.56	7.89	9.81	11.86	14.22	85.4
Laborers	12.99	17.67	21.79	24.11	22.37	20.93	24.28	86.9
Letter Carriers, National Association	2.85	3.58	2.72	3.16	2.65	3.25	5.62	96.9
Letter carriers, rural	5.38	5.05	5.33	7.70	11.80	13.16	14.87	176.4
Longshore and Warehouse Union	19.63	21.38	23.42	25.31	22.11	21.88	25.43	29.5
Longshoremen's Association	27.74	17.74	19.06	20.83	14.79	18.01	14.59	−47.4
Machinists	10.04	9.84	12.11	12.56	14.24	16.69	18.29	82.2
Mine workers, united	36.89	25.77	8.30	15.48	11.51	19.18	20.36	−44.8
Musicians	11.38	10.36	11.56	10.17	11.45	11.78	11.93	4.8
National Education Association	12.96	13.08	14.58	17.98	17.01	15.12	15.93	22.9
Novelty and Production Workers	9.94	7.93	6.53	13.06	5.79	6.22	6.12	−38.4
Office and professional employees	9.47	10.65	10.57	12.63	15.47	17.72	20.83	119.8
Painters	9.18	13.59	13.81	18.96	13.24	15.97	18.52	101.8
Plasterers and cement masons	13.54	11.87	28.06	27.77	21.69	20.22	22.89	69.1
Plumbers	13.15	9.53	11.81	11.27	9.46	8.71	15.36	16.8
Postal workers, American	9.56	13.30	11.99	16.95	16.71	12.81	9.98	4.4
Roofers	19.60	21.25	20.63	22.86	20.92	20.50	18.03	−8.0
Seafarers	2.93	4.10	5.74	7.80	5.62	6.98	6.47	120.5
Security police, fire professional	17.71	14.81	18.05	22.98	22.85	18.68	22.06	24.5
Service employees	6.23	5.97	5.89	5.36	6.53	7.18	5.05	−19.0

(Continued)

Table 11.7 (Continued)

Union	*Cycle*							*% Change from 2006–2007 to 2018–2019 (%)*
	2006–2007 (%)	*2008–2009 (%)*	*2010–2011 (%)*	*2012–2013 (%)*	*2014–2015 (%)*	*2016–2017 (%)*	*2018–2019 (%)*	
Sheet metal, air, rail, and transportation workers	9.05	16.15	16.67	28.11	13.79	19.30	16.48	82.1
Stage and picture operators	3.91	2.18	0.00	0.00	7.81	6.76	6.49	66.0
State, county, and municipal employees	10.43	8.31	9.60	9.81	11.05	11.65	12.14	16.3
Steelworkers	9.86	27.60	25.41	28.15	22.83	25.93	17.04	72.9
Teachers	6.79	7.11	7.85	5.42	5.65	6.12	7.61	12.1
Teamsters	17.11	17.54	18.57	23.10	22.89	22.79	24.97	46.0
Transit Union	13.86	31.93	31.59	26.88	3.06	7.07	9.44	−31.9
Transport workers	6.87	11.37	11.14	9.21	15.72	4.14	3.82	−44.3
Treasury Employees Union	7.08	8.05	6.83	6.85	10.62	10.37	10.83	53.0
Unite Here	13.43	13.79	8.11	12.02	11.34	11.05	9.62	−28.4
University Professors	8.32	8.34	9.72	8.86	9.73	8.59	7.42	−10.9
Utility workers	15.21	15.21	10.54	12.92	12.99	14.45	15.33	0.7
Writers Guild West	4.99	4.49	4.32	5.41	4.70	4.60	4.59	−8.0
Average	**12.91**	**13.48**	**14.02**	**15.07**	**14.36**	**13.38**	**13.71**	**6.2**

Benefits

The 53 national unions' percentage of net disbursements allocated to benefits appears in Table 11.7. Only one union (UFCW) devoted more than one-third of its net disbursements to benefits in 2018–2019. Nine unions spent more than 20 percent, while 20 allocated less than 5 percent in this two-year interval. The average percentage of net disbursements going to benefits climbed from $12.91 million in 2006–2007 to $13.91 million at the end of the period, or 6.2 percent. The average expenditure peaked at $15.07 million in 2012–2013. Seventeen unions spent relatively less on benefits in 2018–2019 than in 2006–2007.

12 Union Corruption

This chapter examines the issue of union corruption. A common public perception is that unions often suffer from corruption involving the misuse of union funds. Several federal (and state) laws exist to prosecute such malfeasance. The 1947 Taft-Hartley Act includes provisions which proscribe corporate officials from attempting to influence union officials through bribery. The Labor-Management Reporting and Disclosure Act of 1959 (LMRDA) imposes on unions extensive reporting requirements, as previously noted, as well as fiduciary obligations upon officials. The 1970 Racketeer Influenced and Corrupt Organizations (RICO) law adds another layer of prosecutorial pursuit which has been used to indict and convict union officers for conspiring to corrupt their organizations through multiple criminal acts. We examine the extent of prosecution of union wrongdoing reported by the US Department of Labor (DOL)'s Office of Labor-Management Standards (OLMS). The US DOL investigates wrongdoing among unions through its Office of Investigations [Labor Racketeering and Fraud] of the Office of Inspector General. We examine in some detail a major recent union scandal involving the United Auto Workers (UAW), particularly in relation to joint training centers with the Detroit 3 auto companies (General Motors [GM], Ford, and the former FCA [Fiat Chrysler of American/now Stellantis specifically]). A significant aspect of the scandal, often overlooked in news reporting, is the way the centers were funded and the interdependencies it created between the union and the companies.

In this chapter, we examine the nature and scope of corruption in unions, focusing on cases where money is involved. In theory, corruption manifests itself in various aspects of union affairs, from the election of officers, hiring of personnel, influencing politics, investing union funds, managing welfare and benefit funds, awarding contracts to vendors, negotiating and administering collective bargaining agreements, and managing day-to-day operations. With respect to matters involving union money, corruption tends to fall into one or more of these buckets: bribery; extortion; embezzlement; and falsification of records.

We review relevant laws and regulations pertaining to the financial operations of unions. In so doing, we report on the mechanisms used at the federal level to

DOI: 10.4324/9781003335474-13

enforce relevant legal standards. Data on the scope of relevant misconduct as compiled by one of the key enforcement entities, namely, OLMS, are provided to show trends in illegal activities. We turn then to the application of the RICO statute to labor unions. A somewhat distinguishing though troubling aspect of improper conduct in unions in the United States is the presence historically of organized crime. We use the recent scandals enveloping the UAW to underscore the potential scope of financial misconduct and the continual need to be on guard against such impropriety. This specific UAW case provided a point from which to examine the possible remedies available to prevent and deter the recurrence of unethical and illegal behaviors. Our analysis also taps into the potential hazard of undue corporate influence in union affairs through cozy collaborative arrangements that involve a company's financial subsidization of union operations.

Federal Laws

Three sets of federal laws regulate the conduct of unions and their officers and employees in the realm of managing finances: (1) labor laws such as the National Labor Relations Act (NLRA), Taft-Hartley (LMRA), and the Labor Management Reporting and Disclosure Act (referred commonly to Landrum-Griffin); (2) the RICO statute; and (3) miscellaneous laws which prohibit activities used to facilitate crimes, such as filing false tax returns or using electronic transactions for money laundering. We present the key provisions of the labor and RICO laws in Table 12.1.

Enacted to protect workers' rights to form unions and bargain collectively, the NLRA establishes public policy to ensure the status of unions as independent organizations, free of undue corporate influence. Specifically, Section 8(2) makes it an unfair labor practice for companies "to dominate or interfere with the formation or administration of any labor organization or contribute financial or other support to it." This provision effectively bans the creation of so-called company unions, which are dominated by employers with which a union may bargain on behalf of its members. Corporate domination breaches the independence of unions and thus compromises the interests of the rank and file. A caveat to this restriction, however, permits companies and unions to negotiate provisions to a collective bargaining agreement allowing union officials paid leave to conduct business representing employees in labor-management relations. The parties may contract for the company's support of office space and equipment to enable a union to represent employees accordingly. As we will show later, the UAW-connected scandal, which has resulted in the conviction of 15 officials of the union and FCA, involved in a substantial part of the misuse of corporate funds contributed to joint labor-management training programs created in the 1980s to improve workforce productivity and product quality. To a certain extent, the training centers also subsidized the unions' operations financially, which raises the specter of "company unionism."

Table 12.1 Selected Provisions of the LMRDA (and Amended Taft-Hartley Act)

LMRDA/Taft-Hartley *Provision*	*Statutory language*
Report of labor organizations Section 201	(b) Every labor organization shall file annually with the Secretary a financial report signed by its president and treasurer or corresponding principal officers containing the following information in such detail as may be necessary accurately to disclose its financial condition and operations for its preceding fiscal year.
Criminal provisions	(a) Any person who willfully violates this title shall be fined not more than $10,000 or imprisoned for not more than one year, or both.
Section 209	(b) Any person who makes a false statement or representation of a material fact, knowing it to be false, or who knowingly fails to disclose a material fact, in any document, report, or other information required under the provisions of this title shall be fined not more than $10,000 or imprisoned for not more than one year, or both.
Fiduciary responsibilities of officers of labor organizations	(a) The officers, agents, shop stewards, and other representatives of a labor organization occupy positions of trust in relation to such organization and its members as a group. It is, therefore, the duty of each such person, taking into account the special problems and functions of a labor organization, to hold its money and property solely for the benefit of the organization and its members and to manage, invest, and expend the same in accordance with its constitution and bylaws and any resolutions of the governing bodies adopted thereunder, to refrain from dealing with such organization as an adverse party or on behalf of an adverse party in any matter connected with his duties and from holding or acquiring any pecuniary or personal interest which conflicts with the interests of such organization, and to account to the organization for any profit received by him in whatever capacity in connection with transactions conducted by him or under his direction on behalf of the organization. A general exculpatory provision in the constitution and bylaws of such a labor organization or a general exculpatory resolution of a governing body purporting to relieve any such person of liability for breach of the duties declared by this section shall be void as against public policy.
Section 501	(c) Any person who embezzles, steals, or unlawfully and willfully abstracts or converts to his own use, or the use of another, any of the money, funds, securities, property, or other assets of a labor organization of which he is an officer, or by which he is employed, directly or indirectly, shall be fined not more than $10,000 or imprisoned for not more than five years, or both.

Amendment to Taft-Hartley Labor Management Relations Act of 1947 with reference to employer aid to union representatives and labor organizations Section 301	(a) It shall be unlawful for any employer or association of employers or any person who acts as a labor relations expert, adviser, or consultant to an employer or who acts in the interest of an employer to pay, lend, or deliver, or agree to pay, lend, or deliver, any money or other thing of value. 1. to any representative of any of his employees who are employed in an industry affecting commerce; or 2. to any labor organization, or any officer or employee thereof, which represents, seeks to represent, or would admit to membership, any of the employees of such employer who are employed in an industry affecting commerce; or 3. to any employee or group or committee of employees of such employer employed in an industry affecting commerce in excess of their normal compensation for the purpose of causing such employee or group or committee directly or indirectly to influence any other employees in the exercise of the right to organize and bargain collectively through representatives of their own choosing; or 4. to any officer or employee of a labor organization engaged in an industry affecting commerce with intent to influence him in respect to any of his actions, decisions, or duties as a representative of employees or as such officer or employee of such labor organization.

The LMRA included additional provisions to restrict conduct which might compromise the institutional integrity of the parties and their bargaining relationships. Section 301 forbade company representatives "to pay, lend, or deliver, or agree to pay, lend, or deliver, any money or other thing of value" to union officials or representatives. This 1947 Act also required labor organizations to make limited financial disclosures to the US DOL, though there was no obligation that these reports be made available to the general public. It made a union's eligibility for the services of the National Labor Relations Board contingent on making this disclosure. The law stipulated that union members had a right to obtain a copy of union financial reports.

The LMRDA required additional financial and organizational disclosures, including a provision for public accessibility. It also imposed fiduciary responsibilities on unions and their officers. Section 501(a) of this statute states:

> The officers, agents, shop stewards, and other representatives of a labor organization occupy positions of trust in relation to such organization and its members as a group. It is, therefore, the duty of each such person, taking into account the special problems and functions of a labor organization, to hold its money and property solely for the benefit of the organization and its members and to manage, invest, and expend the same in accordance with its constitution and bylaws and any resolutions of the governing bodies adopted thereunder, to refrain from dealing with such organization as an adverse party or on behalf of an adverse party in any matter connected with his duties and from holding or acquiring any pecuniary or personal interest which conflicts with the interests of such organization, and to account to the organization for any profit received by him in whatever capacity in connection with transactions conducted by him or under his direction on behalf of the organization.

In addition, Section 501(c) of the LMRDA makes it a crime for any such person

> who embezzles, steals, or unlawfully and willfully abstracts or converts to his own use or the use of another, any of the money, funds, securities, property, or other assets of a labor organization of which he is an officer, or by which he is employed, directly or indirectly.

Such misconduct is punishable by a fine of "not more than $10,000 or imprisonment for not more than five years, or both."

In 1970, Congress passed the RICO Act to fight organized crime. RICO defined four new federal crimes. Specifically, it became illegal (1) to invest the proceeds of racketeering activity in any legal entity or association; (2) to take an interest in a legal entity through a pattern of racketeering activity; (3) to participate in the affairs of such an entity through a similar pattern; and (4) to conspire to violate any of the three preceding crimes. It defined racketeering as engaging in a variety of illegal activities chargeable and punishable under State laws and numerous enumerated federal laws. The RICO statute elaborated that a pattern of racketeering activity involved

> at least two acts of racketeering activity, one of which occurred after the effective date of this chapter and the last of which occurred within ten years (excluding any period of imprisonment) after the commission of a prior act of racketeering activity.

Operationally, the RICO statute involves building a case against individuals who conspire to commit wrongdoing, which are termed "predicate offenses." Through racketeering activities, these individuals infiltrate otherwise legitimate entities, causing them to become essentially illegal enterprises.

On top of the national labor laws and the RICO law, a litany of other statutes may be invoked to prosecute wrongdoing in labor-management contexts, though they are of broader application. These include statutory prohibitions on filing false income tax forms, refusing to file tax forms, mail fraud, wire fraud, honest services fraud, and financial institution fraud.

Enforcement

Several federal agencies investigate and prosecute union financial corruption. The OLMS enforces provisions of labor laws regulating union finances, elections, and disclosure requirements. It conducts audits and may file criminal complaints when it finds illegalities, resulting in potential indictments and convictions. Within the US DOL's Office of Inspector General, the Office of Investigations (OI)—Labor Racketeering and Fraud pursues allegations of RICO violations in relation to labor unions. Both of these DOL agencies may refer matters to the Federal Bureau of Investigation (FBI), lodged with the US Department of Justice, to investigate and compile evidence of possible criminality. The agencies may bring their findings to the attention of a US Attorney's office to seek indictments and convictions under applicable statutes. In the case of the aforementioned UAW scandal, the former US Attorney for the Eastern District of Michigan, Matthew Schneider, whose term in office ended in 2021, led the prosecution of wrongdoing for several years.

Nature and Scope of Union Financial Corruption

As mentioned, union financial corruption manifests itself in the forms of extortion and kickbacks, embezzlement, bribery, and the illegal subsidization of union operations. Corruption may occur at the organizational and individual levels, with the difference being that the former typically involves a conspiracy among individuals in the use of money or power. If the activities involve the commission of a specified State or federal crime, then racketeering is alleged, with two or much such incidents constituting a pattern. In this realm, the perpetrators may be associated with organized criminal elements, which have infiltrated various labor organizations to certain degrees (Jabobs 2006; Jacobs and Cooperman 2011).

In the early 1980s, President Reagan created a Presidential Commission on Organized Crime and charged it to report on the nature and scope of such criminal activity, including its penetration of labor organizations. The Presidential Commission on Organized Crime issued a report in 1986 titled: *The Edge*:

> Labor racketeering is the infiltration, domination, and use of a union for personal benefit by illegal, violent, and fraudulent means, Although labor racketeering can be conducted by anyone, the history of the labor movement shows that the most substantial corruption of unions is conducted by organized crime families and syndicates.... Traditional rackets include raiding workers' benefit funds, entering into sweetheart labor deals with employers, and exacting strike insurance payments from vulnerable businesses.... The Commission has found that organized crime can use unions in four principal ways: First, it can convert union resources—members' dues, union assets, or worker benefit funds—to its own use. Second, it can use unions to exact payoffs from businesses in the form of sweetheart contracts or strike insurance. Third, it can use the union as a way to influence an entire market. This last use may generate the same kind of payoffs that come from the sweetheart deal or strike insurance. Indeed, these rackets may be part of a general market corruption scheme. Finally, organized crime can use unions as a means of access to and protection from the political and governmental process.

The scope of union corruption is difficult to determine. Enforcement statistics of the OLMS provide one set of relevant data. In its annual reports, the OLMS details the number of criminal investigations conducted, the indictments and convictions resulting from the investigations, and the number of compliance audits completed (e.g. https://www.dol.gov/sites/dolgov/files/olms/regs/compliance/annualreports/highlights_20.pdf). Between 2006 and 2020, the number of criminal investigations ranged from a high of 339 in 2006 to 223 (2018). Indictments peaked at 144 in 2011, dropping to a low of 73 in 2018, while convictions plateaued at 129 in 2006 before falling to 60 in 2019. Audit completions peaked, for the selected years reported, at 748 in 2006 but fell to 215 in 2018.

The UAW Scandal: A Case Study in Recent Union Corruption

On July 26, 2017, *The Detroit Free Press* reported that US Attorney Matthew Schneider's office had filed a criminal complaint implicating a top-ranking official of FCA and selected other company and UAW-connected representatives of violating labor law by embezzling funds from the company-funded joint UAW-FCA National Training Center (NTC) for personal gain (Goeddeke and Masters 2021). [The scandal involving the NTC represented the first in three major sets of illegal activities that also implicated the training center at GM and the International UAW itself and its Region 5; see Tables 12.2–12.4.] The complaint implicated the deceased former UAW International Vice President, General Holiefield, in this scandal. Over several years, these UAW and FCA representatives illegally siphoned roughly $4.5 million of these joint training center funds to spend on a luxurious lifestyle. Since the investigation began in 2015 by the US Attorney's office, 15 union and corporate officials have been convicted of crimes,

Table 12.2 UAW Scandal: FCA and UAW

Dimensions	*Description*
Narrative	This scandal involving the FCA and UAW, operating principally through the joint UAW-FCA NTC, had two related components. The first component involved efforts on the part of UAW and corporate officials to divert NTC funds for their personal use; the second involved a concerted effort by FCA executives to "buy" influence with the UAW to influence labor-management relations to the financial advantage of the company
Players	Sergio Marchionne, former CEO of FCA, deceased; Alphons Iacobelli, former Vice President of Employee Relations, FCA; General Holiefield, the deceased former UAW International Vice President; Norwood Jewell, former UAW International Vice President; Michael Brown, former FCA Director of Employee Relations; Monica Morgan-Holiefield (UAW vendor and girlfriend/spouse of General Holiefield); Virdell King, former UAW official; Keith Mickens, former UAW official; Nancy A. Johnson, former UAW official; Jerome Durden, former FCA Financial Analyst
Organizations	UAW Solidarity House; UAW-Chrysler NTC; FCA
Time period	2009–2017
Crimes	Embezzlement; wire and mail fraud; filing false tax returns; conspiracy to violate Labor Management Relations Act; making illegal payments to influence union officials and labor organizations in labor-management relations
Financial value	Over $4.5 million for personal gain and over $10 million in UAW-FCA NTC "chargebacks" to UAW

Table 12.3 UAW Scandal: UAW-GM The East Coast Connection

Dimensions	*Description*
Narrative	Joe Ashton, former International Vice President, UAW, and two of his assistants conspired with a vendor in the Philadelphia, PA area to grant a fraudulent contract and receive "kickbacks" for payment, which was made by the UAW-GM Center for Human Resources; two other vendor contracts were let for which Grimes and/or Pietrzyk received kickbacks
Players	Joseph Ashton, former UAW International Vice President; Michael Grimes, former UAW administrative assistant; Jeff Pietrzyk, former UAW administrative assistant
Organizations	UAW-GM Center for Human Resources
Time period	2006–2016
Crimes	Honest services fraud; conspiracy to commit wire fraud and money laundering
Financial value	>$2 million

Table 12.4 UAW Scandal: Solidarity House and Region 5

Dimension	*Description*
Narrative	The crux of this scandal is the systematic embezzlement of union funds to finance a lavish lifestyle that was concealed as part of regular leadership conferences held by Region 5 in Palm Springs, CA. Three successive Region 5 Directors, including Gary Jones, who eventually became UAW president, conspired to channel union-connected funds to selected resorts who paid for meals, entertainment, housing, and recreation by these three officials, plus Dennis Williams and Norwood Jewell. They established "Master Accounts" at these resorts from which the parties could direct bill their expenses, which were falsified to hide their real purpose. Parenthetically, the UAW paid for improvements in the cottage used by former President Williams and to build a new cottage for him, which has since been sold for nearly $1.3 million
Players	Dennis Williams, former UAW President; Gary Jones, former UAW President and Region 5 Director; Norwood Jewell (former International Vice President, UAW); Vance Pearson (former Region 5 Director, UAW); Jim Wells (former Region 5 Director, UAW, deceased); Edward "Nick" Robinson, former president UAW Midwest CAP
Organizations	UAW Solidarity House; UAW-Chrysler NTC; Renaissance Palm Springs Hotel (RPSH), UAW Southwest CAP, UAW Midwest Cap, Loews Coronado Bay Resort, Lodge of Four Seasons; UAW Region 5
Time period	2009–2017
Crimes	Embezzlement; Mail and Wire Fraud; Filing False Reports; Money Laundering; Aiding and Abetting; Conspiracy
Financial value	Over $1.5 million

including two former UAW International Presidents (Dennis Williams and Gary Jones), two former International UAW Vice Presidents (Joseph Ashton and Norwood Jewell), and the former Vice President of Employee Relations of FCA (Alphons Iacobelli).

The US Attorney's office began its nearly seven-year investigation of the UAW and its joint training centers in 2015. In addition to the corruption unearthed at the UAW-FCA NTC, US Attorney Schneider's office found corruption involving the joint training center at General Motors, wherein a former International UAW Vice President, Joseph Ashton, and at least two of his aides extorted kickbacks from vendors who received multi-million dollar contracts to procure watches and jackets for UAW members employed by GM.

The third set of improper activity which involved both the use of UAW treasury funds and the NTC occurred among union officials connected with the now-defunct Region 5 and the very top leadership of the union. Using accounting falsifications, these officials charged the international for expenses for private villas, lavish meals, golf outings, sports clothing, and other forms of entertainment. Two International UAW Presidents plus others have pled guilty to participating in these illegal schemes. The perpetrators masked their expenses through third-party vendors by claiming the charges were incurred in connection with training programs held at resort areas in Palm Springs and the Ozarks of Missouri.

In the more than five years that have passed since the US Attorney's office began its investigation of financial misconduct at the UAW and the selected joint training centers, 15 union and corporate representatives have been indicated or convicted (see Table 12.2). These include two former International Presidents (Gary Jones and Dennis Williams), two International Vice Presidents (Joseph Ashton and Norwood Jewell), a Regional Director (Vance Pearson), a Vice President of Employee Relations and Director of Employee Relations of FCA, and several lower-level union and company representatives. Many of these have been sentenced to prison, serving or having already served their sentences.

GM added a twist to this maze of scandals by filing a RICO civil suit against FCA, alleging that the company and its joint training center essentially became racketeer-influenced enterprises. Top FCA officials, included the deceased former CEO, Sergio Marchionne, allegedly conspired to bribe UAW officials to effect favorable changes in the collective bargaining relationship and hence the company's labor cost structure. The motivation behind the conspiracy pertained to make FCA more attractive to GM as a potential candidate for a merger, which Marchionne had favored for several years before his unexpected death.

A central argument of the GM RICO suit is that FCA, through its top leaders, tried to corrupt the collective bargaining process through bribery to secure cost advantages compared to GM and Ford (Goeddeke and Masters 2021). It used the NTC as a source of funds to bribe top union officials and, in at least one case, a spouse of an International UAW Vice President, who was offering services as a vendor. The bribes, according to the prosecutors' theory of the case, resulted in the UAW granting the FCA greater flexibility to hire more lower-paid workers, implement higher-performance production systems, and smooth day-to-day labor relations by minimizing grievances.

The most potentially disturbing aspect of the entire set of improprieties involved the financial subsidization of the UAW by the joint training centers. As noted, these centers received their funding from the companies based on provisions negotiated in the collective bargaining agreements that ties the allotments to workers' hours of work. Nominally, the training centers existed to improve worker skills and abilities to work productively and efficiently in manufacturing high-quality products. In reality, however, the centers operated as social welfare as well as training centers. They lent contracts to procure swag for workers, which channeled money to vendors who are pressured to give kickbacks to union leaders and top staff. The centers also funded a variety of community-based programs that had nothing to do with training. In the process, the centers at all three companies subsidized the UAW through so-called "chargebacks," which compensated the union for personnel it assigned to the training programs. During a period in which the UAW was suffering from financial stress because of massive downsizing occasioned by the Great Recession and attendant bankruptcies at GM and FCA, it relied on these chargebacks to support partially their operations.

As Adams (2019) has written, the labor-management cooperative regime conceived between the UAW and the Detroit 3 evolved into an inherently corrupt enterprise that compromised the institutional independence and integrity of the UAW, reflecting a somewhat wider phenomenon in the labor movement:

> What follows is a somewhat complex tale of what happens when a labor union, structured to be unaccountable to the rank-and-file membership, embraces a system of labor-management cooperation rather than a class-conscious understanding that workers and their employers are adversaries with fundamentally opposed goals and desires. Unfortunately, what is true of the UAW is true for many US labor unions. That the UAW, an iconic union, born of heroic class struggle, could sink into corruption, with a bloated and dictatorial bureaucracy, only shows in microcosm what ails much of organized in the United States. And just how difficult it will be to rebuild a labor movement worthy of the name.

Parenthetically, a RICO suit brought by GM against FCA argues the same point:

> In 2015, with the cooperation of UAW leadership purchased through bribes, Marchionne schemed to use the collective bargaining process to harm GM by becoming the lead in negotiations and attempting to force a merger of the companies. For years, Marchionne had made clear to GM his desire to merge companies, voluntarily or through force. In the spring of 2015, Marchionne formally solicited GM for a merger and was rejected. In the ensuing months, with the purchased support of certain former UAW officials including then-President Dennis Williams, Marchionne proceeded to orchestrate a negotiation of the 2015 CBA designed, through the power of pattern bargaining, to cost GM billions. These negotiations were conveniently timed, as Williams and Marchionne were aware the federal government was actively investigating past FCA-UAW agreements and potentially other misconduct. Through a self-described "rich" FCA-UAW labor contract, Williams and certain corrupt UAW leaders could seek to convince government investigators that they had obtained significant FCA concessions, while Marchionne could impose unanticipated costs on GM in order to force a merger. While GM ultimately resisted the takeover scheme, in the process Marchionne and FCA Group negotiated a 2015 CBA that, as designed, directly damaged GM as a result of the pattern of racketeering.

Thus, as described more fully in this lawsuit, FCA Group and its executives have engaged in a classic pattern of racketeering for the better part of a decade, including committing multiple violations of the Labor Management-Relations Act of 1947 ("Taft-Hartley Act"), wire fraud, and mail fraud. GM seeks to recover its damages from FCA Group and its corrupt executives for the benefit of GM and its employees.

Remedies Adopted to Deter Future Wrongdoing at the UAW

As the evidence of misconduct in the scandal unfolded in the new media, the UAW faced mounting public pressure to take remedial steps. In addition, the US Attorney's office weighed what actions needed to be taken to reform the UAW on top of prosecuting the individuals who committed crimes. One consideration it weighed involved the potential government takeover of the UAW, a precedent for which was set in the federal government's RICO-based actions to rid the International Brotherhood of Teamsters (IBT) of its criminal element the resulted in nearly 30 years of official monitoring of the IBT's operations under the supervision of the federal courts.

Eventually, the top leadership of the UAW has adopted a series of reforms in financial policies and practices which have required additional oversight of the how the union makes expenditures and issues contracts with vendors. It has placed further limitations on expenditure of union funds on entertainment. In their 2019 collective bargaining agreements, each of the Detroit 3 and the UAW negotiated provisions for converting their joint training centers into voluntary employee beneficial associations (VEBAs) with additional restrictions on financial practices to ensure transparency, including regular independent auditing. In late 2020, the US Attorney's office negotiated a consent decree with the UAW that provided for limited government oversight of the union, including the appointment of a government-appointed monitor to approve personnel policies and practices, union elections, and financial operations. In this vein, the consent decree required that the UAW hold a referendum among rank and file on whether it should reform its election procedures to require the direct election of the union's international officers (president, vice presidents, and regional directors) by a secret ballot among the membership. At the end of November 2021, the recently installed election monitor of the UAW reported the results of the referendum, in which the voting members approved of the direct election of International Executive Board (IEB) officers. The election will take place in the fall of 2022.

13 The Top Ten

This chapter recognizes that despite the considerable variation in financial resources across unions, there is nonetheless a substantial degree of concentration of wherewithal among a few unions. We review the concentration of resources among the top-ten ranked unions on the various financial measures. The top-ten ratio or percentage of resources held by the ten highest-ranked unions on the dimension, to which we add membership, is compared to the percentage of such resources held by the bottom 50 ranked unions. We show that resources are relatively concentrated in the highest ranked with the so-called lower 50 have a comparatively small reserve. A lopsidedly distribution in financial capacity is thus indicated which has implications for how unions might restructure to improve organizational performance in the future.

We array the data on selected financial indicators to show the relative concentration of membership and money among the 53 unions. Despite the demonstrated variation among unions in their financial resources, we anticipate that a significant share of the available money is concentrated in a relative few. The resulting concentration influences where labor as a whole must look to find the resources to finance expensive campaigns that involve multiple unions. We also report the top-ten performers on the financial ratios and on which unions demonstrated the most growth in financial resources, comparing end to beginning periods across the seven two-year intervals.

Union Membership Concentration Ratios

To provide a benchmark for examining the concentration of financial resources among the 53 unions in the top-ten organizations for 2018–2019, we report the rank order of unions by their membership for that last interval (from largest to smallest). Table 13.1 shows this rank order and reveals that the top ten in the listing had a total membership of slightly over 13 million of the nearly 18.8 million for the 2018–2019 average. This amounted to a concentration ratio of over 69 percent (Figure 13.1).

The unions' membership concentration ratios for the top ten and bottom 50 percent of the sample over the seven two-year intervals also appear in Figure 13.1.

DOI: 10.4324/9781003335474-14

Table 13.1 Membership Rank Ordered by 2018–2019 Cycle

Union	*Member*
NEA	29,89,225
SEIU	19,40,557
AFT	16,81,160
IBT	13,56,978
AFSCME	13,33,579
UFCA	12,39,213
IBEW	6,75,150
CWA	6,44,489
USW	5,78,501
IAM	5,76,502
LIU	5,72,995
CARP	4,36,769
IUOE	3,98,242
UAW	3,97,266
PLUMBERS	3,52,072
AFGE	3,28,131
IAFF	3,16,837
UNITE	3,04,888
NALC	2,89,086
APWU	2,29,583
SHEET METAL	2,04,964
TU	2,00,816
STAGE	1,42,371
TWU	1,37,187
IRON	1,29,194
NRLCA	1,15,754
PAINTERS	1,11,988
OPEIU	94,745
NTEU	79,914
JOURNEY	77,458
BRICK	73,477
MUSIC	72,797
BAKERY	64,773
ALPA	61,813
UMW	59,795
EPT	58,502
BOILER	49,264
UTILITY	44,745
AAUP	44,305
PLASTERS	44,262
ILWU	36,156
ILA	32,142
SIU	29,469
ELEVATOR	28,706
WRITERS	24,124
ROOFERS	22,450
INSULATE	22,404
NATCA	18,496
SPFP	18,061
DIRECTOR	17,988
NOVEL	16,906
ALPA	14,332
AMA	3,546
Average	**3,54,606**
Total	**1,87,94,114**

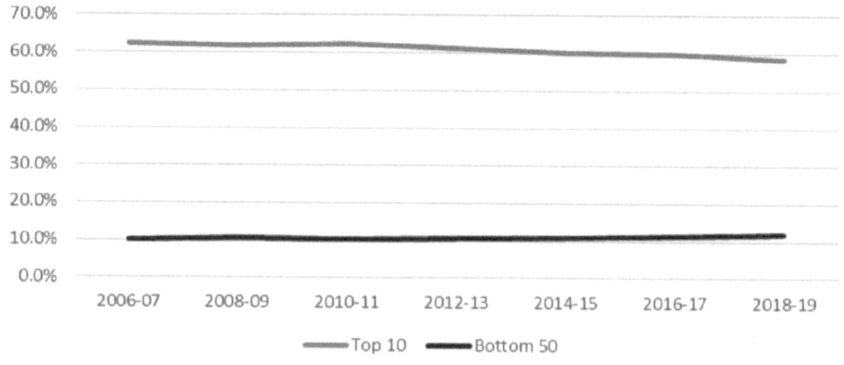

Figure 13.1 Top Ten and Bottom 50 Concentration Ratios Membership.

The top-ten ratio peaked at 69.8 percent in 2012–2013, with the low point occurring 2006–2007 at 66.97 percent. In contrast, the bottom 50 held comprised somewhere between 6.6 and 7.15 percent of overall membership among the 53 nationals. These ratios thus remained relatively steady throughout the time period examined.

Concentration Ratios in Financial Resources

We report the top-ten unions in terms of net assets, net receipts, member-based income (MBI), business income (BI), and working capital (current assets minus current liabilities) during the 2018–2019 interval. We compute the concentration ratio of the top ten in each category to the overall amounts among the 53 unions and compare it to the amount of the overall financial resource held by the bottom 50 percent. In addition, we show the trends in concentration ratios for each of these five financial measures over the seven two-year intervals.

Table 13.2 reports the unions' net assets rank ordered from largest to smallest for the 2018–2019 period. The top-ten unions reported net assets of slightly over $4.8 billion compared to a total of almost $8.17 billion. The concentration ratio

Table 13.2 Net Assets 2018–2019 Rank Ordered

Union	*Net assets*
UAW	999.5074
CARP	736.0541
USW	578.3415
IBEW	420.6717
UFCA	364.4646
NEA	355.7989
SEIU	346.7313
IBT	344.1992
IUOE	337.9486
NALC	316.5039

(*Continued*)

Table 13.2 (Continued)

Union	*Net assets*
CWA	313.0897
PLUMBERS	271.2323
LIU	264.6039
IAM	230.8762
ALPA	206.6666
UNITE	174.024
TU	170.6905
AFSCME	167.6965
UMW	141.4054
SHEET METAL	137.5743
IRON	117.0552
APWU	115.4074
BRICK	95.53593
PAINTERS	83.26023
WRITERS	72.46083
TWU	65.39737
DIRECTOR	64.71014
ILA	56.82238
BOILER	54.19755
STAGE	50.14264
ALPA	48.76783
AFT	39.69898
PLASTERS	39.26056
ROOFERS	37.40741
NTEU	35.77759
BAKERY	27.44437
IAFF	24.32341
ELEVATOR	23.57256
OPEIU	23.35
INSULATE	22.66077
MUSIC	20.35424
UTILITY	16.47282
SPFP	10.27854
NATCA	8.74467
NRLCA	7.897166
ILWU	6.056889
AAUP	4.771683
EPT	3.191928
JOURNEY	2.930496
AMA	2.084513
NOVEL	1.988286
SIU	0.691365
AFGE	–43.7191
Average	**151.2656**
Total	**8168.343**

for the top ten amounted to 58.8 percent for the last two-year interval. It peaked at over 74 percent in 2010–2011. In contrast, the bottom half of the union sample held less than 4 percent of the net assets in 2010–2011. It rose to nearly 7.4 percent in the last interval (Figure 13.2).

The unions' rankings in 2018–2019 working capital (current assets minus current liabilities) appear in Table 13.3. The top-ten unions on this list possessed

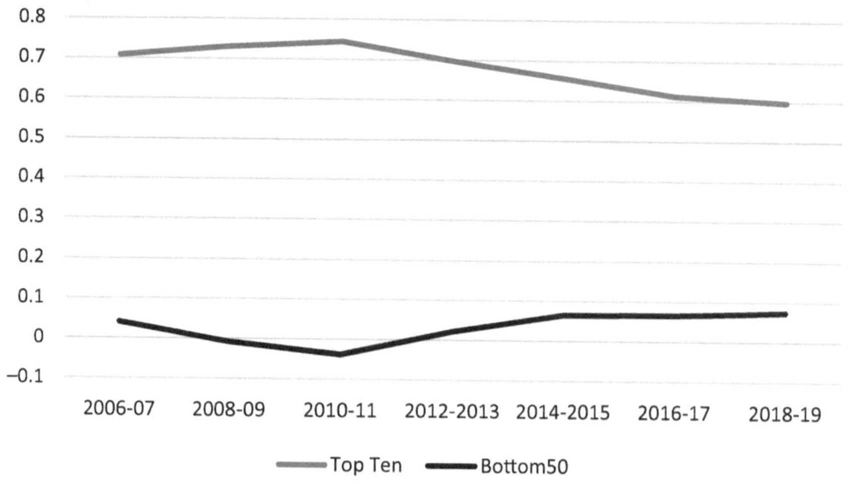

Figure 13.2 Concentration Ratios for Net Assets.

Table 13.3 Working Capital 2018–2019 Rank Ordered

Union	*Working capital*
AFSCME	255.2742
USW	234.8092
SEIU	232.7835
UAW	214.6345
NEA	207.9218
UFCA	138.0901
PLUMBERS	110.6909
CARP	90.28891
IBEW	81.57858
WRITERS	56.39283
LIU	48.79906
UNITE	48.57961
AFT	48.52888
BRICK	47.90122
NALC	43.83928
TWU	41.55108
CWA	35.6521
DIRECTOR	35.18952
SHEET METAL	34.90751
IRON	34.39287
IBT	32.15822
ILA	30.90098
IAM	26.00468
MUSIC	25.6319
STAGE	25.17862
OPEIU	22.44536
ELEVATOR	21.53847
BAKERY	19.92118

(*Continued*)

Table 13.3 (Continued)

Union	*Working capital*
APWU	18.5225
PAINTERS	17.15187
SPFP	16.35759
ALPA	15.90647
AFGE	15.70768
ALPA	15.58778
IUOE	15.33123
IAFF	14.17984
PLASTERS	12.89362
NRLCA	11.82507
INSULATE	10.97128
BOILER	8.514546
AAUP	8.301192
ILWU	7.609232
UTILITY	7.244504
TU	7.158097
ROOFERS	6.292403
NTEU	5.318666
UMW	4.9771
JOURNEY	2.766141
NATCA	2.062797
EPT	1.674129
NOVEL	1.610566
SIU	1.435326
AMA	1.063448
Average	**46.71789**
Total	**2476.048**

slightly more than $1.62 billion in working capital of the nearly $2.48 billion across the 53 nationals, yielding a concentration ratio roughly 65.5 percent.

The top-ten ratio peaked at over 72 percent in 2006–2007 before falling to 60.66 percent in 2012–2013 (Figure 13.3). For the bottom 50 percent, the ratio peaked at just under 12 percent in 2016–2017 after rising from about 8.9 percent in 2012–2013. In 2018–2019, the bottom 50 percent of the unions in the sample held less than 11 percent of the overall working capital.

Table 13.4 presents similar rank-ordered data on the 53 unions' receipts. The top-ten unions garnered a total of $2.99 billion in net receipts, compared to the overall of $5.86 billion, for a concentration ratio of just above 52 percent. The top-ten ratio peaked at 64 percent in 2006–2007. In contrast, the bottom half of the sample generated only 12.15 percent of the total in 2018–2019, which was significantly higher than the 9 percent at the beginning of the 14-year span.

The rank-ordered MBI data for 2018–2019 appear in Table 13.5. The top-ten unions reported MBI of $2.27 billion or about 57.5 percent of the total of nearly $4 billion raised. The ratio peaked at about 62.5 percent in 2006–2007. The bottom half raised just 11.9 percent of the MBI in 2018–2019, compared to just above 10 percent in 2006–2007 (see Figure 13.5).

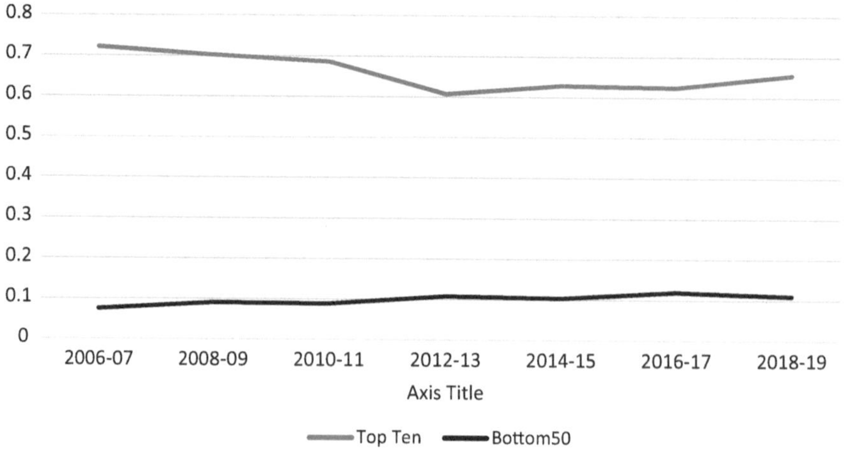

Figure 13.3 Concentration Ratios for Working Capital.

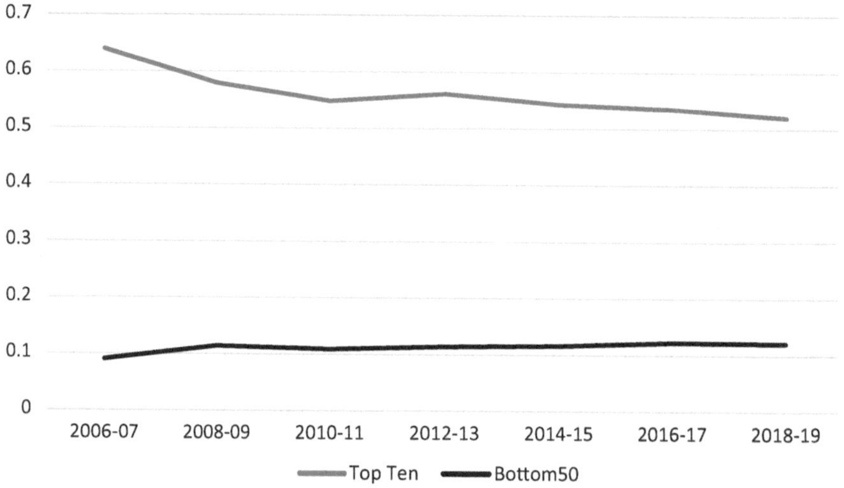

Figure 13.4 Concentration Ratios for Net Receipts.

Table 13.4 Net Receipts 2018–2019 Rank Ordered

Union	*Net receipts*
USW	391.7265
NEA	390.7036
SEIU	372.9871
ALPA	302.7197
UFCA	292.8836

(*Continued*)

Table 13.4 (Continued)

Union	*Net receipts*
UAW	279.7397
IBEW	267.0209
AFT	263.4432
IRON	223.7047
IBT	207.5262
IUOE	203.8153
AFSCME	197.0068
PLUMBERS	172.0981
IAM	163.0493
CARP	152.563
CWA	151.8921
TWU	142.0361
NALC	116.8805
UNITE	116.5417
LIU	108.3244
SHEET METAL	107.1932
STAGE	96.69497
AFGE	89.88612
BOILER	84.44767
IAFF	76.98134
TU	76.79014
WRITERS	74.35575
APWU	67.52117
DIRECTOR	65.38192
PAINTERS	50.69472
ALPA	49.4995
BRICK	48.98773
NRLCA	39.35452
NTEU	38.67603
UMW	32.79601
NATCA	30.63981
ILA	25.87288
ELEVATOR	22.93176
PLASTERS	20.21591
OPEIU	17.72974
INSULATE	15.34471
UTILITY	13.99318
MUSIC	13.90893
BAKERY	11.98024
AAUP	11.56786
ROOFERS	10.32607
ILWU	8.326829
JOURNEY	7.634991
SPFP	6.458784
EPT	5.256035
NOVEL	4.211146
AMA	3.149679
SIU	1.696784
Average	**108.4371**
Total	**5855.606**

Table 13.5 MBI 2018–2019 Rank Ordered

Union	*MBI*
NEA	371.3696
USW	298.2284
SEIU	280.6685
UFCA	226.0175
ALPA	211.8295
IBT	190.2694
AFT	187.8029
AFSCME	182.1219
UAW	180.6756
IBEW	145.1526
IAM	142.4811
CWA	124.5586
PLUMBERS	101.9546
LIU	92.06211
AFGE	80.28655
SHEET METAL	76.42813
CARP	72.78948
IUOE	66.54146
UNITE	62.56486
APWU	57.58114
IAFF	50.99042
IRON	49.74029
NALC	43.93803
BOILER	43.0951
ALPA	41.08053
BRICK	40.79242
NRLCA	35.13048
WRITERS	35.07812
PAINTERS	32.61995
STAGE	32.49712
NTEU	29.77491
TU	29.57356
DIRECTOR	29.42662
NATCA	26.66472
TWU	25.41504
ILA	22.76934
ELEVATOR	21.48997
PLASTERS	18.69899
OPEIU	16.53023
UMW	14.7674
INSULATE	13.82303
UTILITY	12.94959
MUSIC	9.518971
BAKERY	9.017206
ROOFERS	8.710799
ILWU	8.126671
AAUP	7.365712
JOURNEY	6.348848
SPFP	5.900176
EPT	4.996211
SIU	1.565363
AMA	1.510296
NOVEL	0.928024
Average	**73.2494**
Total	**3955.467**

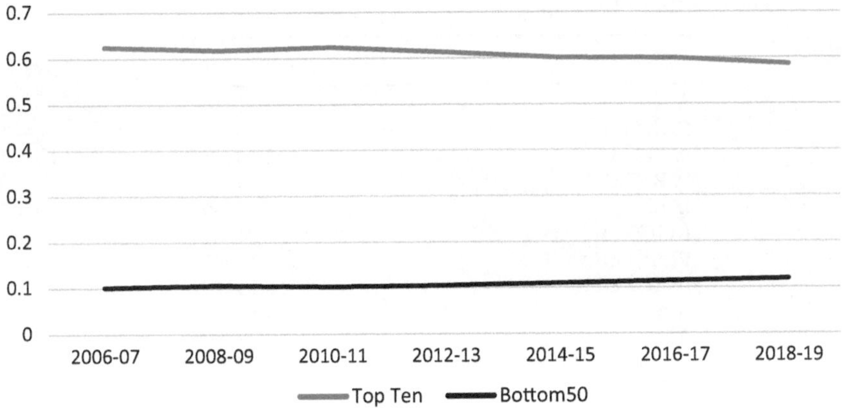

Figure 13.5 Concentration Ratios for MBI.

Table 13.6 Business Income 2018–2019 Rank Ordered

Union	*Business income*
IRON	161.605
TWU	111.6005
IBEW	107.6638
IUOE	82.63509
NALC	70.82581
UAW	68.51007
ALPA	68.03818
PLUMBERS	65.67741
STAGE	62.30203
USW	57.40605
SEIU	55.5494
TU	46.66813
UFCA	44.29537
CARP	43.36954
UNITE	37.53886
SHEET METAL	25.98944
CWA	16.13006
AFT	13.30835
UMW	12.07585
IBT	9.726783
APWU	9.108628
DIRECTOR	8.420727
ALPA	8.011056
LIU	7.889088
PAINTERS	6.798702
IAM	6.517605
BOILER	5.751289
NTEU	5.648645
NEA	5.200413
AFSCME	3.687837
NOVEL	3.281699

(*Continued*)

Table 13.6 (Continued)

Union	*Business income*
AFGE	2.515949
BAKERY	2.489876
NATCA	2.268202
WRITERS	2.09905
IAFF	1.748895
ROOFERS	1.2469
PLASTERS	1.120225
INSULATE	1.104702
ILA	0.864283
AMA	0.787004
ELEVATOR	0.472037
UTILITY	0.417683
MUSIC	0.351613
BRICK	0.338586
NRLCA	0.313464
OPEIU	0.170411
SPFP	0.167972
AAUP	0.068222
EPT	0.051362
JOURNEY	0.030243
ILWU	0.0064
SIU	0.000405
Average	**23.58236**
Total	**1273.447**

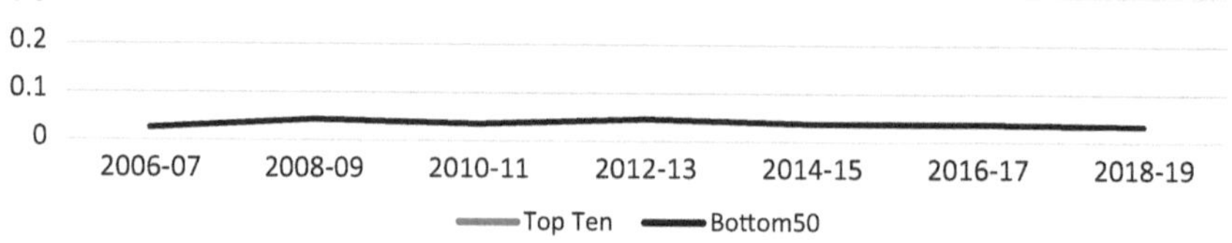

Figure 13.6 Concentration Ratios for Business Income.

Table 13.6 reports the unions' rank-ordered BI. It shows that the top ten yielded \$826 million in BI or more than 67 percent of the total of \$1.27 billion. The bottom half generated less than 4 percent in 2018–2019, which was significantly higher than the 2.5 percent reported for 2006–2007. The concentration ratio for the top ten peaked at 82.8 percent in 2006–2007 before falling to its low point of under 70.6 percent in 2012–2013 (Figure 13.6).

14 Strike Activity

The ability to wage a strike constitutes an important aspect of the union's power vis-à-vis employers and in society at large. The effectiveness of the strike depends to a certain extent on the willingness of the union and its members to sustain the stoppage. Strike benefits are used to provide at least some economic assistance to strikers for this purpose. Over the past several decades, union strike activity has fallen dramatically as labor's position in society has deteriorated, though there has been an uptick in 2021. We estimate the amount of money, based on their "working capital (WC)," that unions have to support strike benefits for a given level of strikers on strike for a designated period of time. Based on data for 2020, our estimates show that three of the 53 nationals have more than 50 times the amount of money needed to fund a one-week strike. Another six have WC sufficient to fund a strike of between 25 and 49 weeks. Seven, in contrast, have liquid reserves to pay for between one and two weeks.

The ability to wage a strike constitutes an important aspect of the union's power vis-à-vis employers and in society at large. To a certain extent, strikes are a protected form of activity exercised to influence the outcome of impasses at the bargaining table. Regardless of their legality, strikes impose potentially significant costs on strikers, employers, labor organizations, and broader interests in the community. The strikers themselves suffer a loss in income by walking off their jobs. While they may seek alternative employment opportunities, they are not typically entitled to unemployment compensation. The unions whose members are on strike lose their dues payments. To offset the strikers' loss of wages, these organizations may provide strike benefits to workers, generally in the form of a nominal weekly payment. (They may also negotiate bargaining agreements which require employers to maintain healthcare benefits for strikers for at least a portion of the strike's duration.) Thus, labor unions may incur the loss of dues revenues and cost of striker benefits during a strike. Their legal costs may also rise with ensuing litigation over the rights and obligations of the parties in a strike.

As mentioned, the effectiveness of a strike depends to a certain extent on the willingness of the union and its members to sustain a strike. Strike benefits are used to provide at least some economic assistance to strikers for this purpose. From an

DOI: 10.4324/9781003335474-15

institutional standpoint, a union's capacity to sustain a strike depends partly on the severity of its loss in revenue from strikers in addition to the cost of paying striker benefits.

We provide insight into the financial capacity of the national unions to withstand a strike. First, we estimate the potential loss of revenue a union might suffer from the strike of a given number of strikers over a stipulated time period. Second, we similarly estimate the cost of paying strike benefits. Unions often set aside assets to pay striker benefits in the so-called strike funds. They may tap into the funds in a strike where benefits are extended. The amount of strike benefits paid depends on the amount of the benefit stipulated per worker, the length of time the strike lasts, and the number of workers involved in the strike. We show the extent unions have the funds in WC to finance a strike by making certain assumptions about strike-benefit pay, the number of workers on strike, and the length of the strike.

Major Strikes (Bargaining Units of 1,000 or More)

Figure 14.1 reports the total number of major strikes (which involve bargaining units with 1,000 or more employees) that occurred between 2010 and 2020 to provide an indicator of overall union strike activism. The data reveal that such strikes range from 7 (2017) to 25 (2019) in number. In 2020, only eight major strikes occurred, five of which involved Service Employees International Union (SEIU), and one the International Brotherhood of Teamsters (IBT). To put these numbers into some historical perspective, the total number of major strikes in 1970 totaled 381.

Over the time period between 2006 and 2020, SEIU recorded the most major strikes among the nationals at 28 in number. The UAW recorded 15 such strikes, followed by the IAM with 11. AFSCME and CWA had nine major strikes in this interval, and USW had six. The IBT and the IBEW each had five major strikes.

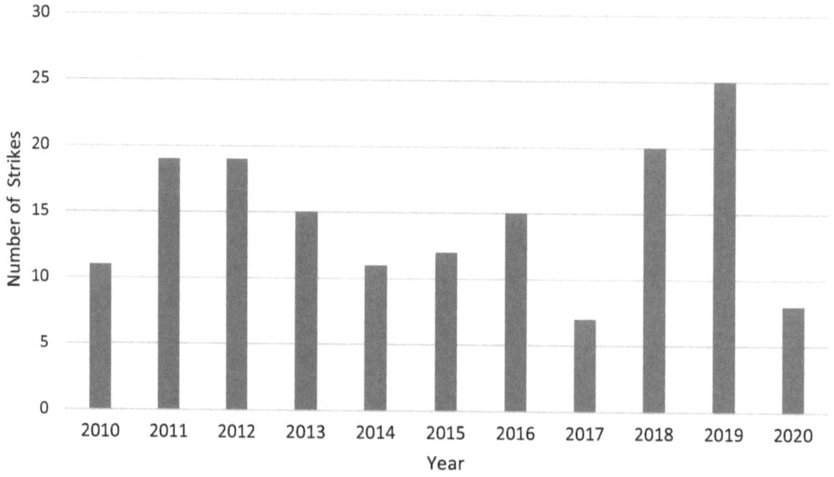

Figure 14.1 Major Strikes 2010–2020.

Major strike is 1,000 or more members.

Strike Benefits

Many unions accumulate strike funds from which they may draw to pay strike benefits to their members who go out on duly authorized strikes. The LM-2 forms do not require the itemized reporting of such funds, though some unions may disclose the relevant amounts in news reports. Specially earmarked strike funds, however, may not accurately measure the full amount of resources that unions have at their disposal to pay stipulated strike benefits without having to divert money from operating budgets. For this purpose, unions may exhaust their current assets, which are relatively liquid by definition, which exceed current liabilities. This reservoir of funds, as previously noted, is "working capital."

Typically, union strike benefits are relatively small in amount. The UAW, for example, provides $275 per week for each striker. In 2019, it incurred a major strike at General Motors involving more than 45,000 workers. We estimate the relative capacity (as of 2020) of the national unions to finance strike benefits by (1) reporting their working capital, (2) estimating the number of members each national would have on strike if 10 percent of its members struck, and (3) stipulating that the benefit per strike is $275 per week for each striker.

Table 14.1 ranks the unions by their capacity to finance one- and four-week strikes for 10 percent of their members at $275 weekly payment per striker.

Table 14.1 Capacity to Fund Strikes using Working Capital

Union	*1 Week*	*4 Weeks*
Directors Guild of America INC NHQ	86.28	21.57
Writers Guild West IND	78.70	19.68
Allied Pilots Association	52.47	13.12
Insulators AFL-CIO	44.61	11.15
Security police, fire professionals, IND	40.52	10.13
Longshoremen's Association AFL-CIO	34.67	8.67
Elevator constructors AFL-CIO	33.78	8.45
Bricklayers AFL-CIO	29.81	7.45
AIR Line Pilots Association AFL-CIO	25.68	6.42
Auto workers AFL-CIO	20.87	5.22
Plumbers AFL-CIO	19.58	4.89
Aircraft mechanics ASN IND	18.08	4.52
Steelworkers, AFL-CIO	17.72	4.43
AIR traffic controllers AFL-CIO	15.93	3.98
Roofers AFL-CIO	13.94	3.48
Musicians AFL-CIO	13.83	3.46
Bakery, tobacco, and grain AFL-CIO	12.41	3.10
Plasterers and cement masons AFL-CIO	12.32	3.08
Carpenters IND	11.90	2.97
Longshore and Warehouse Union	11.30	2.82
Unite Here	11.07	2.77
Office and professional employees AFL-CIO	10.71	2.68
Boilermakers AFL-CIO	10.38	2.59
SHEET metal, air, rail, and transportation workers	8.65	2.16

(*Continued*)

Table 14.1 (Continued)

Union	*1 Week*	*4 Weeks*
Utility workers AFL-CIO	8.26	2.07
State county and municipal employees AFL-CIO	8.23	2.06
Iron workers AFL-CIO	8.19	2.05
Stage and picture operators AFL-CIO	7.53	1.88
Painters AFL-CIO	6.82	1.70
Letter carriers, rural, IND	6.45	1.61
Novelty and production workers AFL-CIO	5.55	1.39
Mine workers, united, AFL-CIO	5.24	1.31
Service employees	4.99	1.25
Letter carriers, Natl Association, AFL-CIO	4.86	1.22
Postal workers, American, AFL-CIO	4.52	1.13
University professors, IND	4.14	1.03
Electrical workers IBEW AFL-CIO	4.13	1.03
Food and commercial workers	3.41	0.85
Government employees AFGE AFL-CIO	3.31	0.83
Treasury Employees Union IND	3.11	0.78
Machinists AFL-CIO	2.90	0.73
Laborers	2.89	0.72
Firefighters AFL-CIO	2.42	0.61
Journeymen and allied trades IND	2.39	0.60
Seafarers AFL-CIO	2.32	0.58
Transport workers AFL-CIO	2.14	0.54
Communications workers AFL-CIO	1.84	0.46
National education ASN IND	1.79	0.45
Transit Union AFL-CIO	1.78	0.44
Engineers, operating, AFL-CIO	1.73	0.43
Engineers, professional and technical, AFL-CIO	1.44	0.36
Teamsters	1.40	0.35
Teachers AFL-CIO	1.23	0.31

It shows that three of these nationals have more than 50 times the amount of money needed to fund a one-week strike. Another six have WC sufficient to fund a strike of between 25 and 49 weeks. Seven, in contrast, have liquid reserves to pay for between one and two weeks. In the case of a four-week strike, five unions have more than ten times the amount to fund strike benefits for 10 percent of their members. Four of the nationals have sufficient WC to fund five to ten times the amount needed to pay the strikers for four weeks, while ten have one to two times such capacity. As noted, 16 of the nationals lacked sufficient WC to pay for a full four weeks of strike payments to 10 percent of their memberships.

15 Financing a New Wave of Unionism

In this chapter, we examine how organized labor today can finance an ambitious plan to organizing workers in industries and companies historically resistant to any such effort. Our analysis starts with a review of the recent wave of organizing activity and success, focusing particularly on workers at Amazon, Apple, and Starbucks. After documenting the scope of certification drives, we turn to how the economic, legal, and political climate has moved favorably for labor, making the timeliness of any concerted effort to scale up more critical. This leads to a discussion of the salient labor organizations at the tip of the spear of these new-wave drives, with emphasis on how they are financed and could benefit materially from an infusion of additional money. Given their evident financial needs, the focus moves to how to finance vastly expanded efforts based on information on the financial wherewithal available to major national unions.

During the past year between July 1, 2021 and June 30, 2022, union activism has accelerated on several dimensions. The number of strikes increased significantly as the national began emerging from the COVID-19 pandemic and its widespread lockdowns, which depressed the economy and forced sweeping changes in workplaces with remote work proliferating and enduring. At the same time, organizing activity in the form of petitions to hold certification elections sponsored by the National Labor Relations Board (NLRB) climbed by 57 percent in the first half of the fiscal year 2022 (October 1, 2021 to March 31, 2022). Several newly formed unions emerged to organize corporate giants such as Amazon, Apple, and Starbucks, scoring impressive victories at a time in which economic, legal, and political conditions blended to labor's favor. With unions being the doldrums for so long, this rising activism breathed hope in union supporters and occasioned discussion about how organized labor might capitalize on the evident mobilization. The long-term labor reporter Steven Greenhouse has argued that unions stand at a pivotal point, with the future of their movement lying on how they exploit this opportunity. In particular, Greenhouse (2022) has advocated that major national unions invest in the nascent unions and organizing drives to accelerate the pace of success in workforce mobilization:

DOI: 10.4324/9781003335474-16

Many bottom-up unionization efforts seem ready to sprout at other companies, like Trader Joe's, where workers at one store have filed for recognition for an independent union they've established. Such efforts badly need more money and resources, however. Established unions can provide that support, with the goal of maximizing union growth and worker power, while eschewing the old jurisdictional game of which union gets the members and dues money. Lewis and Hillman understood this when they formed the CIO to create new unions like the United Auto Workers and the United Steelworkers.

Rising Wave of Union Organizing

To appreciate the significance of the recent uptick in union organizing, we need to put the spurt of activity in a historical perspective. Under the National Labor Relations Act of 1935, as amended, unions rely heavily on duly established certification-election procedures to gain bargaining representation. They petition the NLRB to hold such elections based on a showing of sufficient support for representation. If the NLRB sanctions an election, eligible workers cast secret ballots to determine the outcome, with a union emerging victorious if it secures a majority of the votes cast. Formal certification occurs when any legal challenges to the vote are settled. Once certified, the union so recognized seeks to negotiate a collective bargaining agreement, though employers are not bound to reach an agreement if negotiating in good faith. The trend in the frequency of certification elections and the volume of workers involved mirrors the decline in union membership over the past several decades.

Figure 15.1 reports the number of certification elections held by the NLRB in selected fiscal years between 1953 and 2021. It shows the dramatic drop in the frequency of such activity, from a peak of 9,472 in 1973 to 980 in 2021, which represents a nearly 90 percent decrease.

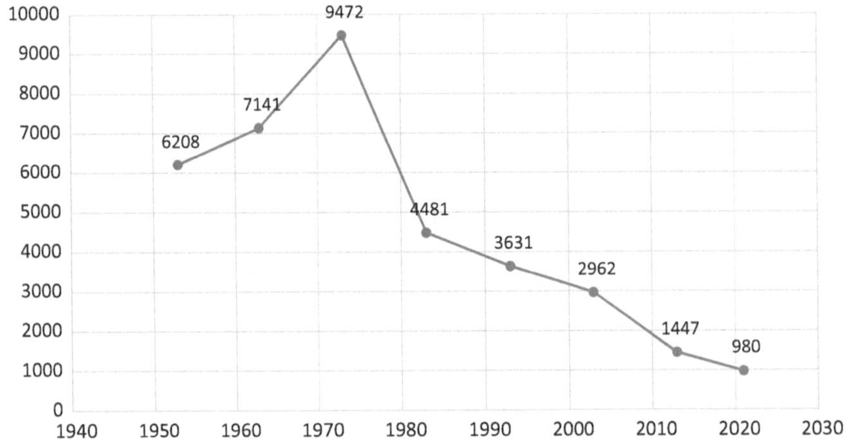

Figure 15.1 # NLRB Elections, Selected Year 1953–2021.

The downturn in the total number of eligible voters in the election units that voted mirrors this trend. Eligible voters constitute the base from which the unions can draw members in potential bargaining units should the members approve recognition by a majority of ballots cast. Figure 15.2 reveals that the number of eligible voters shrank from more than 750,000 in 1953 to under 60,000 in 2021, or 92 percent. The correlated drop in the frequency of elections and the number of eligible voters pose a double-whammy threat.

Given the plummeting amount of certification-election activism, labor has fallen increasingly behind in its effort to enlarge its footprint in the workforce. Just to keep pace with annual turnover in union ranks, labor as a whole must recruit about one million new members in the workplace. Even with such a level of success, unions would experience continued drops in its relative presence, as the labor force increases with rising levels of population and labor-force engagement.

Against this backdrop occurs what many perceive as a sudden burst in new organizing. NLRB data indicate that 1,932 petitions have been filed during October 1, 2021 through July 8, 2022, compared to 1,233 for a similar period in the prior year, which reflects a 57 percent increase. Labor sympathizers had taken heart in this uptick as a sign of rekindled labor activism, which has led Greenhouse (2022) to observe that "This is the first time in decades that America's workers have a real opportunity to increase their power after it has steadily eroded for half a century."

Within this context, labor supporters in the media have focused on the proliferation of petitions filed by groups of baristas working at Starbucks sites across the nation. Table 15.1 shows the number of petitions filed by Starbucks' employees,

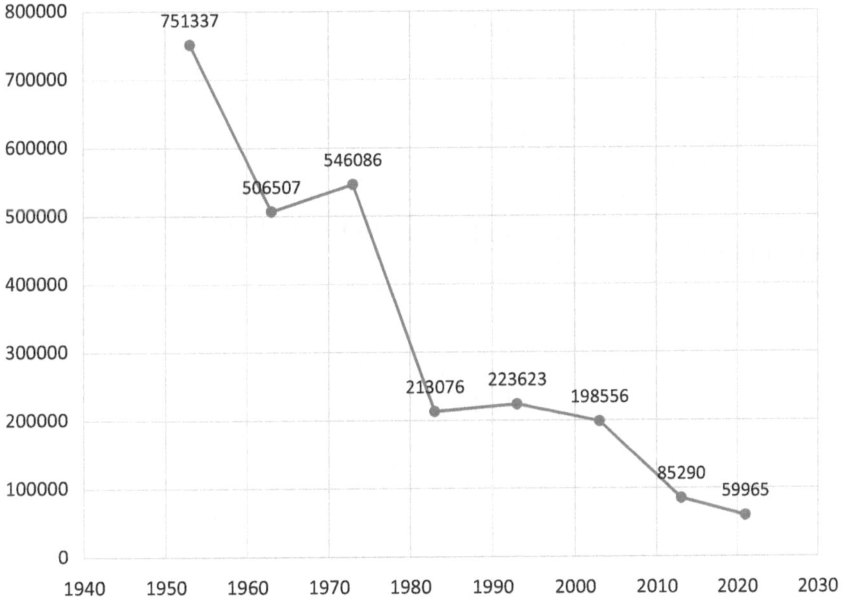

Figure 15.2 NLRB Election Eligible Voters, Selected Years 1953–2021.

organizing through the Starbucks Workers United, an affiliate of the Service Employees International Union (SEIU).

Organizing @Amazon, Apple, Starbucks, and More

Within this context, labor supporters in the media have focused on the proliferation of petitions filed by groups of baristas working at Starbucks sites across the nation, as well as the break-through organizing victory workers achieved in organizing a large Amazon warehousing unit in Staten Island in fall 2021. Bear in mind that the overwhelming majority of companies remain opposed, clandestinely or openly, to having a unionized workforce. Such is generally the case with even the most "progressive" companies eager to tout their Environmental Sustainability and Governance (ESG) proclivities. Top executives in such high-profile companies as Amazon, Starbucks, and Apple argue that their companies do not need third-party representation through unions to deal effectively with their employees, who may be paternalistically labeled associates or partners. But is more than they view unions as unwanted intermediaries. They believe they can do more for their workers in terms of offering higher wages, better benefits, more flexible working arrangements, and opportunities for advancement without having to bargain these terms with a formally recognized labor organization. Thus, in some instances, these corporate leaders have promised to offer better wages and other working conditions for employees who remain non-union than their counterparts who chose union representation.

Table 15.1 shows the number of petitions filed by Starbucks' employees, organizing through the Starbucks Workers United, an affiliate of the SEIU. During this period, a total of 367 petitions have been filed, and elections were held in 169, with the union, Starbucks Workers United, winning in 149 cases, or 89 percent. While this level of activism measured by petitioning and election victories seems quite impressive, it is important to recognize that the total number of workers involved is relatively small. Each Starbucks location, of which there are more than 15,000 in the US, employs about 15–35 baristas. Thus, even if the baristas at all of these sites were to unionize, the total of newly represented employees would amount to about 525,000 at the high end. Thus, amounts to substantially lower than one percent of the total workforce.

Another cautionary note about the degree of activism lies in the gap between union petitions and certification elections. While the number of petitions has

Table 15.1 Number of NLRB Petitions Filed by Workers at Starbucks to Hold NLRB-Certification Elections, AAAA, 2021 through JULY 2022

Status	*Number*	*Total Employees*	*Votes for Union*	*Votes Against*
Open	177	4702	425	194
Withdrawn	18	495	0	0
Unionized	149	4004	1933	410
Voted Failed	20	506	127	233
Other	3	59	0	0

Table 15.2 NLRB FY 2020 Elections and Eligible Voters by Month

Month	*Total Elections*	*% Union Victory*	*Eligible Voters*
May	144	78	8,074
April	110	73	8,612
March	90	51	6,037
February	63	60	2,297
January	86	73	2,404
December	95	85	4,406
November	82	74	3,262
October	76	86	3,511
Total	746		38,603

increased significantly comparing fiscal years 2022 and 2021, the frequency of elections has increased more modestly. During the first two-thirds of FY 2022, the number of certification elections held during the first two-thirds of the latter year totaled 746, compared to 652 based on a pro-rata calculation during the equivalent in FY 2021, which represents a nearly 14.5 percent hike (Table 15.2). The number of eligible workers has remained more or less flat. On a pro-rata basis, the number of eligible workers in units with certification elections in FY 2021 stood at about 39,750, compared to the 38,603 in FY 2022. Based on this comparison, one could deduct that the hoopla over labor's supposed rapid acceleration in union activism has more to do about the breakthroughs at a few corporate behemoths known for their union-avoidance stances than the actual pace of certifications and implied growth in membership. Yet, these developments at Amazon and Starbucks as well as in other companies that have long seemed impenetrable should not be minimized. In addition to Amazon and Starbucks, unions have achieved recognition at Apple among retail employees and initiated organizing efforts at Chipotle, Alphabet, Microsoft, and Wells Fargo. The sheer boldness, coupled with the symbolic value of breaking a few barriers, of these efforts provides unions with an opportunity to strike when the proverbial iron is hot. As we note later, the economic, legal, and political environments have aligned to give cause for more optimism among the ranks of union supporters than has been witnessed for decades on end.

Nascent Unions and Grassroots Activism

Several labor organizations have been involved in attempts to unionize Amazon, including the more recently formed Amazon Labor Union, an independent union which successfully won recognition at Staten Island, New York. In the case of Starbucks, as noted, the dominant union is Starbucks Workers United, which is part of the SEIU-affiliated Workers United. In the past, the Retail, Wholesale, and Department Store Union has sought recognition at Amazon. Locally based organizations affiliated with the International Association of Machinists (IAM) and Communications Workers of America (CWA) have sought recognition at retail sites of Apple. We profile each of these organizations to gauge their relative capacities to exploit the opportunities for growth which loom on the horizon (Table 15.3).

Table 15.3 Selection Characteristics of Localized Unions Associated with Major Companies

Union	*Affiliation*	*Membership*	*Net Assets*	*Total Receipts*	*Founding*
Amazon Labor Union	Independent				2021
Starbucks Workers United	Workers United, SEIU, AFL-CIO	WU: 48,501 SBWU: 1,600	WU: $1,71,932,826	WU: $6,366,264	2004
Apple Coalition of Organized Retail Employees (a.k.a. AppleCore)	IAM, AFL-CIO				2022
Apple Retail Union (a.k.a. Apple Workers Union)	CWA, AFL-CIO				2022

- *The Amazon Labor Union (ALU) was founded on April 14, 2021, to organize warehouse workers employed by Amazon in the New York City metropolitan area, where it is headquartered. It is an independent union, which has yet to file an LM-2 financial disclosure report. Its LM-1 report indicates that its annual receipts exceeded $250,000.*
- *Founded in 2004, the Starbucks Workers United is affiliated with Workers United, an affiliate of SEIU. WU includes about 48,500 members, and the SBWU website indicates that it has won more than 180 certification elections (though not all have been formally certified yet by the NLRB) with more than 1,600 union supporters.*
- *Founded in 2022, the Apple Coalition of Organized Retail Employees, AppleCore, is affiliated with the IAM.*
- *Founded in 2022, the Apple Retail Union, referred also as Apple Workers Union, is an affiliate of the CWA.*

Leveraging Opportunity: Aligning with the Favorable Environment

The successes achieved at Amazon, Apple, and Starbucks occurred at a time in which the environment seemed more favorable to organized labor than has been the case for several decades. First, the COVID-19 pandemic generated a massive set of fiscal and monetary stimuli which have contributed to a combination of low unemployment and labor shortages. The resulting situation has forced upward pressures on wages and emboldened workers who are more willing to take the risks associated with union organizing.

Second, public opinion has become more supportive of unions, particularly among younger workers. Millennials and Generation Zs have insisted more on having a voice in the workplace, recognizing in the process that unions through collective bargaining provide a viable means toward this end. A recent Gallup Poll has shown that a full 68 percent of the American public supports unions and an even greater 77 percent of younger workers do so.

Third, the election of President Biden has led to the appointment of new members of the NLRB who have taken a much more favorable disposition to unions. The recently appointed General Counsel (GC) of the NLRB has proved willing to file unfair labor practice charges against employers such as Amazon and Starbucks which have resisted organizing drives. The GC has also taken the bold step of issuing memoranda to challenging employer's anti-union practices, such as captive audiences, which has previously had judicial and board support. These forces have converged to lead some that a tipping point is within reach if an aggressively coordinated labor campaign to exploit these recent successes materializes.

Financial Need and Wherewithal

Given existing levels of employer opposition to unions and the panoply of legal devices that can be used in resistance, the costs of organizing workers in the United States can be heavy, not only in direct financial terms but also in the legal and economic risks borne by union activists. It is not known how much it costs a group of workers to launch and win an organizing campaign and then translate that into the successful negotiation of a first contract. But we know that employers spend vast sums to resist unions and bargain combatively. For example, xxx. To surmount this magnitude of determined opposition, labor supporters need to mobilize substantial resources to protect workers' rights, communicate effectively with employees and the community, litigate disputes, and assemble a qualified and well-prepared negotiating team. The level of commitment required to offer such support rises commensurately with the scope of effort contemplated. If unions want to export the successes experienced recently, they will need first to hone the recipe and expend the resources needed for wider application. In formulating the secret sauce and making it widely available to viable opportunities, unions will need to acquire the money to front such an operation. Obviously, relatively localized, small, and nascent organizations, such as ALU and SBWU, may not be adequately financed for this scale of endeavor. Herein lies the potential that more established labor organizations can offer.

We examine the potential pool of money unions have available to invest in new-wave organizing without diverting their recurring streams of revenue needed to finance ongoing operations. For the most part, unions generate just sufficient revenues to support disbursements for their operating functions and a minimal level of investment needed to some provide cushion and fund striker benefits. Over time, they accumulate both assets of various types and liabilities. Their net assets offer one measure of the money unions have available to invest in special projects along the lines we describe. The summary indicator, however, includes assets that range in ready accessibility. Fixed assets need to be sold before they can yield the cash for immediate expenditure. Current assets represent the immediately disposable money unions have for discretionary spending, if they so choose. They include cash, accounts receivable, and investments in Treasury securities. The degree to which current assets exceed current liabilities (as measured by the loans payable by the union) refers to a unions' working capital.

As shown in Table 15.4, the roughly 100 labor organizations filing LM-2 financial disclosures with the US Department of Labor in 2021 reported having $11.5 billion in net assets and more than $3.6 billion in working capital. The unions are listed from highest to lowest amounts in working capital. The top ten ranked unions possessed more than $2.34 billion or 65 percent of the grand total. They include the American Federation of State, County, and Municipal Employees (AFSCME), United Auto Workers (UAW), United Steelworkers (USW), United Food and Commercial Workers (UFCW), the plumbers, service employees (SEIU), and the carpenters. If unions were to "pool" a portion of these funds into a new operational enterprise to support organizing campaigns spawned by indigenously based workers, then organized labor might facilitate the replication of successful efforts that have witnessed Amazon, Apple, and Starbucks. The question arises as to how such an enterprise might operate.

Table 15.4 Working Capital and Net Assets (in thousands)

Union	*Working ($)*	*Net Assets ($)*
Professional athletes	46,20,16,444	71,83,26,305
State, county, and municipal employees AFL-CIO	33,87,91,793	24,61,55,508
SAG-AFTRA	30,14,39,254	(1,67,32,666)
Auto workers AFL-CIO	23,48,13,936	1,08,68,02,397
Steelworkers, AFL-CIO	23,46,72,153	1,06,53,14,880
Plumbers AFL-CIO	21,09,25,047	41,40,58,630
Service employees	20,84,81,765	42,01,17,706
Carpenters IND	15,74,84,620	72,85,74,698
National Education Association IND	11,84,47,234	34,79,27,626
Food and commercial workers	8,18,74,926	49,50,33,990
Teachers AFL-CIO	7,45,95,201	5,50,28,873
Sheet metal, air, rail, and transportation workers	6,31,72,927	24,43,78,481
Letter carriers, National Association, AFL-CIO	5,94,12,973	36,20,37,585
Electrical workers IBEW AFL-CIO	5,86,51,389	57,50,44,616
Teamsters	5,78,01,605	52,53,62,002
Laborers	5,50,50,958	38,00,25,150
Unite Here	5,48,67,857	10,11,76,089
Writers Guild West IND	5,26,59,468	8,77,39,569
Directors Guild of America INC NHQ	5,04,67,107	6,83,10,582
Bricklayers AFL-CIO	4,49,15,107	12,10,15,090
United Service Workers Union, IUJAT	4,07,87,294	5,14,59,205

(*Continued*)

Table 15.4 (Continued)

Union	*Working ($)*	*Net Assets ($)*
Machinists AFL-CIO	4,07,09,834	28,57,93,800
AFL-CIO	4,05,17,159	6,06,26,912
National Nurses United	3,96,54,146	3,90,74,997
Office and professional employees AFL-CIO	3,69,75,865	3,74,89,687
Longshoremen's Association AFL-CIO	3,69,54,920	7,53,24,815
Letter carriers, rural, IND	3,35,15,724	2,84,40,878
Government employees AFGE AFL-CIO	3,02,69,119	(60,78,609)
Communications workers AFL-CIO	2,95,34,916	31,36,42,997
Iron workers AFL-CIO	2,87,46,790	12,96,04,945
Musicians AFL-CIO	2,77,08,836	2,10,11,306
Elevator constructors AFL-CIO	2,68,36,346	2,43,91,220
Stage and picture operators AFL-CIO	2,57,27,080	5,73,94,392
Air Line Pilots Association AFL-CIO	2,41,40,687	36,97,82,717
Security police, fire professionals, IND	2,24,33,886	1,26,60,263
Firefighters AFL-CIO	2,23,62,797	3,08,44,036
Insulators AFL-CIO	2,15,49,697	4,95,13,895
Postal workers, American, AFL-CIO	2,06,20,383	15,55,33,919
Bakery, tobacco, and grain AFL-CIO	2,04,64,501	3,77,54,677
Government employees NAGE SEIU AFL-CIO	1,87,21,172	2,26,18,551
Plasterers and cement masons AFL-CIO	1,78,35,998	5,75,14,509
Painters AFL-CIO	1,77,72,679	9,22,38,102
New York State Nurses Association	1,71,96,328	5,87,74,774
Postal mail handlers, LIUNA	1,54,06,474	2,13,41,622
Air traffic controllers AFL-CIO	1,23,67,569	2,41,54,379
Boilermakers AFL-CIO	1,17,72,847	7,05,38,031
Utility workers AFL-CIO	1,17,08,709	2,40,07,752
Transport workers AFL-CIO	1,13,90,562	6,29,94,076
Transit Union AFL-CIO	1,00,06,311	19,73,13,890
Transportation Communications Union/IAM, AFL-CIO	93,73,942	1,15,73,736
Longshore and Warehouse Union	90,97,331	82,80,367
Roofers AFL-CIO	79,52,923	4,68,48,600
Railroad signalmen AFL-CIO	77,29,272	1,61,11,746
Allied Pilots Association	69,03,754	6,99,86,393
Locomotive engineers, IBT	58,16,623	2,58,81,891
Journeymen and allied trades IND	51,69,175	55,08,174
Strategic organizing center	49,41,185	49,07,749
Police fraternal order, IND	48,02,569	1,17,70,122
Pulp and paper workers UBCJA	41,98,720	1,26,78,420
Musical artists AAAA AFL-CIO	41,72,389	1,52,20,157
Treasury Employees Union IND	40,96,424	4,21,66,289
Writers Guild East AFL-CIO	37,70,480	1,39,47,351
University professors IND	27,79,611	1,09,25,335
Engineers, professional and technical, AFL-CIO	24,10,012	53,88,296
Variety artists AAAA AFL-CIO	21,56,127	21,88,407
Industrial trade unions, IUJAT	17,95,363	62,43,098
Inlandboatmen, ILWU, AFL-CIO	16,42,232	17,34,333
Seafarers AFL-CIO	15,63,683	14,37,023

(*Continued*)

Table 15.4 (Continued)

Union	*Working ($)*	*Net Assets ($)*
Building and construction trades department AFL-CIO	14,44,609	1,55,33,311
Transportation trades department AFL-CIO	13,83,843	46,41,810
Aircraft Mechanics ASN IND	13,48,084	26,54,487
Weather service employees	12,98,696	12,96,660
Alliance of Health Care Unions	10,94,368	28,444
Farm workers, UNITED	10,60,137	66,32,807
Government security officers, IND	10,28,497	15,33,914
Department for professional employees, AFL-CIO	10,16,648	9,32,795
Graphic communications, IBT	9,89,005	41,27,782
Industrial workers of the world	9,30,888	8,02,521
Novelty and production workers AFL-CIO	9,24,636	40,95,220
National Infrastructure Alliance	8,45,334	5,46,225
NLRB Union IND	6,81,812	6,80,893
Christian Labor Union IND	6,51,851	11,86,893
Metal trades department AFL-CIO	5,91,095	9,87,465
Flight Attendants Association, CWA	5,85,522	68,23,656
Federal employees NFFE, DIST 1, IAM, AFL-CIO	5,28,386	37,55,881
Association of Civilian Technicians	5,24,376	20,81,513
National Staff Organization IND	4,53,115	1,22,41,764
American train dispatchers	4,15,974	1,48,29,524
United Workers of America	3,51,530	3,51,530
National Association of Independent Labor	3,00,499	2,99,098
National Women's Soccer League Players Association	2,11,745	2,11,745
Utility Workers Council	1,13,859	80,286
Union Label SVC Trades Department AFL-CIO	61,228	3,91,579
Trabajadores Industriales DE PR IND	34,069	2,72,075
Independent Unions, Congress of	31,398	1,56,737
Familias Unidas Por La Justicia	20,522	50,111
Marine Engineers AFL-CIO	16,404	16,404
Industrial Workers United SIUNA AFL-CIO	(2,06,496)	(1,22,652)
National Production Workers Union IND	(5,12,058)	1,60,871
Mine Workers, United, AFL-CIO	(43,32,009)	13,83,81,370
Maintenance of way employees, IBT	(55,40,718)	3,20,83,505
Workers united, SEIU	(1,09,57,069)	17,19,32,826
Engineers, operating, AFL-CIO	(10,59,18,209)	34,29,47,286
Total	3,61,60,73,779	11,51,68,82,672
Top ten	2,34,89,47,172	
% Top ten	65%	

A New Wave Union Organizing Incubator

We propose that a consortium of unions representing diverse industries collaborate to fund a one-stop-shopping operational center to support a new wave organizing at the grassroots. A New Wave Organizing Incubation Center (NWOIC) would provide hand-on assistance to grassroots activists who want to organize their work sites in an expeditious manner. The enterprise would offer state-of-the-art organizing toolkits to aid these activities on soup-to-nuts matters that arise in organizing campaigns, from petitioning the NLRB for a certification election, protecting workers from mistreatment by managers, filing unfair labor practice charges, negotiating first contracts, communicating with co-workers and the broader community, and ensuring a secure social media network with a rapid-response capability.

We would stress that this new entity would not supplant or duplicate the ongoing work of the AFL-CIO's Organizing Institute, which concentrates on training organizers, or of the multilateral Strategic Organizing Center, which provided cutting-edge research to guide practice. These entities would service the NWOIC, as appropriate.

The labor organizations funding the NWOIC would establish a procedure whereby local grassroots activists would apply for operational support. The gamut of support would be tailored to the industry and occupation targeted by the activists. It would include making them part of a network of activists from work sites that have successfully organized. The NWOIC would be staffed with technicians and experts who can provide hands-on assistance in response to the often rapidly changing needs of the indigenous activists. There would be minimal bureaucracy and immediate accessibility to exploit opportunities as they arise.

Table 15.5 presents a brief description of the vision and mission of the proposed NWOIC as well as some details on how it would be funded and administered. The vision and mission statements are intended to guide the day-to-day operations of the entity so that the funding unions, governing leadership, and operational staff have a lodestar to follow. Sponsoring unions would draw a charter and bylaws for the NWOIC, committing to provide an annual budget and establishing a process

Table 15.5 Selected Dimensions of the New Wave Organizing Incubation Center

Dimension	*Policy*
Vision	To accelerate the pace and volume union of representation to better working people's lives
Mission	To provide operational support to indigenous-based union organizing and initial contract bargaining
Financing	Contributions made by a consortium of labor organizations to provide a dependable budget for allocation among viable organizing campaigns; budgets would rise to the level of success achieved by grassroots organizers
Allocations	Fund-specific organizing campaigns that are indigenous and grassroots, based on the presentation of plans of action to industry-specific review boards from on-the-ground activists on how to spend funding requests
Types of support	Make available to funded projects resources that cover the gamut of services required, from petitioning the NLRB, filing Unfair Labor Practices (ULPs), representing workers subject to employer abuses, mounting public relations campaigns, communicating digitally with workers and community supporters, and negotiating contracts: a one-stop organizing operations service provider.

for allocating support to viable organizing opportunities. The NWOIC would be on guard against just throwing money at a problem. Blank checks would not be written to local organizations or groups of activists to conduct operations. Instead, the NWOIC would engage the activists in a continuing service to maximize success. A premium would be placed on creating a robust network of activists who could exchange practical insights as to what works best in organizing the targeted audience.

16 Future Directions

In this chapter, we explore how organized labor might reposition itself to exploit future opportunities. Repositioning involves a structural realignment through the creation of mega-unions, a redefining of the role of the American Federation of Labor-Congress of Industrial Organizations (AFL-CIO) as the umbrella federation hosting these newly formed conglomerates, remodeling of the relationship between labor organizations and workers to broaden the inclusion of the contingency workforce, and relatedly, the experimentation of new ideas on financing operations. The chapter is organized to address these contemplated changes. Before delving into future directions, however, we pause to summarize several key findings which inform the discussion.

Key Findings

The review of the finances of 53 major national unions over seven two-year intervals covering the 2006–2007 through 2018–2019 period yielded several findings which bear on labor's future capacity to meet the challenges ahead:

- These unions collectively experienced a relatively small loss in membership though vast differences existed across them.
- While the unions suffered financial losses during the depths of the Great Recession in assets and overall receipts, their wherewithal recovered.
- During the entire period examined, the unions' collective position in terms of member-based income (MBI) improved, giving them greater coverage of their operating budgets from this recurring source of income.
- The unions maintained healthy positions, overall, in terms of available working capital and generally improved their financial performance.
- Vast differences exist in the financial wherewithal across unions, with many possessing relatively small levels of assets and revenues.
- Financial wealth and revenue are relatively concentrated among a small number of unions.

DOI: 10.4324/9781003335474-17

- The cost of doing union business, in terms of administration and compensation, continued to increase, notwithstanding significant reductions in the overall number of employees reported who earned at least $10,000 in gross compensation (salary and expenses).
- The unions' business income fell precipitously, which makes them more dependent on members for their revenues. This makes them more vulnerable to recessions and general membership stagnation or decline.

Forming Mega-Unions

These findings raise the possibility that unions might benefit from consolidating their operations to derive economies of scale and other efficiencies. They could, for example, form a set of mega-organizations that correspond with the broad industrial classifications: goods producing; private services; professional/business services; education and health services; leisure and hospitality; and government (federal, postal, state, and local combined). In Table 16.1, we identify the distinct national unions which might consider joining a super-structure to derive economies of scale and other efficiencies to improve operations. We suggest which nationals might align with the different industrial classifications dominant in

Table 16.1 Mega-Unions Bi Industrial Sectors

Industry Sector	*Selected Unions*
Goods producing (21,092) Mining, logging (625) Construction (7,670) Manufacturing (12,797)	UMW, UAW, USW, IAM, LIU, IBEW, SHEET METAL, PLUMBERS, CARPENTERS, ROOFERS, PAINTERS, PLASTERERS, UE, IUOE, IRON
Private service (108,673) Trade, transportation, and utilities (28,746) Information (3,008) Financial activities (8,951) Real estate/rental (23,615)	IBT, UTILITY, RWDSU, CWA, ATU, TWU, SIU, ALPA, APA. ILA, ILWU, Aircraft Mechanics, Writers Guilds, Aircraft Mechanics
Professional/business services (22,273) Professional and technical (10,446) Management (2,385) Administrative (9,443) Waste management (474)	OPEIU, EPT
Education and health services (24,339) Education (3,807) Health service (20,532) Social assistance (4217)	AFT, NEA, UNITED NURSES, ANA, SEIU,
Leisure and hospitality -15,665	UNITE HERE; UFCW
Government (22,215)	AFSCME, AFGE, NALC, IAFF, APWU, NRLCA, NAPFE, NTEU, NATCA, MAILHANDLERS/LIU, FOP

Table 16.2 New Model of Union Representation (Tiered Membership and Services)

Type of Membership	*Level of Service*
Premium	Bargaining, contract administration, legal representation, political representation, training and development, user fee (insurance, credit card, transportation, housing)
Basic	Bargaining, contract administration, political representation, user fee
Associate	Political representation, user fee
Retiree	Political representation, user fee
Contingent	Political representation, legal representation, user fee

today's workforce. The goods-producing sector would include 15 unions with members who work in mining, logging, construction, and manufacturing. In private services, 14 unions could effectively merge to cover the industries of trade, transportation, and utilities. Eleven unions might coordinate efforts in government, with two dominating the leisure and hospitality sector. At least five might be engaged in education and health services, with two assigned to the professional and business services.

The unions might expand their reach in terms of offering membership services if they proposed to connect alternative levels of service. We report on five levels of membership, associated with different degrees of service (Table 16.2). Premium services include bargaining and contract administration, legal and political representation, training and education, and user fees. The basic services packages would include bargaining, contract administration, political representation, and user fees. Associate status is conferred upon those who did not presently have bargaining rights but may aspire to if they can secure such privileges. Retiree membership status would be comparable to the associate type. Contingent membership confers political and legal representation in the hope of convincing the legislatures to grant formal bargaining rights to workers whose attachment to specific employers is looser because of their independent-contractor status.

A Revamped AFL-CIO

As the nation's largest federation of labor organizations, the AFL-CIO, which was formed in the mid-1950s, has provided an array of services, from political representation and public relations to offering assistance at the bargaining table and in litigating disputes, as well as providing discounted services for members. We envision an expanded role for the federation, giving it more operational focus, particularly as it relates to organizing. We also believe that the federation could essentially contract to perform basic services for unions. To capture the current organizational capacity of the AFL-CIO, we present relevant data in Table 16.3.

The federation includes 58 affiliated labor organizations which comprise the bulk of the unionized workforce. Its affiliates have more than 12 million members. The federation employed 244 people who made more than $10,000 in gross compensation (salary and expenses) in 2021. Its net assets exceeded $60 million, while

Table 16.3 AFL-CIO Statistics

Variable	*Value*
Membership	12,033,779
#Employees	244
Net assets	$60,626,912
Total receipts	$146,436,236
Member-based	
Income	$71,565,257
Working capital	$40,517,159
Operating budget	$75,019,110
Total disbursements	$149,539,563
Compensation	$34,771,758
Net receipts	$105,998,046

Source: AFL-CIO LM-2.

Table 16.4 Repositioned AFL-CIO

Core functions	Political representation, legal representation, bargaining/ financial expertise, information technology, payroll/ benefits management, organizing, research, diversity and inclusion, user services, financial management/investments
Organizing portfolio	Strategic Organizing Center (research); NWOIC (operations), Organizing Institute (training and education)

its net receipts (total receipts minus transmittals) were over $105 million. The AFL-CIO draws about $71.6 million in MBI, which does not fully cover its operating budget of just over $75 million. The federation spends about $34.8 million on compensation (gross salaries and benefits) of its employees and officers. Its working capital exceeds $40.5 million.

A repositioned AFL-CIO would serve as a one-stop shopping center which could provide, on fee basis, the capacity to assist affiliates in financial management, bargaining, grievance administration, and information technology, especially data analytics (Table 16.4). It would continue to play a role in coordinated political representation. It would also contribute to upgrading the quality of personnel in the unions, promoting diversity and inclusion as well as training and education in the process. Perhaps the most significant expansion in its supportive role would be in organizing. It would host the previously described New Wave Organizing Incubation Center, with its operational focus. The federation might also absorb the existing Strategic Organizing Center to offer leading-edge research to bolster grassroots organizers. Its ongoing Organizing Institute, which focuses on training, would supplement this enhanced role.

References

Allison, E. K. (1975). "Financial Analysis of the Local Union". *Industrial Relations*, 14 (May): 145–55.

Applebaum, L. (1964). "Financial Structure and Characteristics of Labor Organizations in a Metropolitan Area." *Labor Law Journal*, 15 (January): 30–47.

Applebaum, L. (1965). "An Analysis of the Financial Structure of Local Labor Unions". *Labor Law Journal*, 16 (3): 164–75.

Applebaum, L. (1966)." Officer Turnover and Salary Structure in Local Unions". *Industrial and Labor Relations Review*, XIX (January): 224–30.

Applebaum, L. (1969). "A Comparison of Officer Turnover and Salary Structures in Local Unions." *Labor Law Journal*, XX (December): 795–802.

Applebaum, L. and Blaine, H. R. (1975). "Compensation and Turnover of Union Officers." *Industrial Relations*, 14 (2): 156–57.

Baumol, W. J. (2012). *The Cost Disease: Why Computers Get Cheaper and Health Care Doesn't*. New Haven, CT: Yale University Press.

Baumol, W. J. and Bowen, W. G. (1966). *Performing Arts: The Economic Dilemma*. Cambridge, MA: MIT Press.

Belfer. N. (1949). "Financial Resources of Trade Unions," *Journal of Political Economy*, 57 (2): 157–61.

Belfer, N. (1953). "Trade Union Investment Policies". *Industrial and Labor Relations Review*, 6 (3): 337–51.

Bennett, J. T. (1991). "Private Sector Unions: The Myth of Decline". *Journal of Labor Research*, 12 (Winter): 1–12.

Chaison, G. N. (1986). *When Unions Merge*. Lexington, MA: Lexington Books.

Child, J., Loveridge, R. and Warner, W. (1973). "Towards an Organizational Study of Trade Unions." *Sociology*, 7 (1): 71–91.

Clark, P. F. and Gray, L. S. (2008). "Administrative practices in American unions: A longitudinal study". *Journal of Labor Research*, 29 (1): 42–55.

Ehrenberg, R. and Goldberg, S. (1977). "Officer Performance and Compensation in Local Building Trades Unions." *Industrial and Labor Relations Review*, 30 (2): 188–96.

Estey, M. S., Taft, P. and Wagner, W. (1964). *Regulating Union Government*. New York: Harper and Row.

French, L. J., Hayashi, P. and Gray, D. A. (1983). "The Compensation of National Union Presidents: Moderating Effects of Union Size". *Journal of Labor Research*, 4 (3): 225–37.

Gamm, S. (1979). "The Election Base of National Union Executive Boards". *ILR Review*, 32 (3): 295–311.

Greenhouse. S. (2022). "Is Organized Labor Making a Comeback?" *Atlantic*, April 4.

Griffin, G. and de Rozairo, S. (1993). "Trade Union Finances in the 1970s and 1980s." *Journal of Industrial Relations*, 35 (3): 424–35.

Holgate, J., Simms, M. and Tapia, M. (2018). "The Limitations of the Theory and Practice of Mobilization in Trade Union Organizing." *Economic and Industrial Democracy*, 39 (4): 599–616.

Huntley, P. (1976). *Inside Australia's Top 100 Trade Unions*. Isaac, J. E. and Ford, G.W. (eds.). Middle Cove, New South Wales: Ian Huntley (Aust.) Pty Ltd.

Huntley, P. (1979). *Inside Australia's Top 100 Trade Unions*. Isaac, J. E. and Ford, G.W. (eds.). Middle Cove, New South Wales: Ian Huntley (Aust.) Pty Ltd.

Jacoby, S. (2021). *Labor in the Age of Finance: Pensions, Politics, and Corporations from Deindustrialization to Dodd-Frank*. Princeton, NJ: Princeton University Press.

Kelly, J. (1998). *Rethinking Industrial Relations*. London: Routledge.

Korpi, W. (1985). "Power Resources Approach vs. Action and Conflict: On Causal and Intentional Explanations in the Study of Power." *Sociological Theory*, 3 (2): 31–45.

Kozmetsky, G. (1950). *Financial Reports of Labor Unions*. Andover, MA: Andover Press.

Lafer, G. (2013). *The Legislative Attach on American Wages and Labor Standards, 2011–2012*. Washington, DC: Economic Policy Institute. October 31.

Lafer, G. (2017). *The One Percent Solution*. Ithaca, NY: ILR Press, Cornell University Press.

Latta, G, (1972). "Trade Union Finance." *British Journal of Industrial Relations*, X (November): 392–411.

Masters, M. F. (1997). *Unions at the Crossroads: Strategic Membership, Financial and Political Implications*. Westport, CT: Quorum.

Masters, M. F., Albright, R. and Gibney, R. (2015). "The Attacks on Federal and Postal Unions, 2001-Present." *Employee Rights and Employment Policy Journal*, 19 (2): 301–29.

Masters, M. F., Albright, R. and Gibney, R. (2020). "The Ebb and Flow of Federal Sector Labor-Management Relations Policies under Four Successive Presidents." *Employee Responsibilities and Rights Journal*, 32 (3): 139–66.

Masters, M. F. and Atkin, R. S. (1995). "Bargaining, Financial, and Political Bases of Federal Sector Unions: Implications for Reinventing Government." *Review of Public Personnel Administration*, 15 (1): 5–23.

Masters, M. F. and Atkin, R. S. (1997). "The Finances of Major U.S. National Unions." *Industrial Relations*, 36 (4): 489–506.

Masters, M. F., Atkin, R. S. and Florkowski, G. W. (1989). "An Analysis of Union Reporting Requirements Under Title II of the Landrum-Griffin Act." *Labor Law Journal*, 40 (11): 713–22.

Masters, M. F. and Gibney, R. (2022). *Trade Union Money: How Labor Organizations Raise and Spend It*. New York: Routledge.

Masters, M. F., Gibney, R. and Zagenczyk, T. J. (2009). "Worker Pay Protection: Implications for Labor Political Spending and Voice." *Industrial Relations*, 48 (4): 557–77.

McCarthy, John D. and Mayer N. Zald. (1977). "Resource Mobilization and Social Movements: A Partial Theory." *American Journal of Sociology*, 82 (6): 1212–41.

McNicholas, C., Mokhiber, Z. and von Wilpert, M. (2018). *Janus and Fair Share Fees: The Organizations Financing the Attack on Unions' Ability to Represent Workers*. Washington, DC: Economic Policy Institute.

Moss, A. (1983). "The Finances of Trade Unions in the Australian Government Sector." MBA research report, University of Melbourne. Rawson, D.W.

Olson, M. (1965). *The Logic of Collective Action*. Cambridge, MA: Harvard University Press.

Pfeffer, J. and Salancik, G. R. (1978). *The External Control of Organizations*. Stanford, CA: Stanford University Press.

Roberts, B. C. (1957). *Trade Union Government and Administration in Great Britain*. London: G. Bell.

Robertson, P. J. and Tang, S. (1995). "The Role of Commitment in Collective Action: Comparing Organizational Behavior and Rational Choice Perspectives." *Public Administration Review*, 55 (1): 67–80.

Rosenfeld, J. (2014). *What Unions No Longer Do*. Cambridge, MA: Harvard University Press.

Sakolski, A. M. (1906). *Finances of American Trade Unions*. Baltimore: Johns Hopkins Press.

Sandver, M. H. (1978). "Determinants of Pay for Large Local Union Officers." *Industrial Relations*, 17 (1): 108–11.

Sandver, M. H. and Heneman III, H. L. (1980). "Analysis and Prediction of Top National Union Officers' Total Compensation." *Academy of Management Journal*, 12 (3): 534–43.

Sheflin, N. and Troy, L. (1983). "Finances of American Unions in the 1970s." *Journal of Labor Research*, 4 (2):149–57.

Stieber, J. (1962). *Governing the UAW*. New York: John Wiley and Sons, Inc.

Strauss, G. (1975). "Union Finances Data." *Industrial Relations*, 14 (2): 131–33.

Taft, P. (1946a). "Dues and Fees in Labor Unions." *Quarterly Journal of Economics*, 60 (2): 219–23.

Taft, P. (1946b). "Understanding Union Administration." *Harvard Business Review*, 24 (2): 245–57.

Troy, L. (1975a). "American Unions and Their Wealth." *Industrial Relations*, 14 (2): 134–44.

Troy, L. (1975b). "The Finances of American Unions, 1962–1969." *Explorations in Economic Research*, 2 (2): 232–51.

Wielgosz, J. (1974). "Financial Resources of Australian Trade Unions." *Journal of Industrial Relations*, 16 (4): 314–22.

Willman, P. (1990). "The Financial Status and Performance of British Trade Unions, 1950–1988." *British Journal of Industrial Relations*, 28 (3): 313–27.

Willman, P. and Bryson, A. (2009). "Accounting for Collective Action: Resource Acquisition and Mobilisation in UK Unions." *Advances in Industrial Relations*, 16: 23–50.

Willman, P., Bryson, P. A. and Forth, J. (2020). "UK Unions, Collective Action and the Cost Disease." *British Journal of Industrial Relations*, 58 (2): 447–70.

Willman, P., Morris, T. and Aston, B. (1993). *Union Business: Trade Union Organisation, and Financial Reform in the Thatcher Years*. Cambridge: Cambridge University Press.

Index

Taylor & Francis Group
an informa business
Taylor & Francis eBooks
www.taylorfrancis.com
A single destination for eBooks from Taylor & Francis with increased functionality and an improved user experience to meet the needs of our customers.
90,000+ eBooks of award-winning academic content in Humanities, Social Science, Science, Technology, Engineering, and Medical written by a global network of editors and authors.
TAYLOR & FRANCIS EBOOKS OFFERS:
A streamlined experience for our library customers
A single point of discovery for all of our eBook content
Improved search and discovery of content at both book and chapter level
REQUEST A FREE TRIAL
support@taylorfrancis.com
Routledge Taylor & Francis Group
CRC Press Taylor & Francis Group